IMAGES
of America

AFRICAN AMERICANS IN NACOGDOCHES COUNTY

On the Cover: This is an image of Long Star Primitive Baptist Church established in 1889. This Nacogdoches African American church was often characterized by the religious rituals and traditions its members practiced as part of the worship services. This picture, taken between 1930 and 1940, shows members dressed in white, singing hymns in circles before walking down to a nearby pond to baptize new members. (Courtesy of East Texas Research Center, Stephen F. Austin State University.)

IMAGES
of America

African Americans in Nacogdoches County

Jeri Mills

ARCADIA PUBLISHING

ISBN 978-1-4671-3215-2

Published by Arcadia Publishing
Charleston, South Carolina

Printed in the United States of America

Library of Congress Control Number: 2014932335

For all general information, please contact Arcadia Publishing:
Telephone 843-853-2070
Fax 843-853-0044
E-mail sales@arcadiapublishing.com
For customer service and orders:
Toll-Free 1-888-313-2665

Visit us on the Internet at www.arcadiapublishing.com

This book is dedicated to the early Nacogdoches African American pioneers and leaders who cleared the bushes and paved a path that many walk on today. We gain strength from our successes and contributions and learn lessons from our personal failures. In the words of writer and author Alice Walker, who said it best, "We remember them because it is an easy thing to forget; that we are not the first to suffer, rebel, fight, love or die. The grace in which we embrace life, in spite of the pain, the sorrows, is always a measure of what has gone on before." We humbly embrace you, thank you, and we should never forget you. I would also like to dedicate this book to those, past and present, who contributed to its creation.

Contents

Acknowledgments 6

Introduction 8

1. Surviving the Best They Could 9
2. Believing in the Word 27
3. Reading, Writing, and Arithmetic 41
4. They Lived Quite Well Considering 67
5. Bits and Pieces of History 91

Bibliography 127

Acknowledgments

I would like to thank all who contributed photographs and information toward this project. This book would not have been possible without your participation. Special thanks go to the East Texas Research Center (ETRC) at the Ralph W. Steen Library of Stephen F. Austin State University and to L.C. Chatham for sharing the Mertie Mims Collection. I would also like to thank Rolonda Teal for her valuable assistance and contributions to the creation of this book. My gratitude also goes to Mable Hall, who encouraged me to finish this project and shared her time with me so generously. Finally a thank-you goes to my husband, Adell, for his constant support.

Adell Mills
Almeda Burrell
Amelia Johnson
Anera Randle Martin
Anne Millican
Annie Jones
Annie Reed
Archie Rison Jr.
Barbara Lewis
Betty Wade
Brooks Quinn Jones Elementary School, Nacogdoches Independent School District
Bruce Partain
Bryan Davis
Carolyn Ericson
Carolyn Spears
Charlotte Stokes
City of Nacogdoches
Clara Corr
Dorothy Warren
Dr. Faye Rison
Dr. Jeff Roth
Dr. Patsy Hallman
Dr. Scott Sosebee
Rev. Earl M. Hall
East Texas Research Center, Stephen F. Austin State University
Garrett family
Barbara Govan
Helen Gallon
Helena Patton Abdullah
Iron Wheel Baptist Church
J.B. Derrick
Jennie Mitchell
Jo Frances West
Judge Dorothy Tigner-Thompson
Judy B. McDonald Public Library staff
Kyle Ainsworth
L.C. Chatham
Rev. Leonard Sweat
Linda Reynolds
Juanita Hancock-Dickey
Little Zion Baptist Church
Mable Hall
Marilyn Griffin
Marion Upshaw
Maye Hamm
Maylene Neal
Clarence "Bo" McMichael family
Mertie Mims Photography Collection
Obadiah Johnson
Odessa Preston
Pascal Brown
Charlotte Patton
Peggy Jasso
Rolanda Teal
Robbie Lee Johnson
Samathia Tutt
Shirley Dickerson, Ralph W. Steen Library, Stephen F. Austin State University
Terrence Reeves
The *Nacogdoches Daily Sentinel*
Shirley Washington
William Rogers
Willie Scott
Willie Stegall Sweat
Richard Orton
Hollis James

INTRODUCTION

Nacogdoches is the oldest town in Texas, and the journey of African Americans in Nacogdoches County is just as old. Antonio Gil Y'Barbo is known as the father of Nacogdoches, Texas (1779), where he was instrumental in designing the town layout and creating governmental policies. During his regime, enslaved people from Louisiana and other parts of the country sought Nacogdoches as a safe haven before traveling into interior portions of the territory. Most often their final destination included Bexar, currently San Antonio, and places in northern Mexico.

When we think about the first African American in Nacogdoches, we would have to consider the first African American who arrived in the area we know today as Texas. He was called Estevanico and had exceptional talent, including the ability to speak several languages. He was born in North Africa but captured later by a Spanish explorer who made Estevanico his personal slave. In 1528, he was on an exploring expedition with his master when he landed on the Galveston shores after their ship wrecked with few survivors. He and several other survivors gained their freedom and searched for and found a Spanish settlement in what later became Mexico. Estevanico's arrival and presence on the Texas soil laid the groundwork for future talented African Americans who contributed to the development and growth of Texas, East Texas, and specifically Nacogdoches County.

In a Texas census taken on December 31, 1792, out of a total population of 3,005 residents, there were 34 Negroes and 415 mulattoes listed. No mention was made of slaves in the region. By 1845, however, Texas had officially become a part of the United States, and slavery was in full practice. Although this "peculiar institution" only lasted for 20 years or until the end of Civil War, the fabric of the community of Nacogdoches had changed.

Colonies, written by Thad Sitton and James H. Conrad, describes blacks who dared to form and develop their own independent, rural communities. Blacks in Nacogdoches, freed from the bonds of slavery, formed their own tiny communities and neighborhoods, developing their own unique culture.

One

Surviving the Best They Could

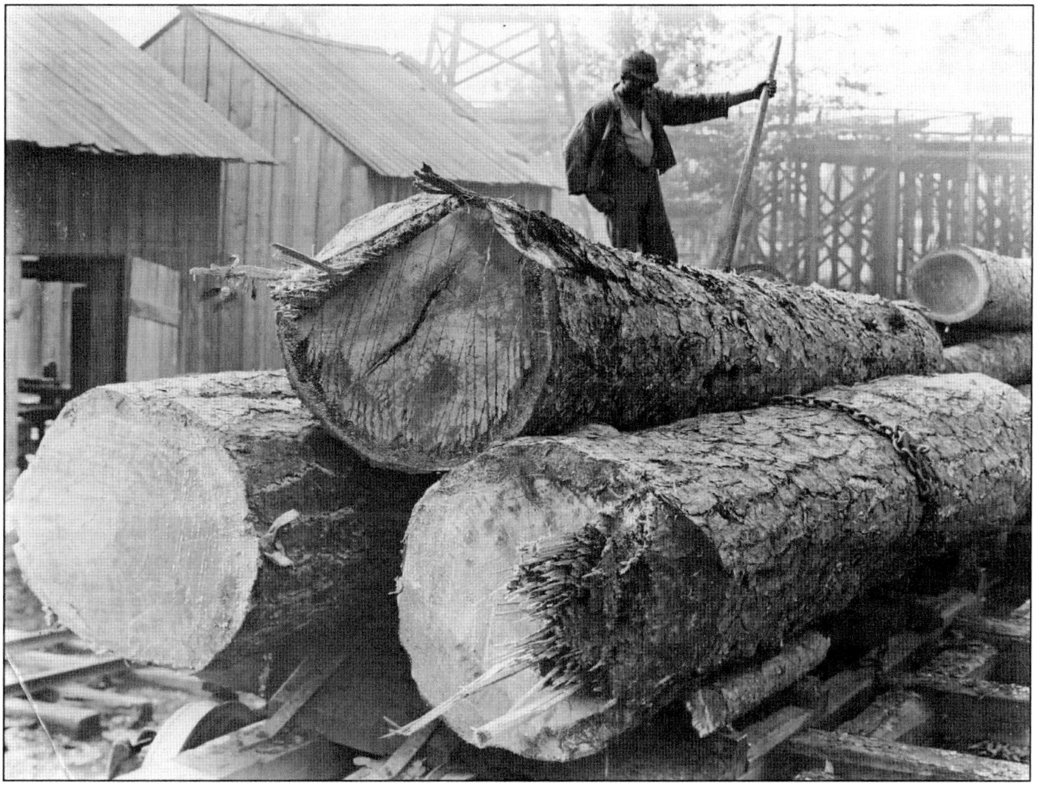

When the railroad companies came to Nacogdoches, the economy was stimulated with rails located near the shipping and industrial center. When the third railroad was established in 1905, Frost Johnson Lumber Company expanded and shipped its goods to Santa Fe Rail lines. Additional black workers were hired to build these rail tracks, providing more jobs in the East Texas area. (ETRC.)

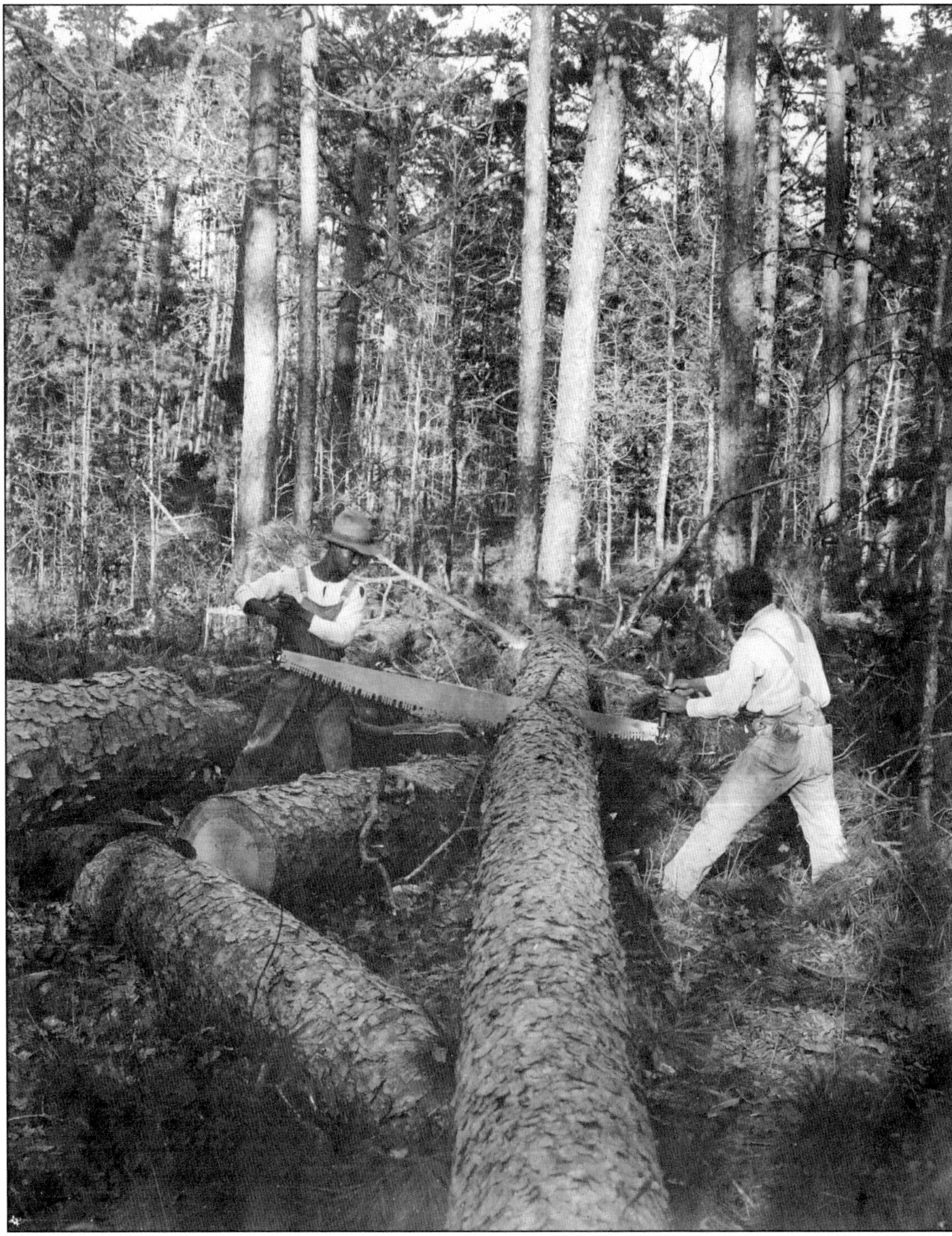

The lumber and logging industry provided jobs for workers from the late 1920s through the early 1950s. The sawmill industry worked alongside the agriculture industry as a primary employer of black men. Hundreds of pine trees were cut and shipped from the region between the late 1800s and the early 1900s. (ETRC.)

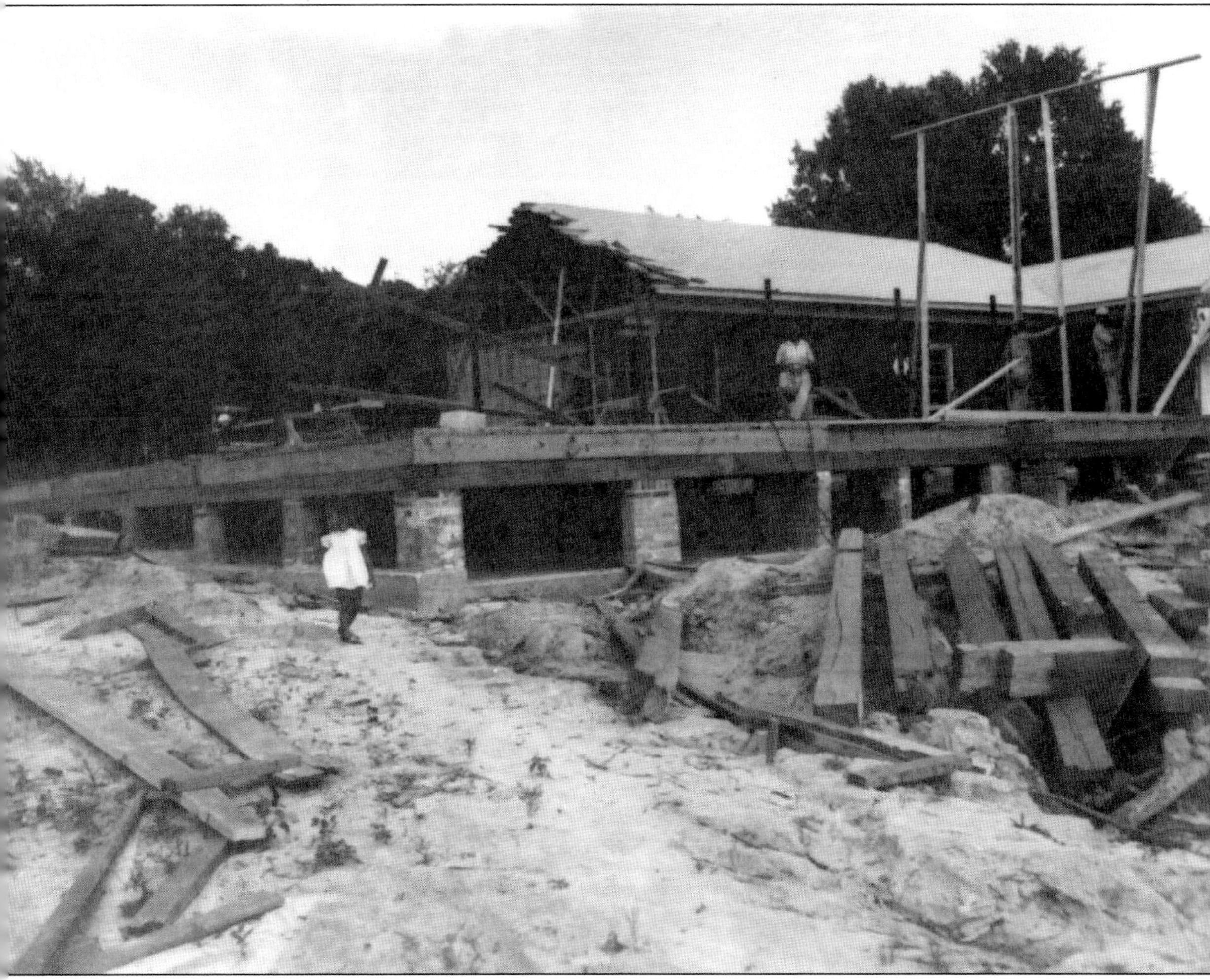

At one point, Nacogdoches was referred to as "Milltown." This was because the Frost Johnson plant covered several acres of the county. The plant provided housing facilities with electricity and water for its workers. It also had a store, commissary, meat market, and church. The millpond community was located near a body of water used to push big logs to loading areas. At one period, a half-dozen lumber mills were providing employment in the Nacogdoches area for unskilled black workers. (ETRC.)

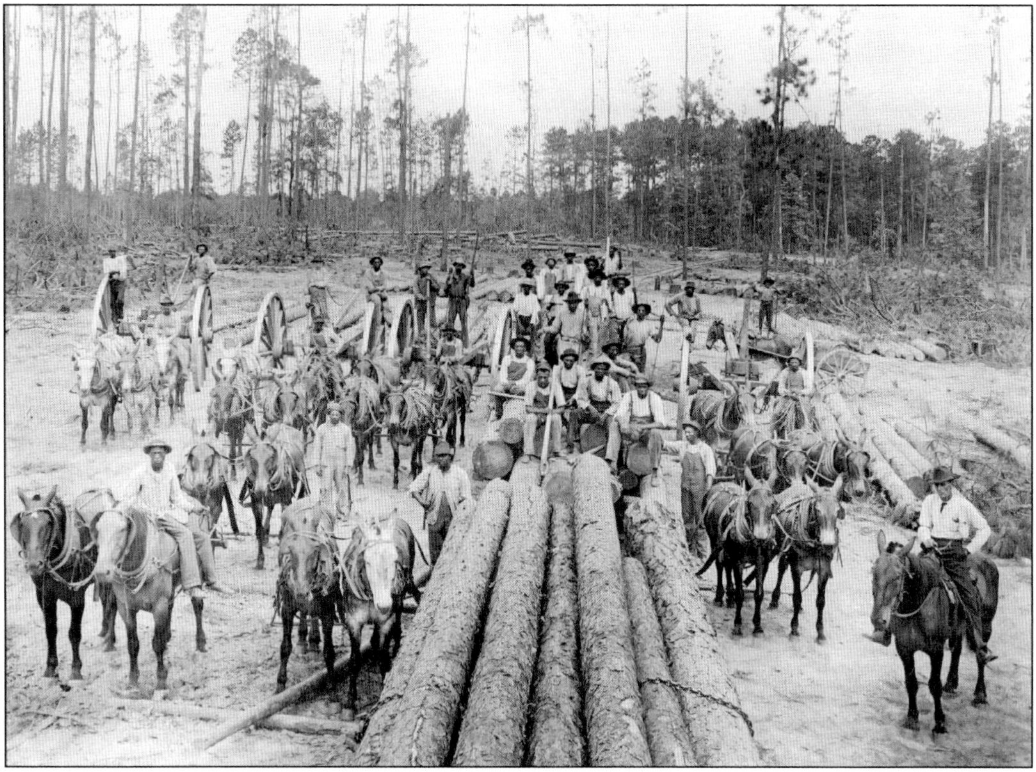

It took several teams of men to handle the amount of work required to successfully run a logging company. In this image are the workers from one such operation. (ETRC.)

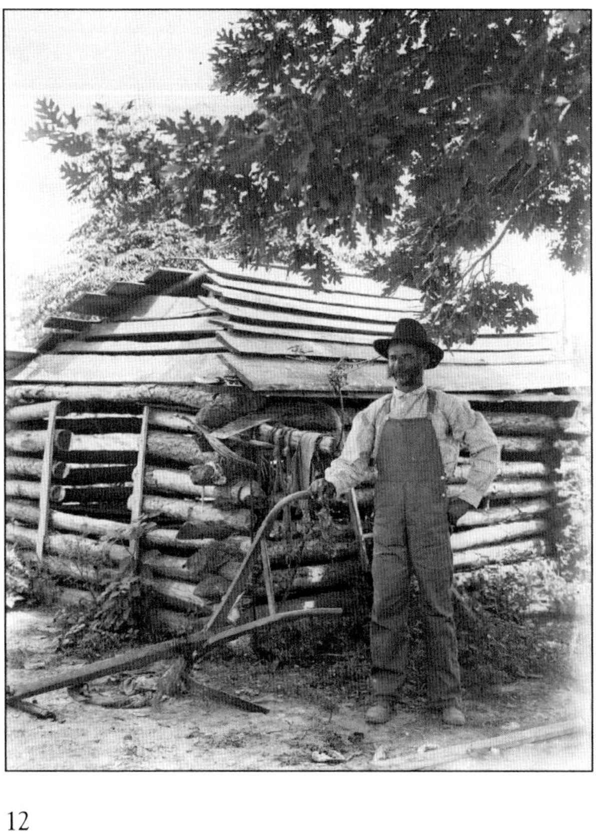

Russ Muckleroy was a former slave of the Thompson Lumber Company family. After emancipation, he worked as a tenant farmer before moving to Rusk County. Many of his descendants still reside in Nacogdoches County. In the background is a log-constructed building that is typical of the architectural style for outbuildings in East Texas. (ETRC.)

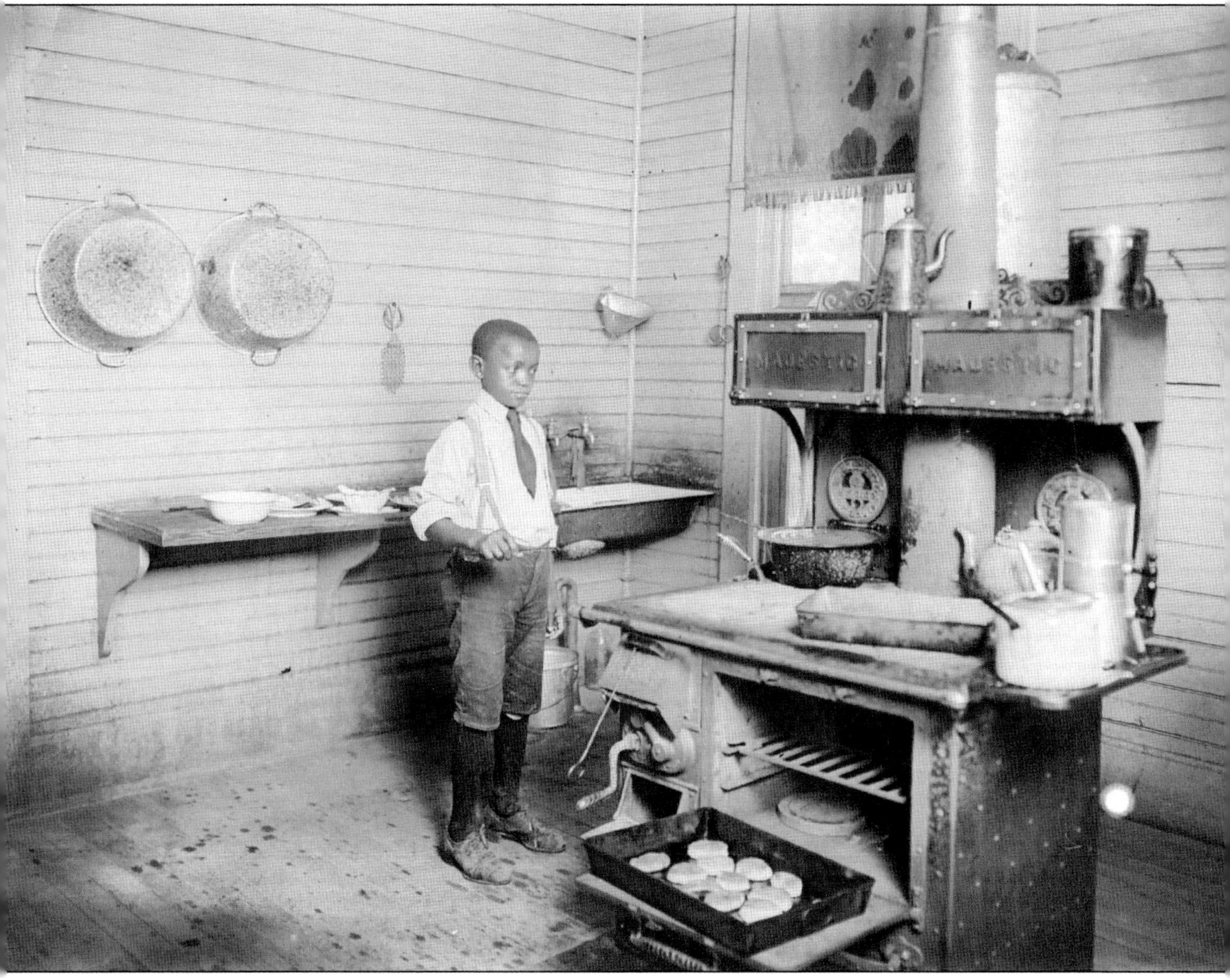

This young boy likely worked as a kitchen helper for the Thompson Lumber Company. His job would have mostly consisted of getting firewood for the stove and carrying food to the company employees once the meal was prepared. (ETRC.)

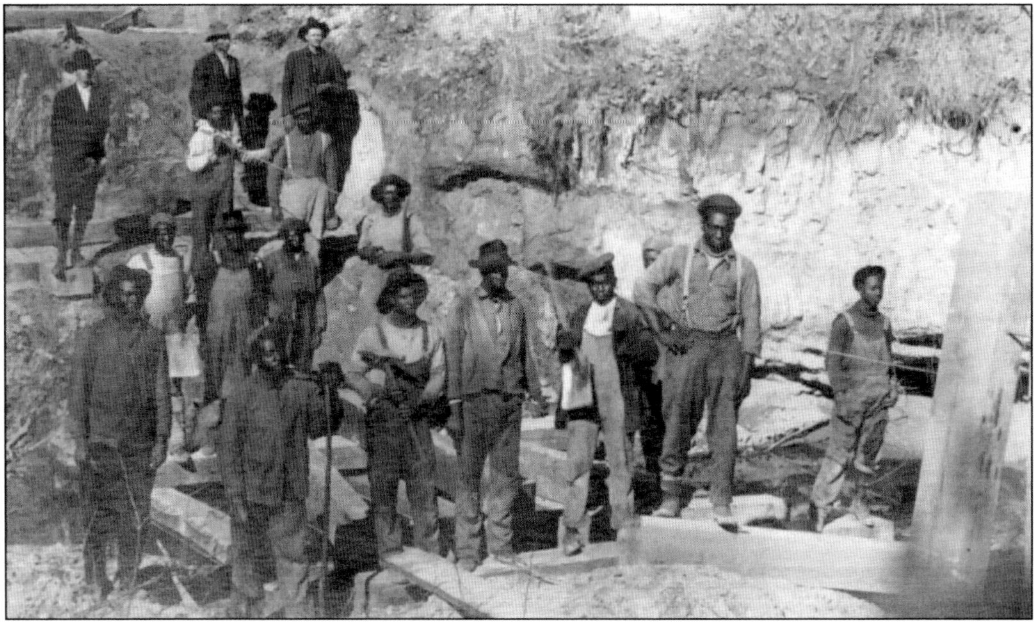

African American railroad workers were often divided into labor gangs. Steel gangs, like the one in this image, were responsible for clearing a path so that train rails could be laid. Section gangs replaced railroad ties and removed debris from the tracks in a specific section. They generally lived in section houses located about every eight miles along the track and returned home at night. Next were extra gang workers who had some of the same job duties as section workers with one major difference—when their work was completed they moved as independent units, with five to six boxcars, to the next location. There were a coach car where the foreman and his family lived, a boxcar for workers, a tanker car that carried water and laundry facilities, and flatcars that carried the equipment needed to perform the jobs. (Both, ETRC.)

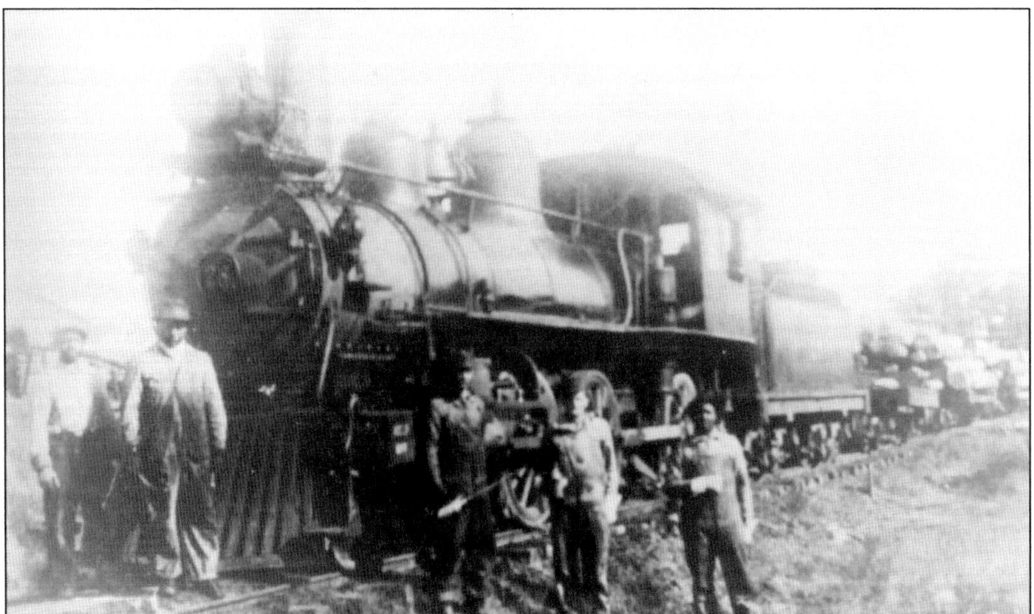

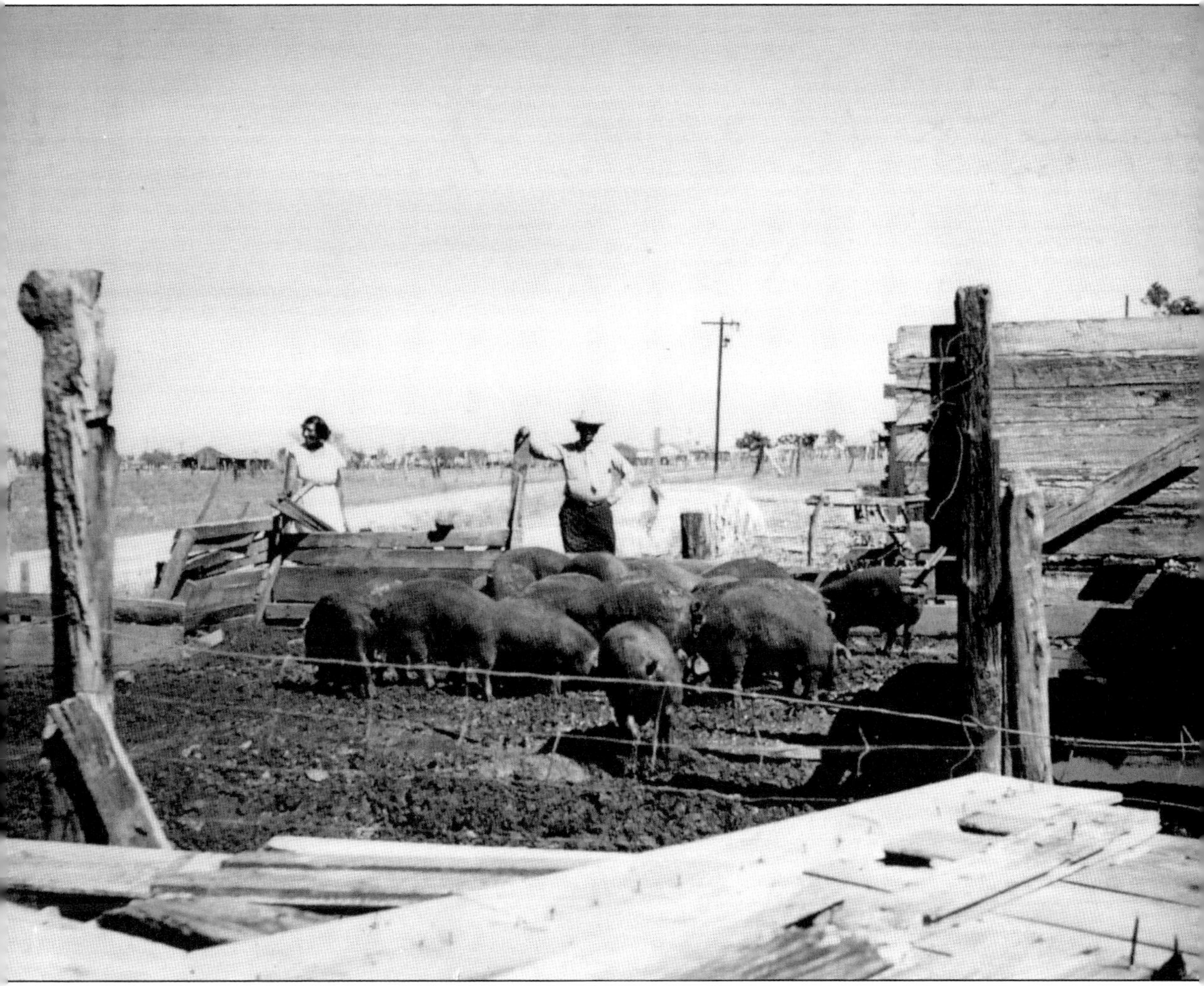

During the early 1900s, many African Americans turned to raising livestock in addition to cotton farming and vegetable crops. The hogs would be butchered and slaughtered, salted and smoked, and consumed by the farmer's family. It was common to store cured pork meat in a smokehouse. (Courtesy of Almeda Burrell.)

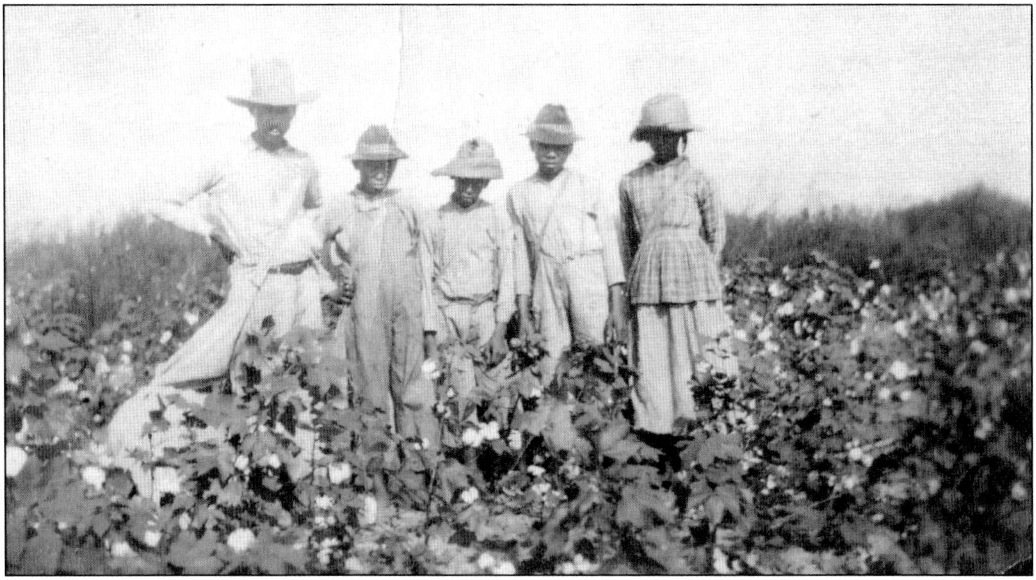

African American history reveals that slave labor was important to the slave owner's cotton crops. Their contributions played a major role in the economic success and lifestyle of the community. After the Civil War and freedom, some African Americans continued working in the cotton fields because other work was not available. Here, Charlie Rusk and his family stop to pose for a picture in the middle of the cotton field. (ETRC.)

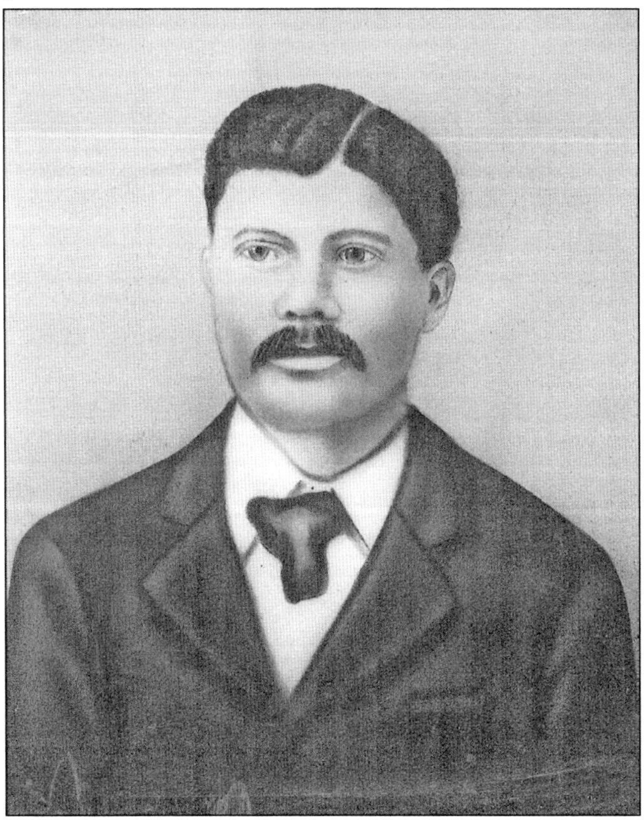

Shown is an image of John Wesley "Jack" Brown at 30-plus years of age. He was a resident of the Sand Hill community when many things were unaffordable for blacks. He made homemade grave markers for deceased family members. Reportedly, his occupations included operating a store, cotton gin, and syrup mill, and he was a carpenter, blacksmith, and farmer. He aided in building the elementary school and Sand Hill Church. He remembered seeing the first Ford Model T passing through Melrose, Texas, driven by Henry Ford himself. (Courtesy of Faye Colston Lampkin.)

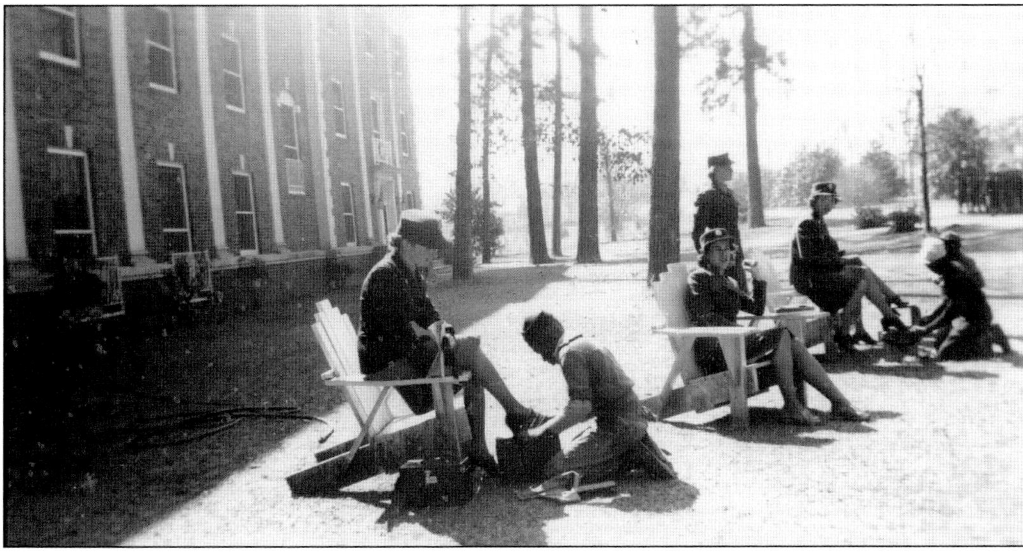

During segregation and Jim Crow laws, African Americans were limited to service jobs such as cooks, yard boys, maids, janitors, chauffeurs, babysitters, and shoeshine boys, as shown in this image. Black women ironed shirts at Price Steam Laundry; some also earned money by "taking in" washing and ironing in their homes. Most white people would deliver and pick up their washed and ironed clothes. (ETRC.)

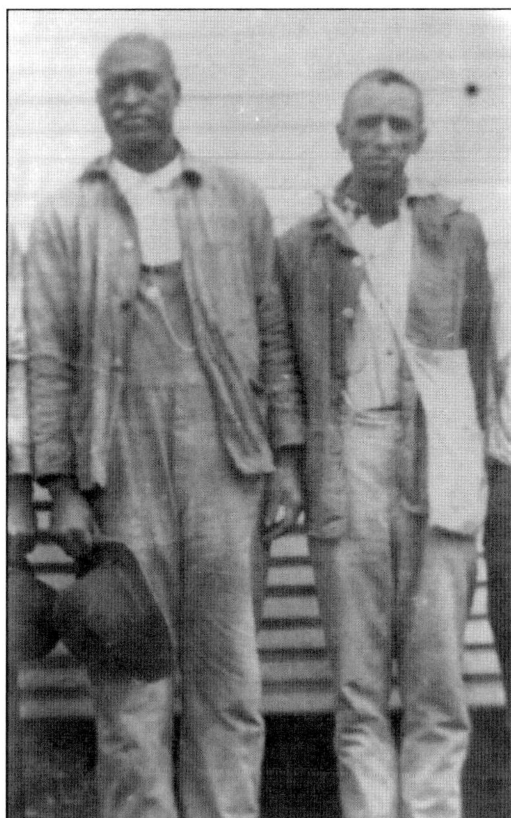

Although agriculture and logging were primary sources of employment for black men, many also found jobs as carpenters. It is unclear how these men made their living; however, the small, white sack that hangs across the one man's shoulder was typical of a carpenter's bag. Hammers, nails, and rulers were easily accessible from these strapped bags. (Mertie Mims Collection.)

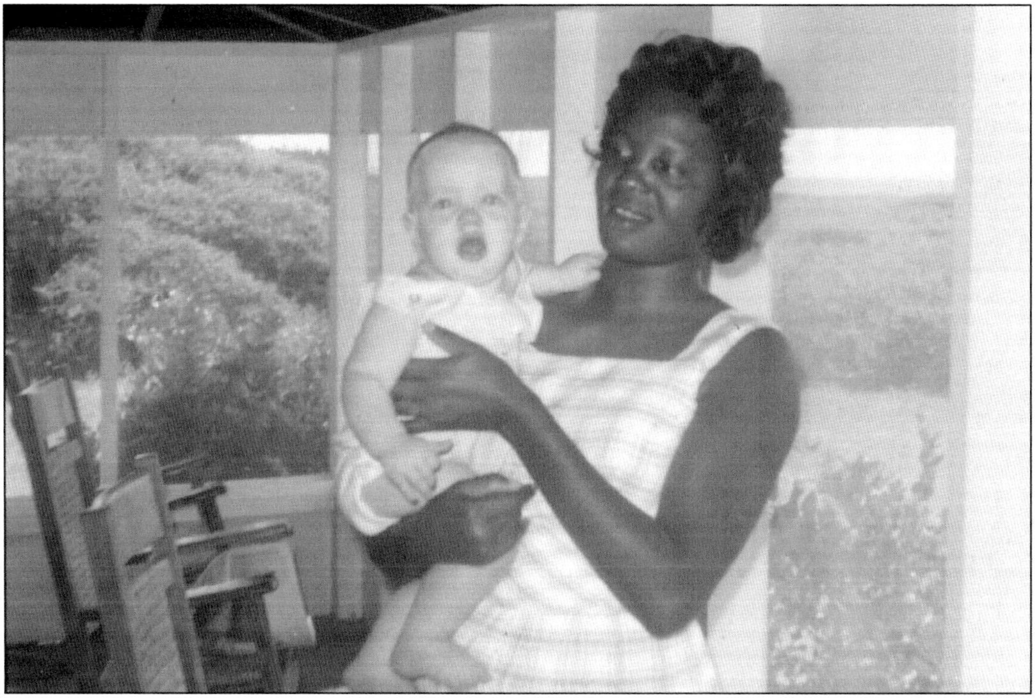

Black women were often employed in homes as caretakers for white children. In addition to caring for the children, they often cooked, cleaned, and ironed. A young Jefferson Davis is shown here with Mamie (unknown last name); she cared for him most of his life. Bryan Davis, Jefferson's son, is now a retired county attorney. (Above, courtesy of Bryan Davis; below, ETRC.)

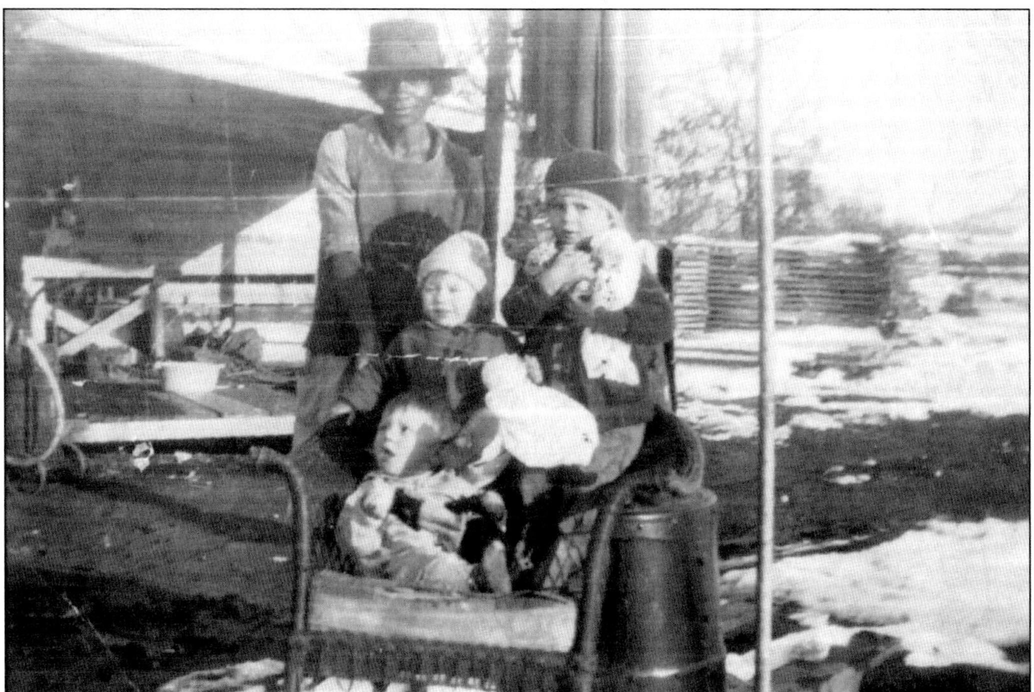

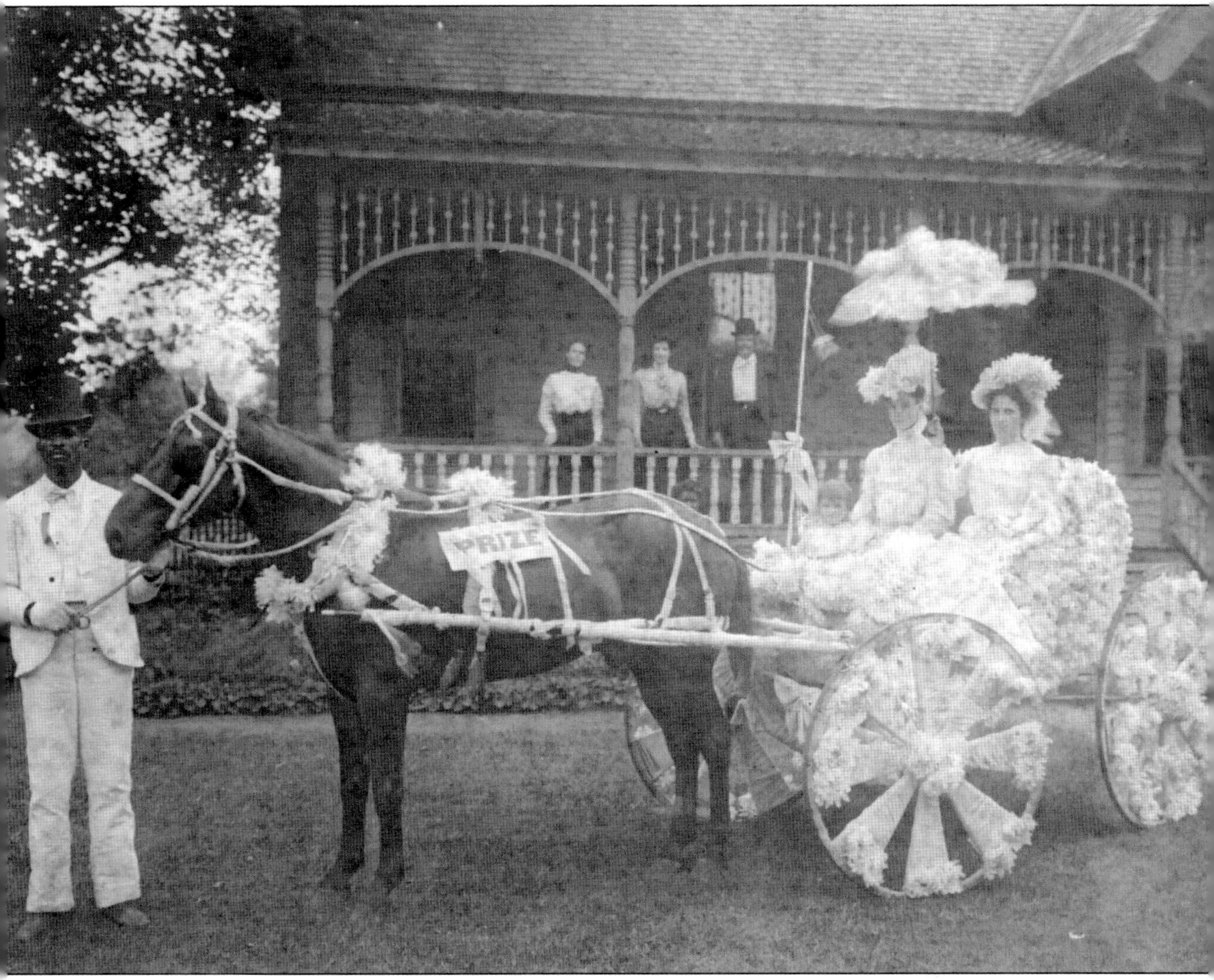

Pictured is an unidentified black driver escorting ladies participating in a parade. Driver positions were usually assigned to "entrusted employees." (ETRC.)

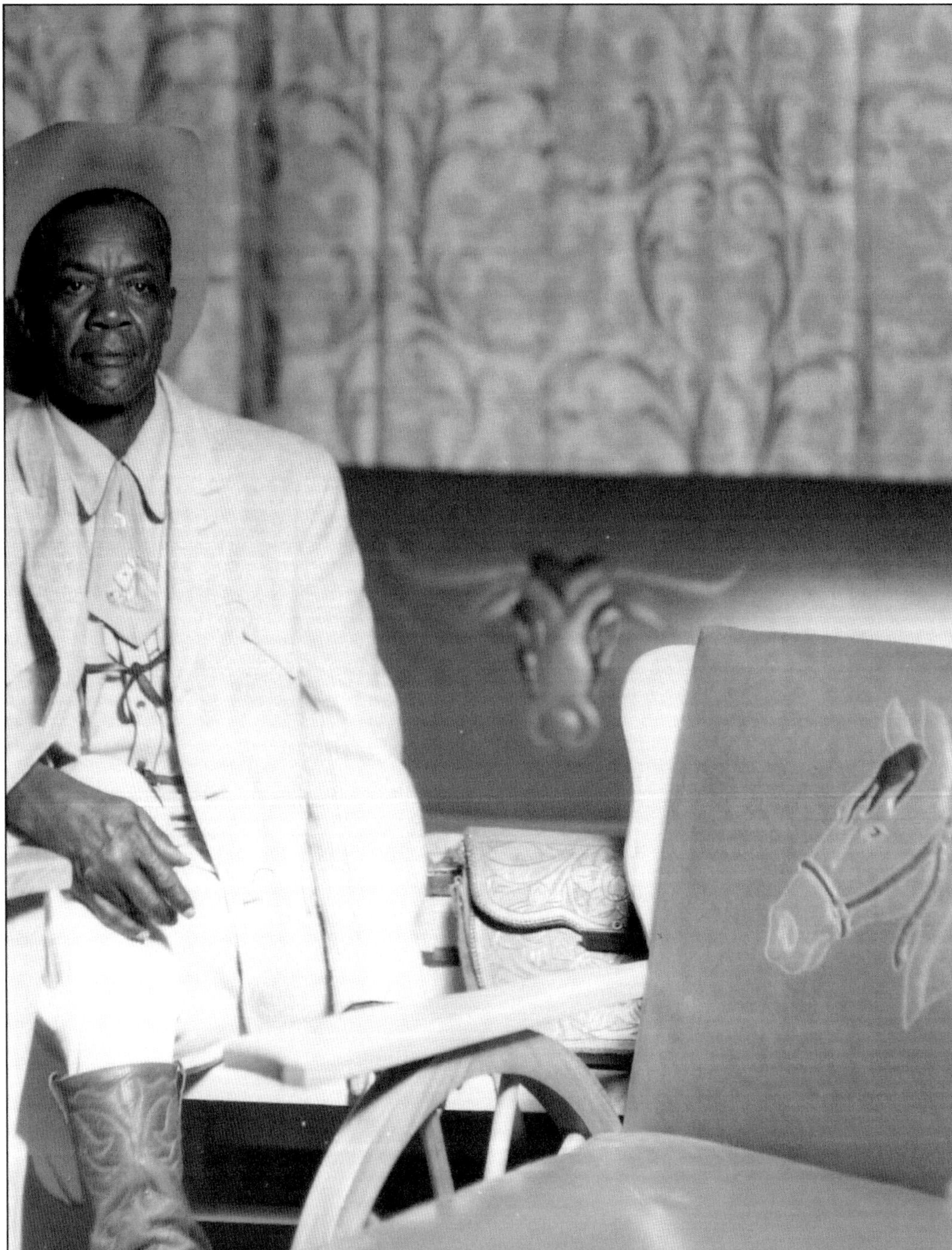

Black Texas cowboys became known when Texas was under Spanish rule. Many black cowboys were born into slavery, and after the Civil War, they were employed as ranch hands and horse breakers. Eugene Garrett, a Nacogdoches cowboy in Western attire, is photographed in a room with Western logos. Rodeos and trail riding were always popular forms of entertainment for the African American community. (Mertie Mims Collection.)

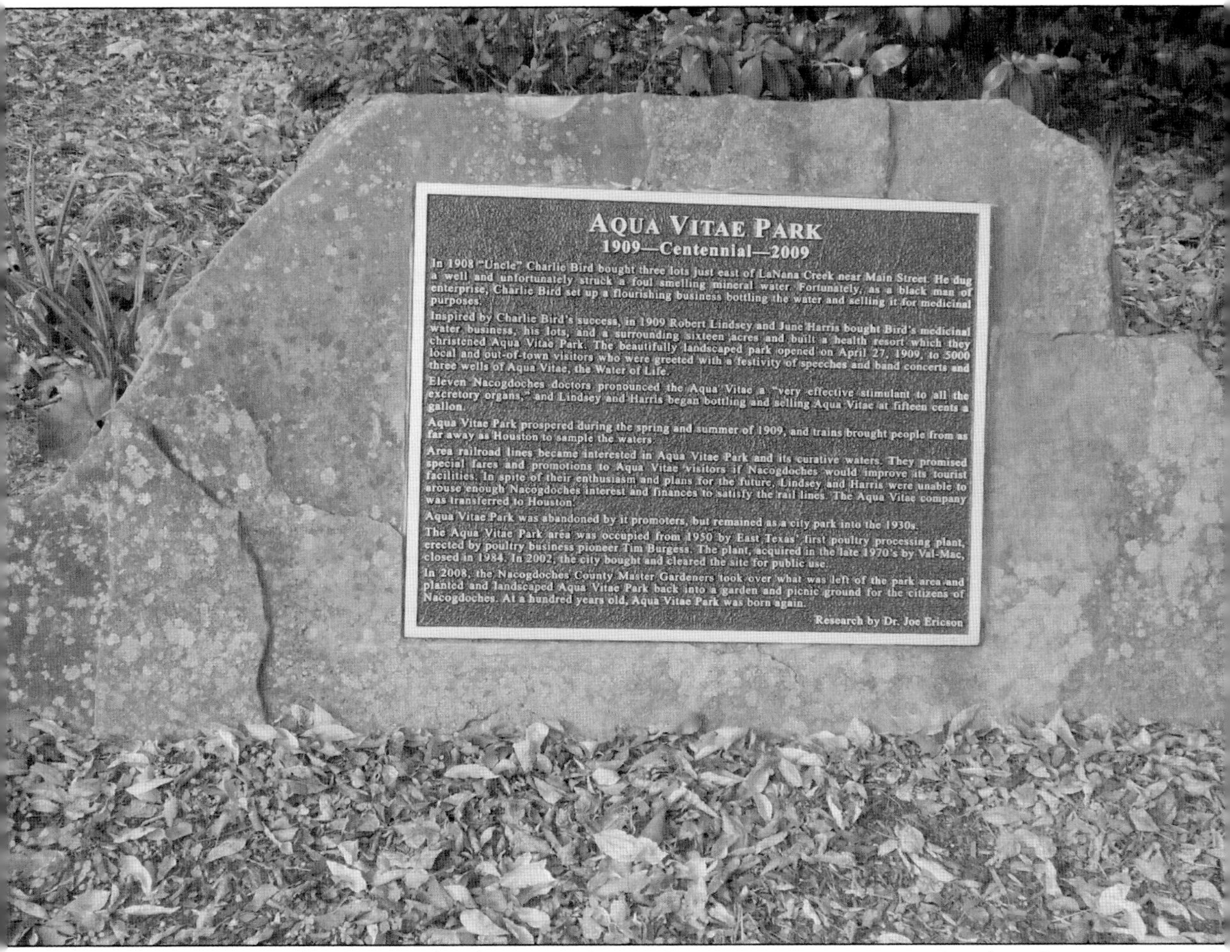

In 1908, "Uncle Charlie" Byrd, a known African American entrepreneur, purchased prime property near Main Street and LaNana Creek. While digging a well, he discovered water with a strange taste and odor, but it had healing properties for bodily ails. He bottled and sold this water over the city with much success. Unfortunately, Uncle Charlie was forced to sell his property to a white couple who created a successful business and sold the same water through Aqua Vitae Park, a resort place on the property. (Author's collection.)

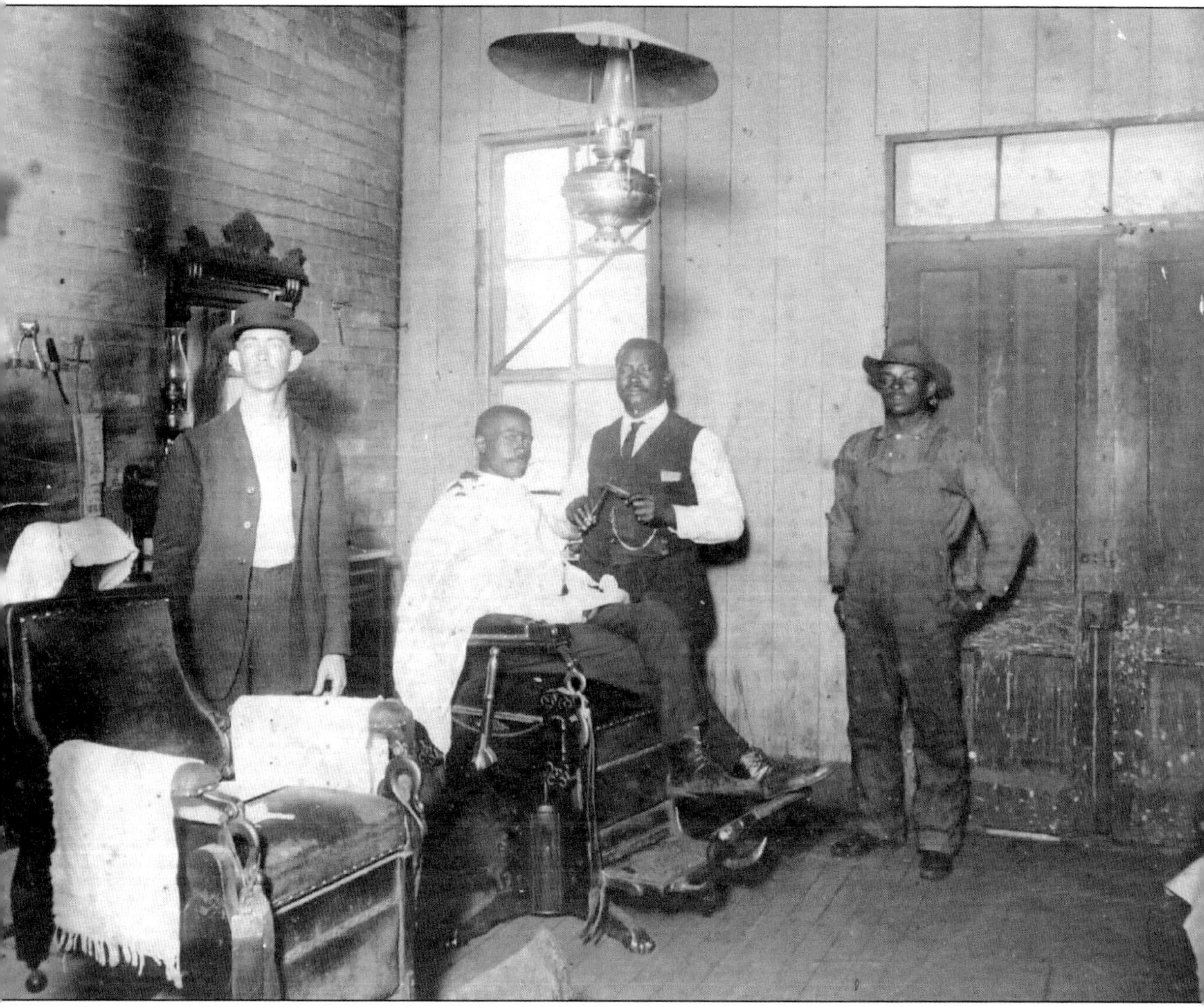

In the early 1920s, racism and Jim Crow laws forced a group of African American businesses from their location at present-day Church Street in downtown Nacogdoches. In August 1924, L.W. Smith went before the Nacogdoches City Council calling for "Moving all Negroes from North Nacogdoches" into a colored ghetto area on the south side of town. The colored businesses in this area included a tailor shop, a barbershop, restaurants, and a silent movie theater. (ETRC.)

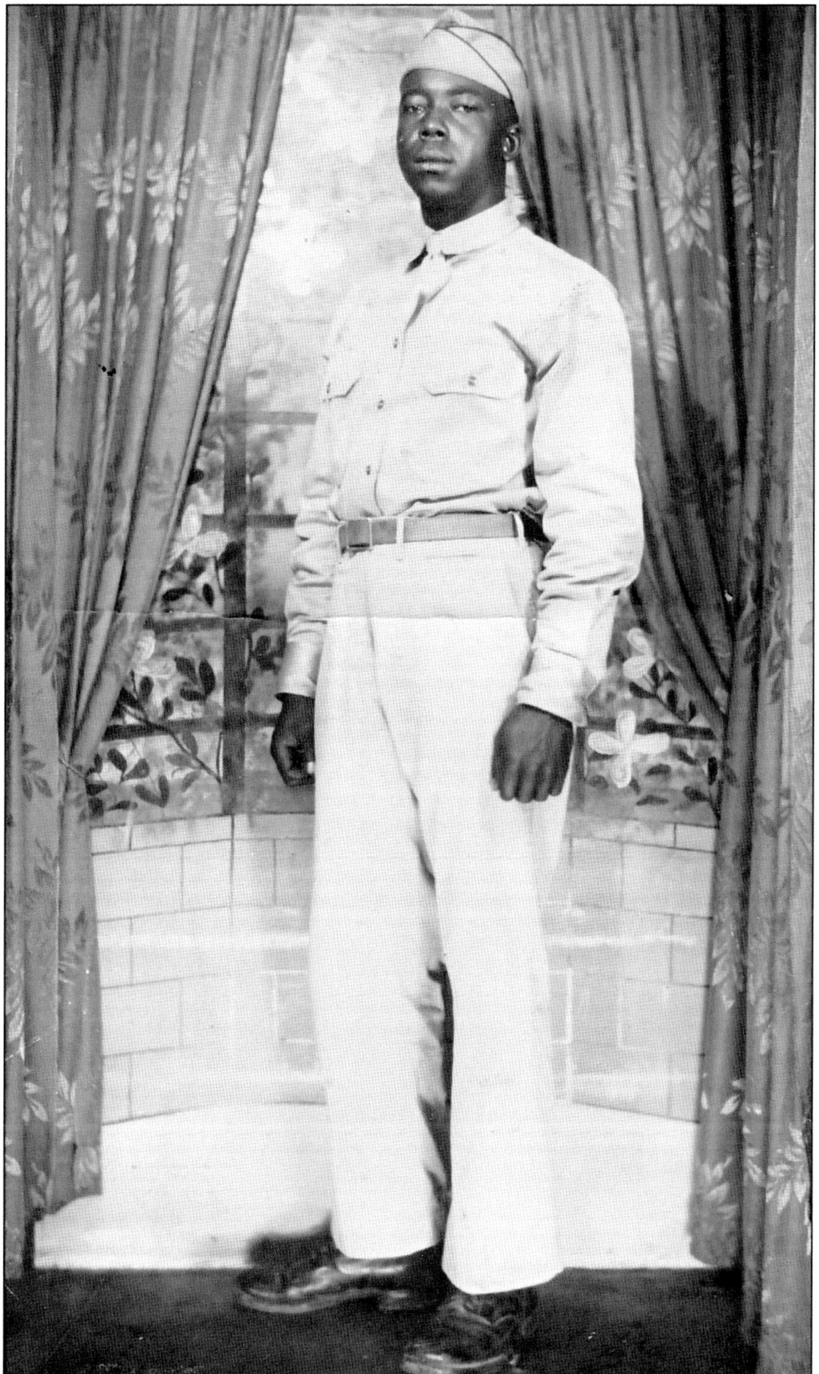

Oran Martin, while stationed in Louisiana, slipped off to Nacogdoches to marry his sweetheart Anera Randle on July 4, 1941. He served as a mechanic in Germany until the end of the World War II. When he returned from the war, he attended school on the GI Bill and worked as a mechanic at Lone Star Feed Company for 35 years. Anera, now age 90, still lives in the house bought with the money she saved from Oran's war pay. (Courtesy of Anera Randle Martin.)

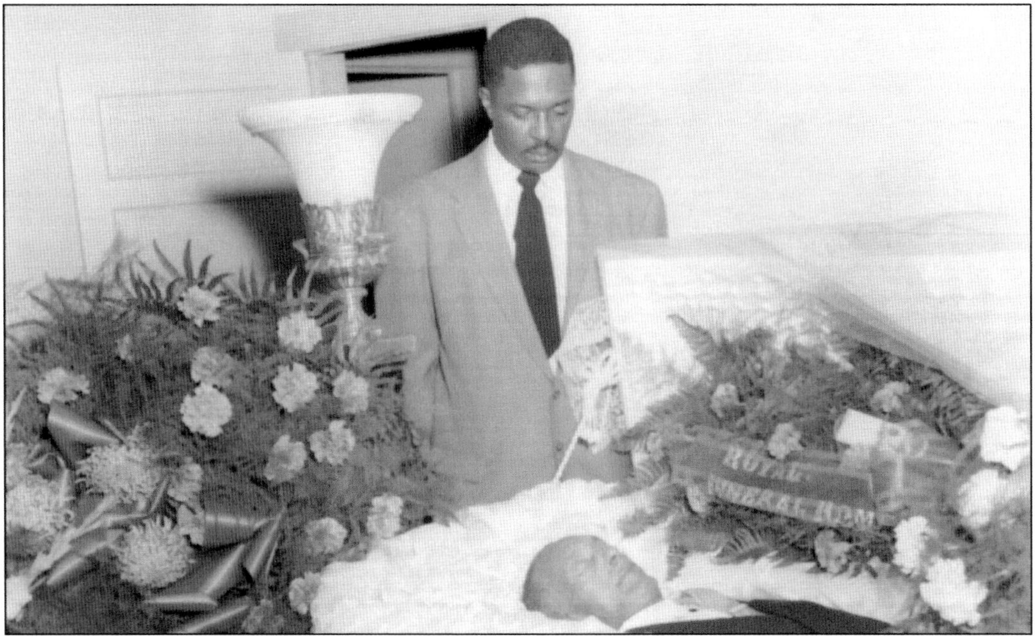

Royal Funeral Home was one of two black funeral homes established in Nacogdoches. In the early 1930s, Sid Roberts opened Royal Funeral Home and, later, moved it into the building once used as a black hospital on Shawnee Street. After Sid Roberts passed away in 1970, the funeral home was named Sid Roberts Funeral Home. The present Sid Roberts Funeral Home is located on Stallings Drive and is owned by Sid Roberts's nephew Noel Cotton. (Mertie Mims Collection.)

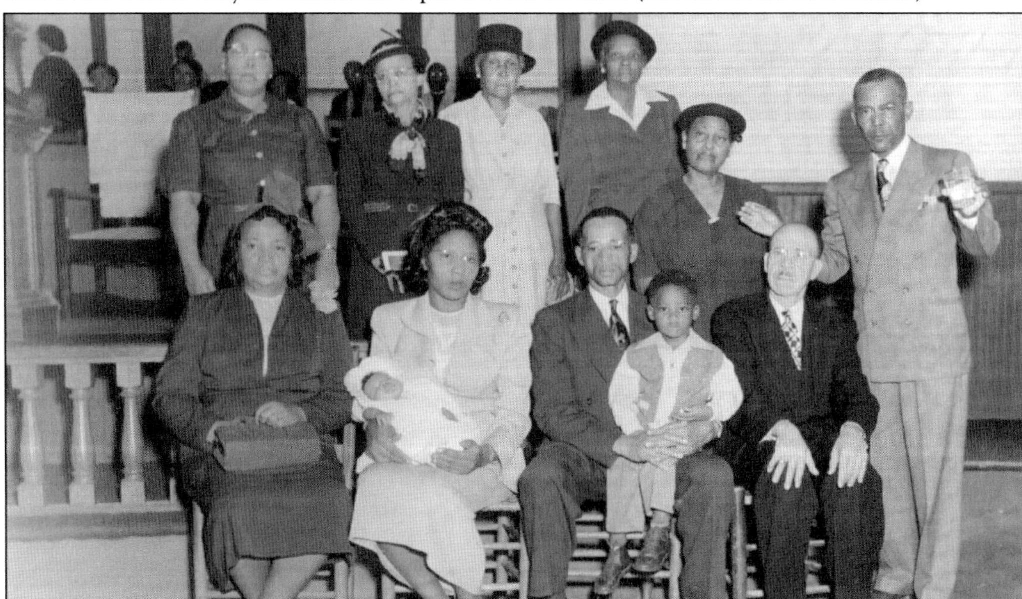

The Sadlers owned one of the two black funeral homes in the area; the funeral home was located on historic Shawnee Street. The first Sadler Funeral Home was established in the early 1930s, and the family still owns this business at the same location today. Otis Sadler Sr. and his wife, L.E. "Tealee" Sadler, holding their infant daughter Jacqueline and son Otis Sadler Jr., were a prominent African American family in the city. (Mertie Mims Collection.)

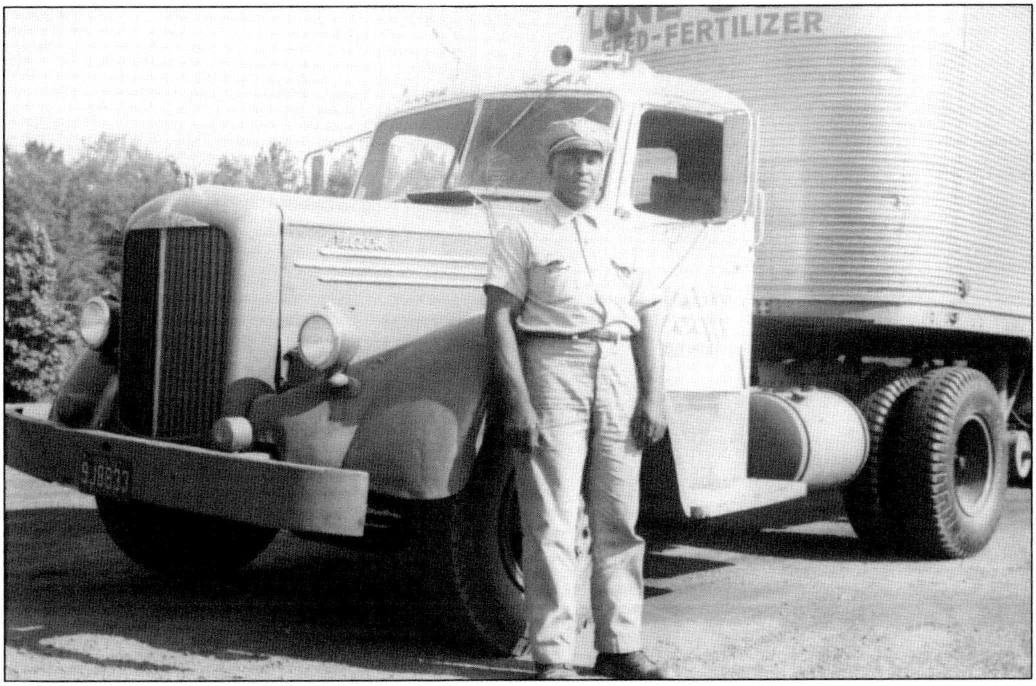

Noel Mims was one of the first employees hired at Lone Star Feed Company, second only to the founder M.S. Wright, who started the company in 1930. Mims was hired to drive the first company-owned truck; he was the company's main driver for 35 years before he retired. He was known for his strength and his ability to "pick up a bale of hay and walk with it." Black men with stable positions working for white people were elevated higher in the black community. (Mertie Mims Collection.)

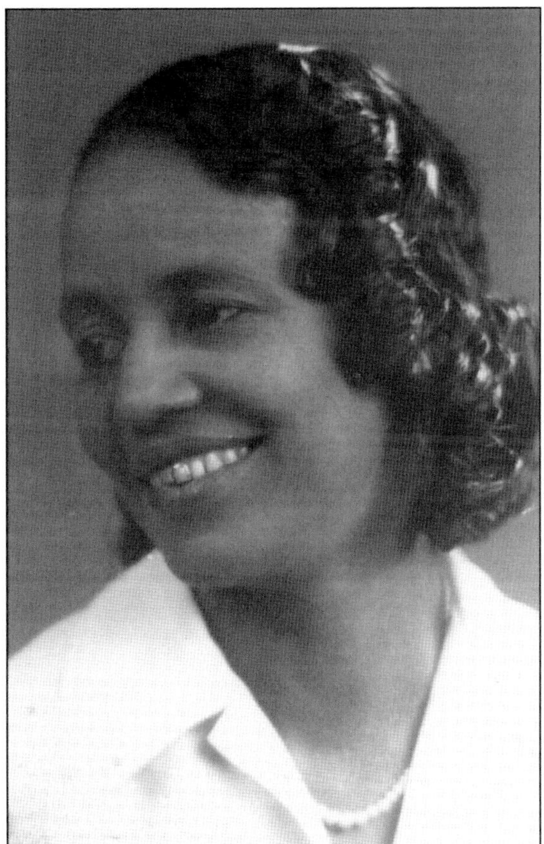

Mertie Jones Mims moved to Nacogdoches after she married Noel Mims in 1935. She worked as a medical assistant at a hospital built for blacks on Shawnee Street in the early 1900s. Mims earned her place in Nacogdoches history as the only African American and female photographer, owning and operating her own professional photography business from a home studio on Orton and Shawnee Streets. She photographed graduations, church groups, weddings, and social events and took individual and family portraits. (Mertie Mims Collection.)

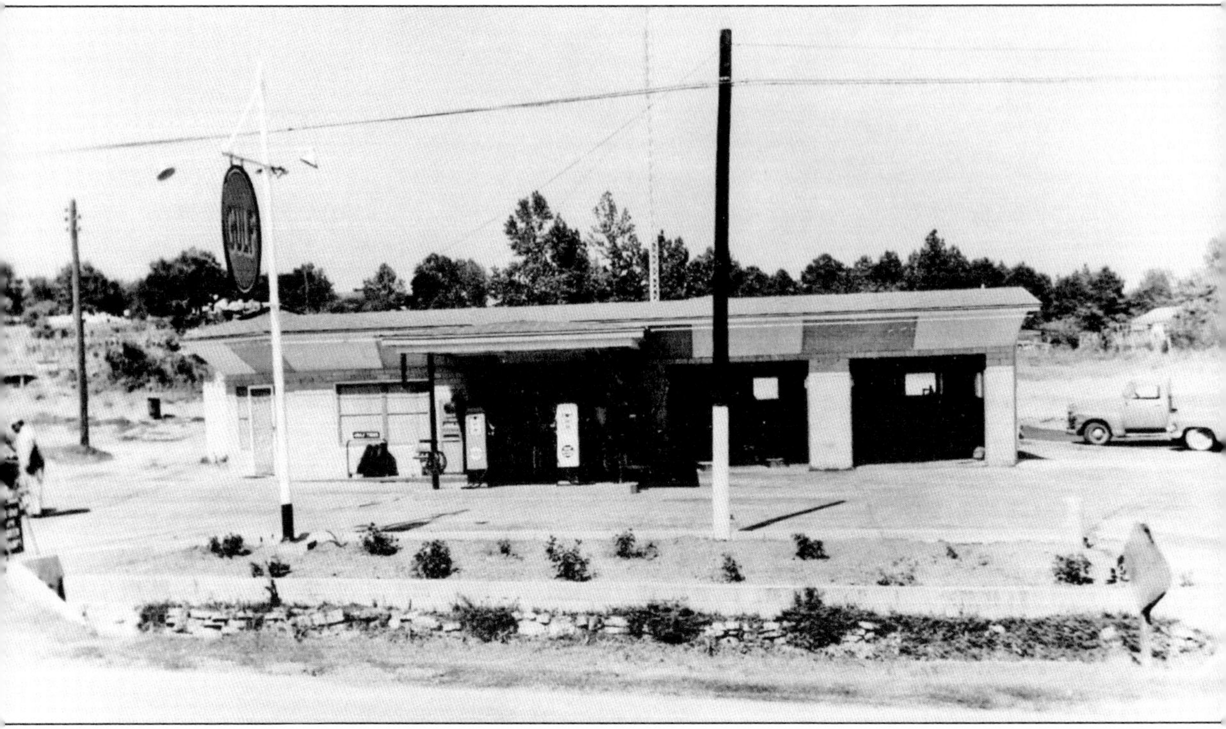

The Colston Gas Station was located on the corner of Butt and Shawnee Streets and was owned by Ira Colston. Prior to that time, the station belonged to Earnest Holman, who is credited for being the first African American service station owner in the city. (Mertie Mims Collection.)

Two

Believing in the Word

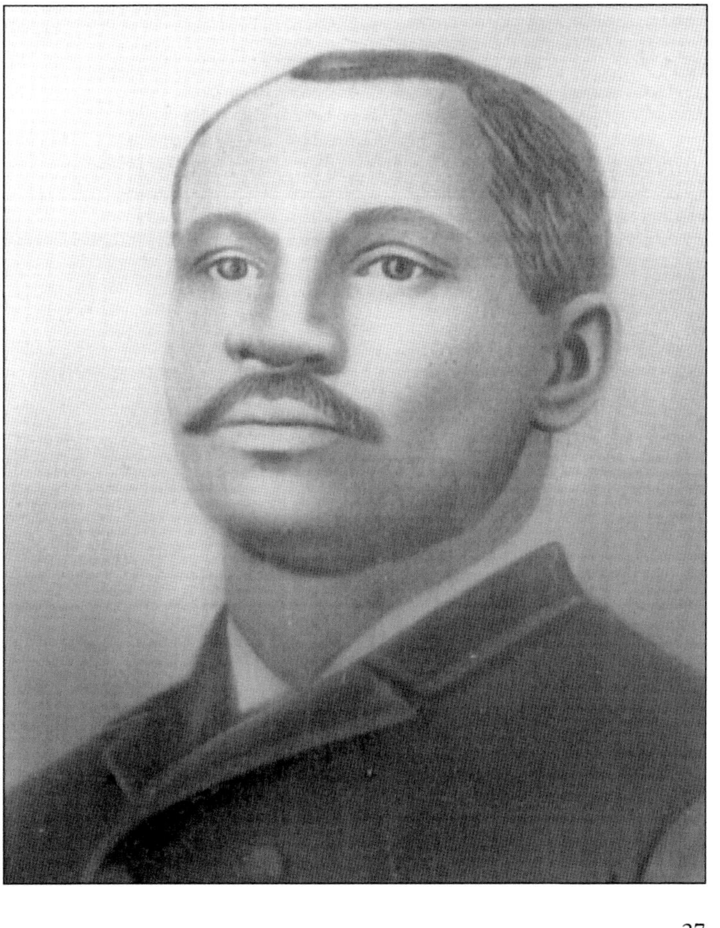

Rev. Lawson Reed contributed means and efforts to establish the first churches for blacks in Nacogdoches. Records reveal that he organized more than 50 African American churches of all denominations in the area. This included the historic Zion Hill Church, where he served as pastor for 25 years until his death in 1924. Clarence "Bo" McMichael, a legendary educator and coach in Nacogdoches, is the grandson of Lawson Reed. (ETRC.)

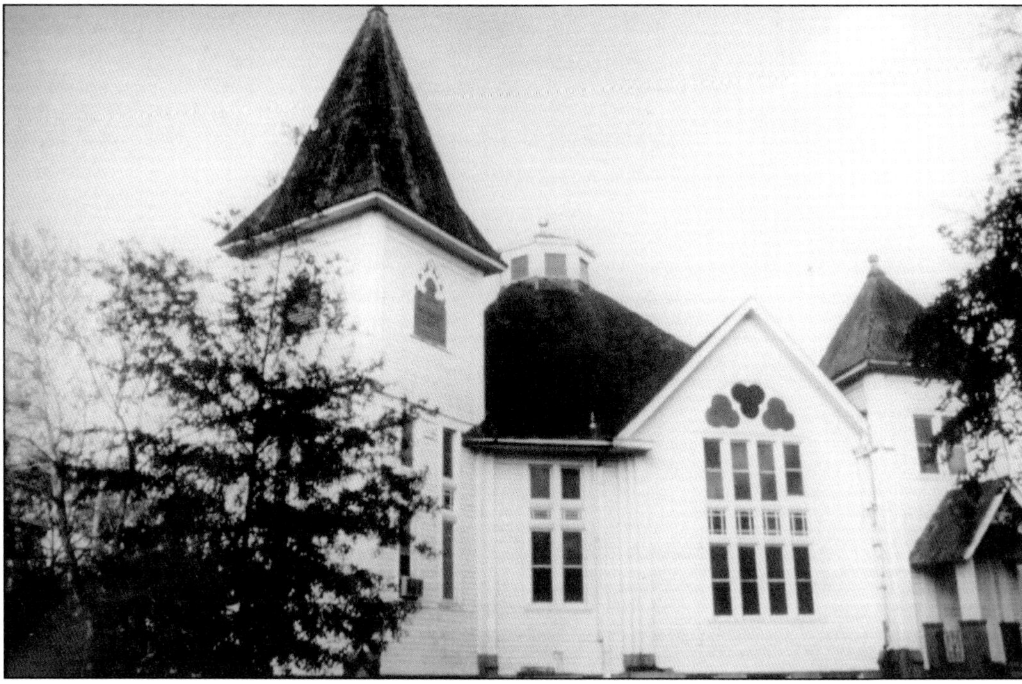

Zion Hill Baptist Church, established in 1878 by Rev. Lawson Reed, was the first organized church for African Americans in Nacogdoches. The church is located in the Zion Hill Historic District and was designed by German architect Dietrich Rulfs. The church's longevity and unusual Victorian features have earned recognition from the Texas Historical Commission and the Nacogdoches Historical Commission. The current Zion Hill congregation is housed in a modern structure on Stalling Drive. (ETRC.)

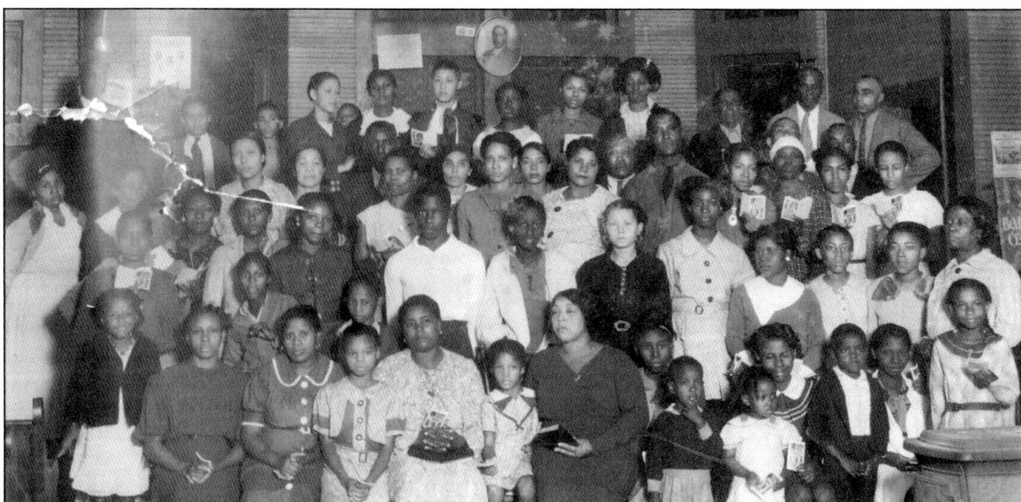

Early Nacogdoches African American churches made up the community's core focus. This image shows one of the early congregations of Zion Hill Baptist Church gathered in front of the church, possibly after Sunday morning services. The church was located on the edge of the established, predominately white, community because most blacks settled near their places of employment. (ETRC.)

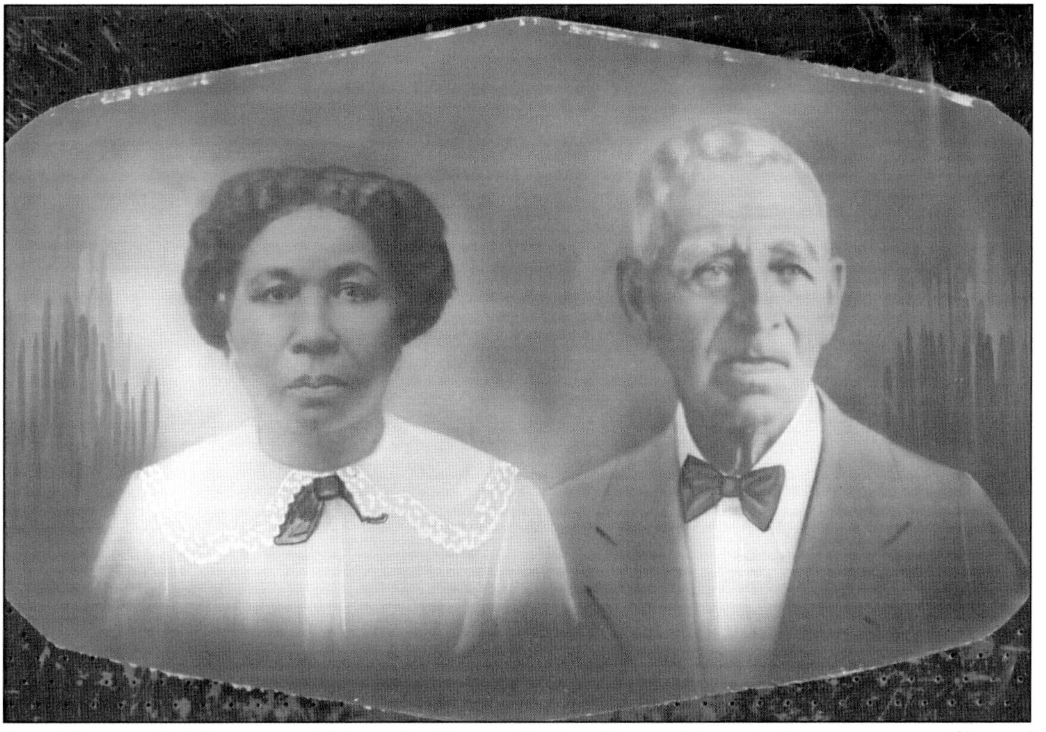

Rev. Horney C. Cleaver and his wife, Nancy Eunice Queen Victoria Burrow, were pillars of the early African American community in Nacogdoches. They held this status until Cleaver's death in 1932. He was the first Negro to teach black children. The school was in a small cabin near Banita Creek. The location of the church-school building is unknown but is believed to have been in the Little Creek community, near the location of the old Southern Pacific Railway Station. (ETRC.)

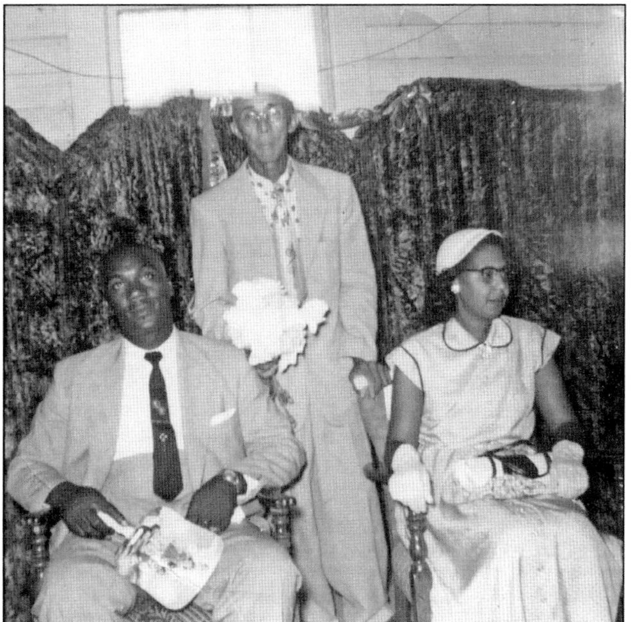

In the early years, rural churches had what were called pastoral Sundays one or two Sundays a month. Pastoral Sunday was the Sunday the preacher or pastor came to preach. The preacher many times travelled quite a distance to get to the church, sometimes spending the night with a member. Pictured are, from left to right, Rev. A.B. Lewis, George Skillern, and Lulu Lewis in 1955. Reverend Lewis pastored Sand Hill Baptist Church for almost a quarter of a century. He had to travel from Henderson or Tyler twice a month to Sand Hill for morning worship and stayed for Baptist Training Union and evening worship as well. (Courtesy of Sand Hill Baptist Church.)

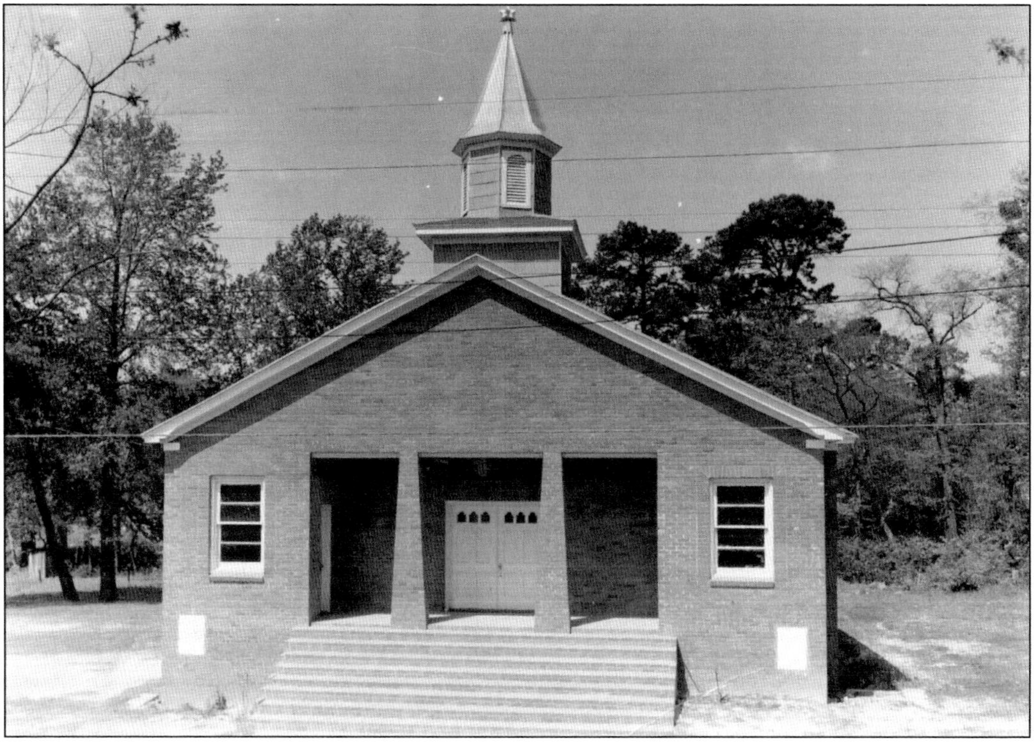

In 1924, Rev. Moran Allen had a vision to establish a church in the new area for blacks in Nacogdoches. The founding members met with Reverend Allen at Curry's Skating Rink, which was used as the first church until 1926. The church later moved to a community domino shack. The current structure was erected near this site and is presently located on First and Orton Street. Rev. James Ervin is the current minister of the new church, which is seen in the image below. (Both, courtesy of Iron Wheel Baptist Church.)

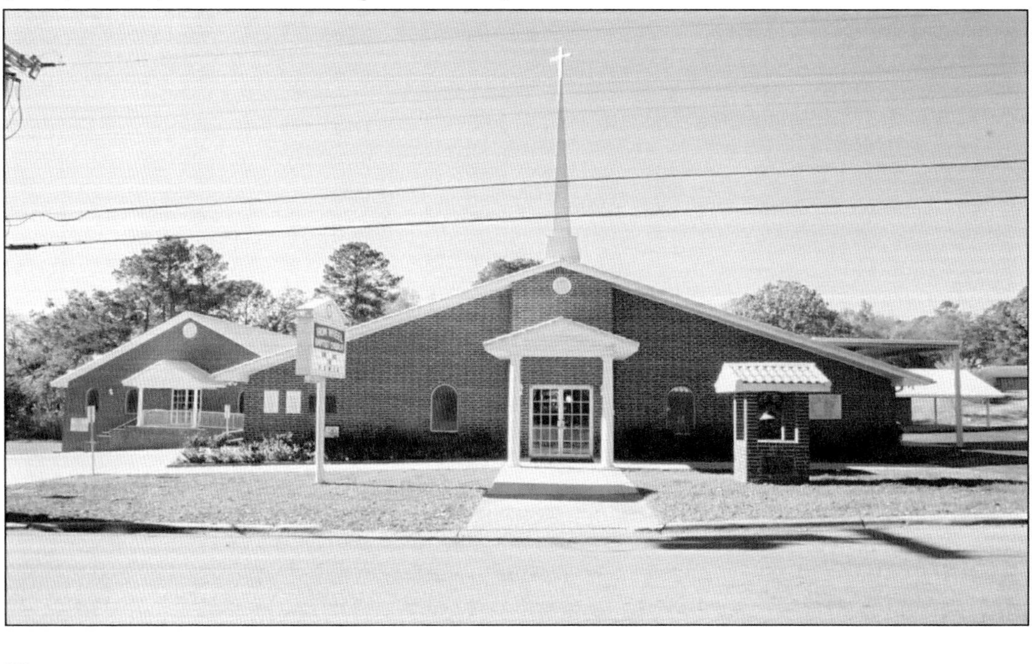

Captured here is a baptism ceremony, one of the most sacred traditions within the black Baptist church. Typically, the minister and a deacon escort the candidate into the water where a prayer is recited before the individual is dunked in the water. The stick in the foreground of the picture was used to determine the depth of the water and when necessary to ward off snakes. (ETRC.)

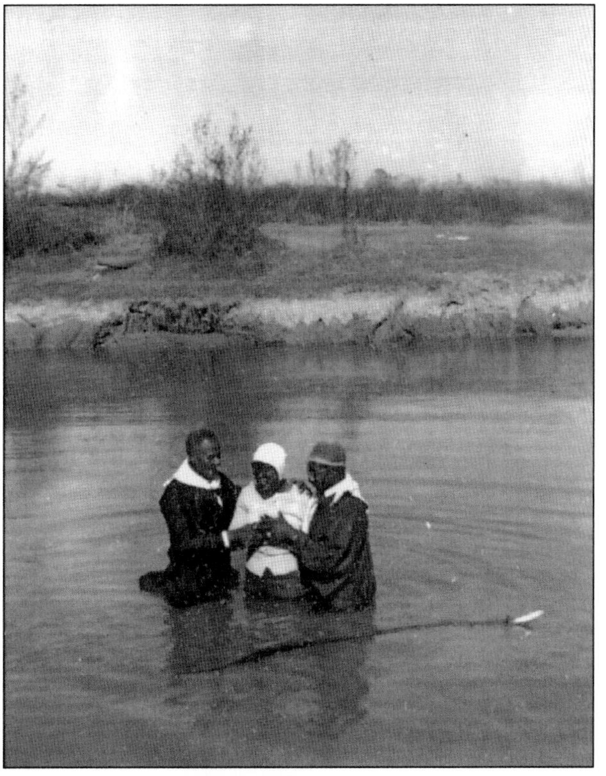

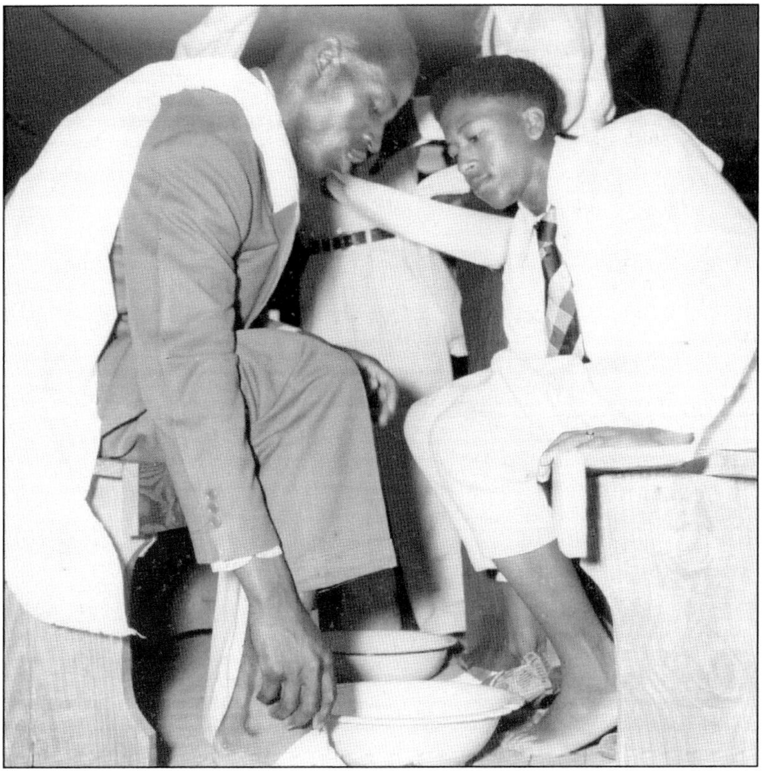

A foot washing ceremony took place inside the church. In John 13: 6–11, Jesus stated, after washing the disciple's feet, "if I then, your Lord and Master, have washed your feet; ye also ought to wash one another's feet. For I have given you an example, that ye should do as I have done to you." Some Christians believe this act was to show hospitality and humility. (ETRC.)

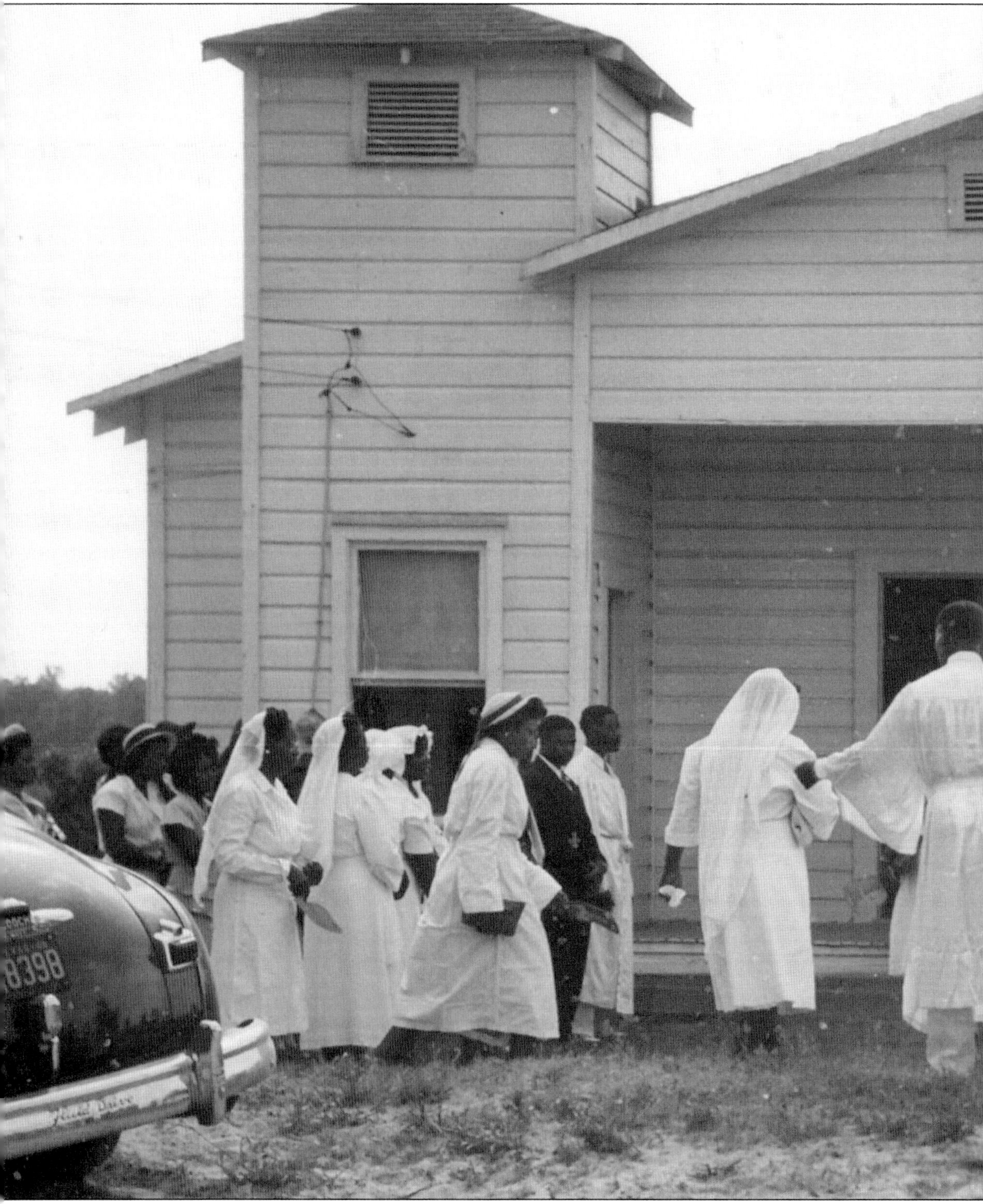

Lone Star Primitive Baptist Church, now known as Lone Star Baptist Church, originally formed in 1889. It was organized, under the direction of Elder F.D. Jackson, Ed McDaniel, and Jerry

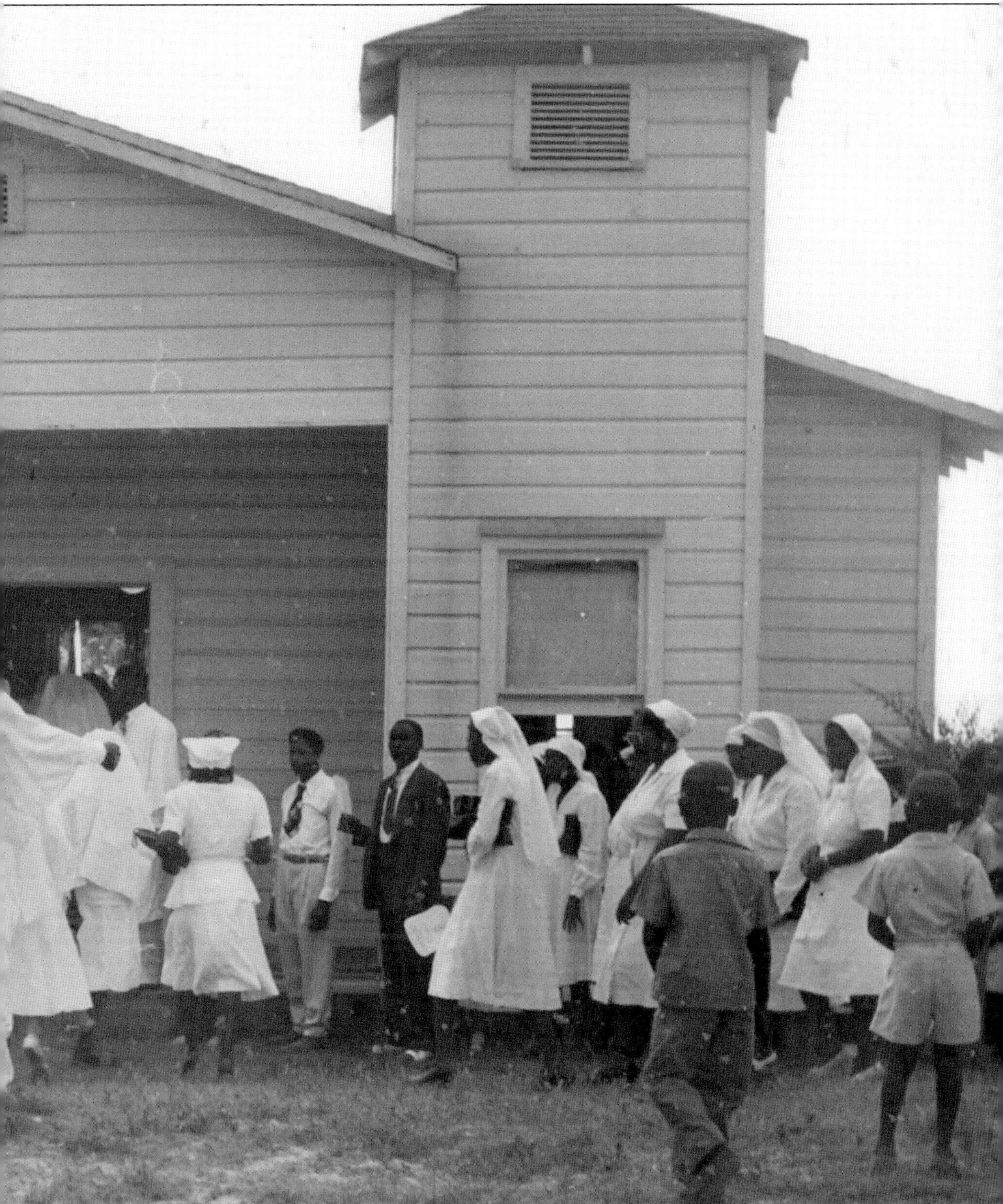

Maise, in the home of Charlie Lee. As of 2013, the church is over 120 years old and still has an active membership. (ETRC.)

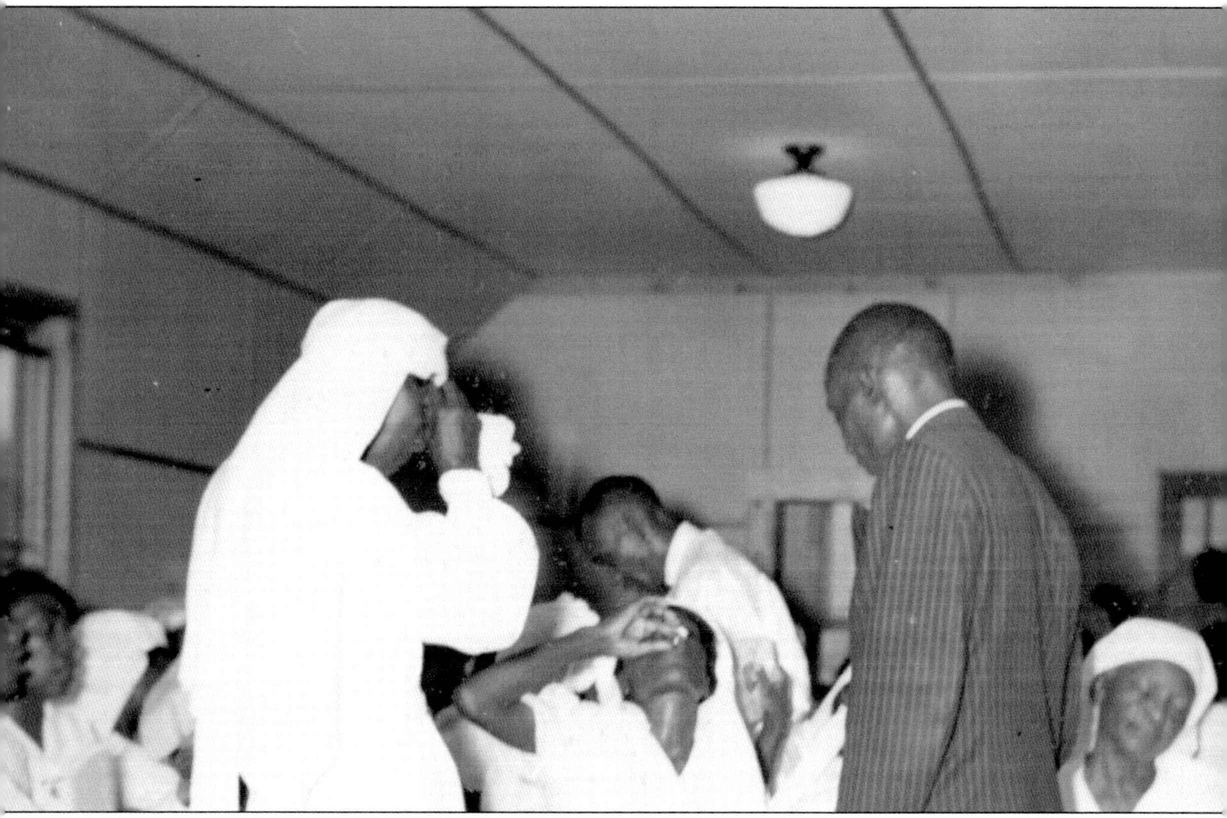

Although it is unclear exactly what is happening in this image, it is likely that church members were participating in a communion service or drinking holy water. Communion is a time when Christians remember Christ's life, death, and resurrection. Holy water is water that has been blessed by any religious authority. (ETRC.)

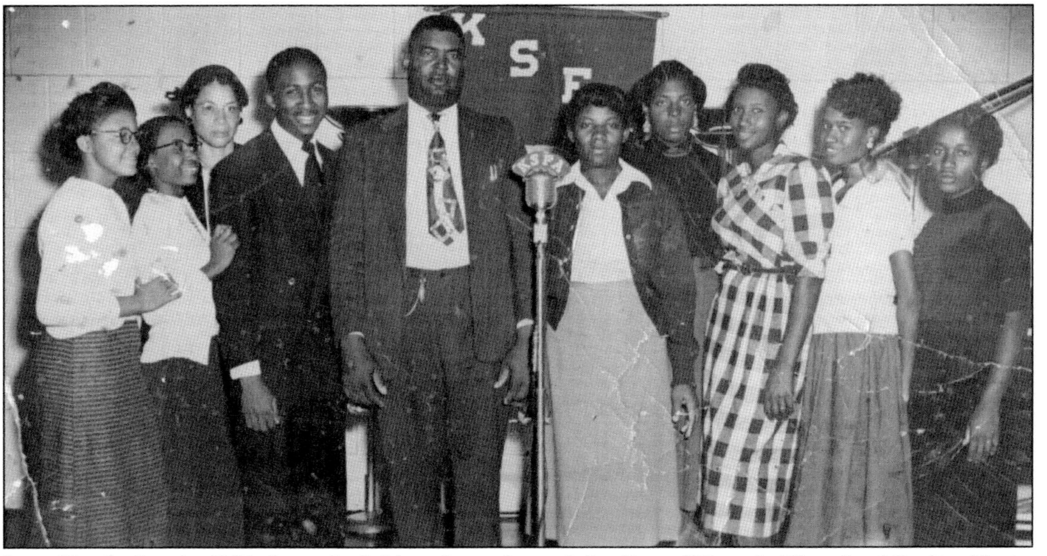

Rev. Charlie Jacobs (fifth from the left) and members of the Gospel Temple Church of God in Christ stand in front of the microphone at their weekly Saturday evening radio program. The broadcast often featured gospel singing, community service announcements, and brief sermons. (ETRC.)

This photograph was taken during performance of an Easter program with the young people in the choir. The homemade flower arrangement on the pillar is a reminder of how people during that era were creative in beautifying their surroundings. A portion of a cross that was a prop for the program can be seen in the foreground. Rev. A.B. Lewis is in the pulpit. (Courtesy of Mable Ferguson Hall.)

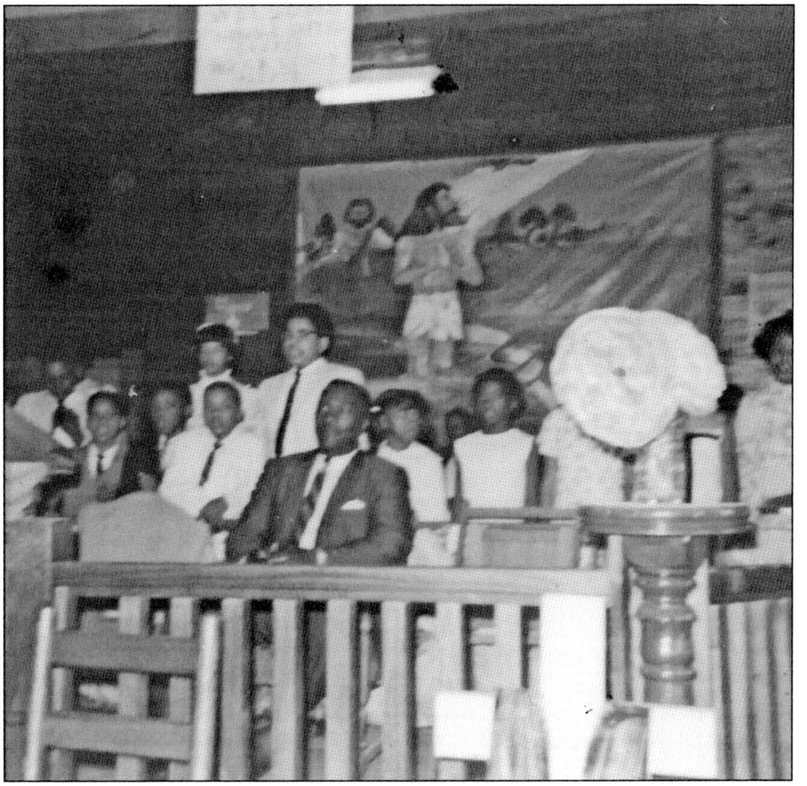

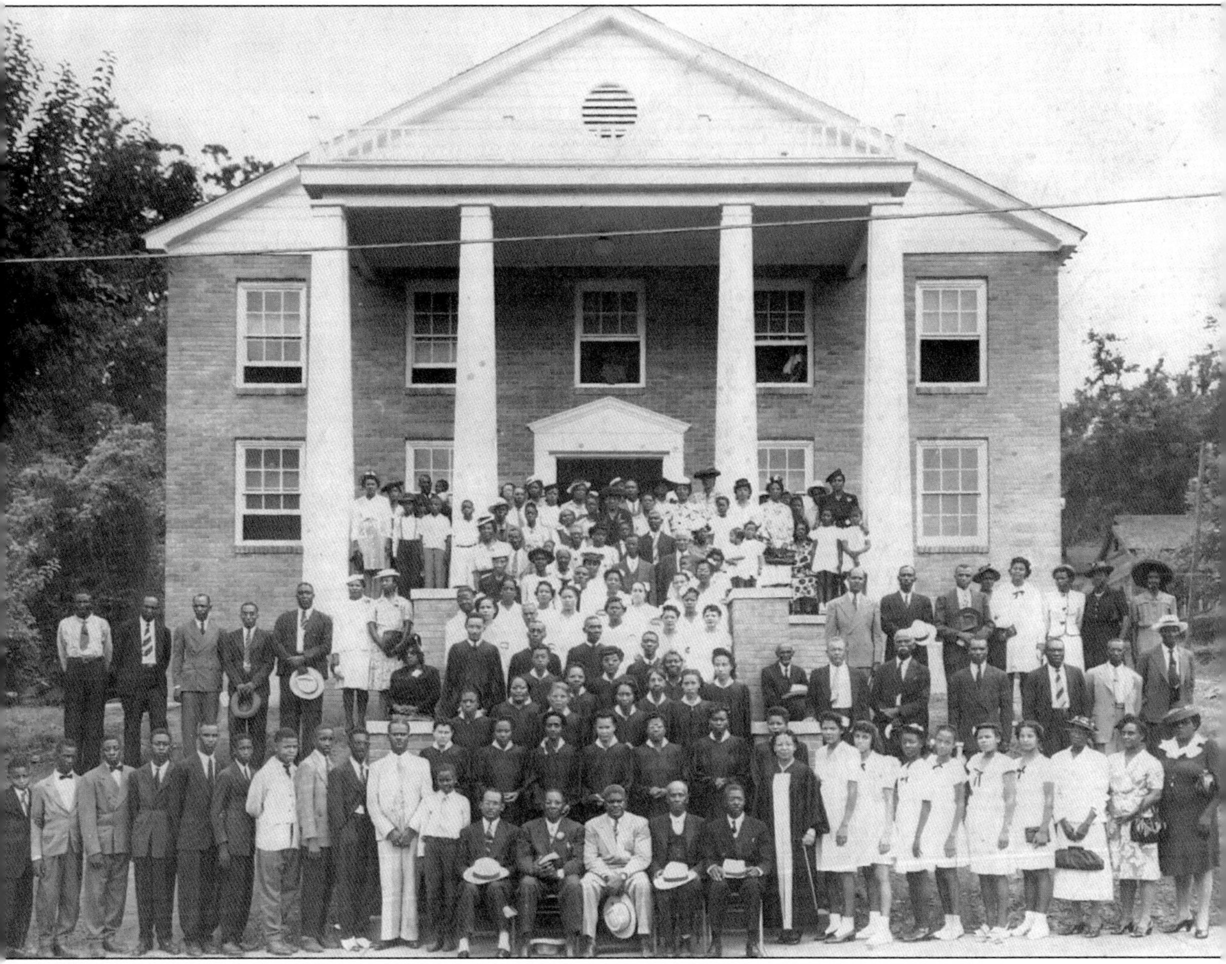

Taken in 1945, this image of Little Zion Baptist Church, located on Shawnee Street, shows the newest church building. The first church, established in 1905, was originally called Second Baptist Church. This church was an outgrowth of the original Zion Hill Baptist Church. Rev. P.M. Rhodes was the first minister, and the current minister is Rev. A.D. Mills. (Mertie Mims Collection.)

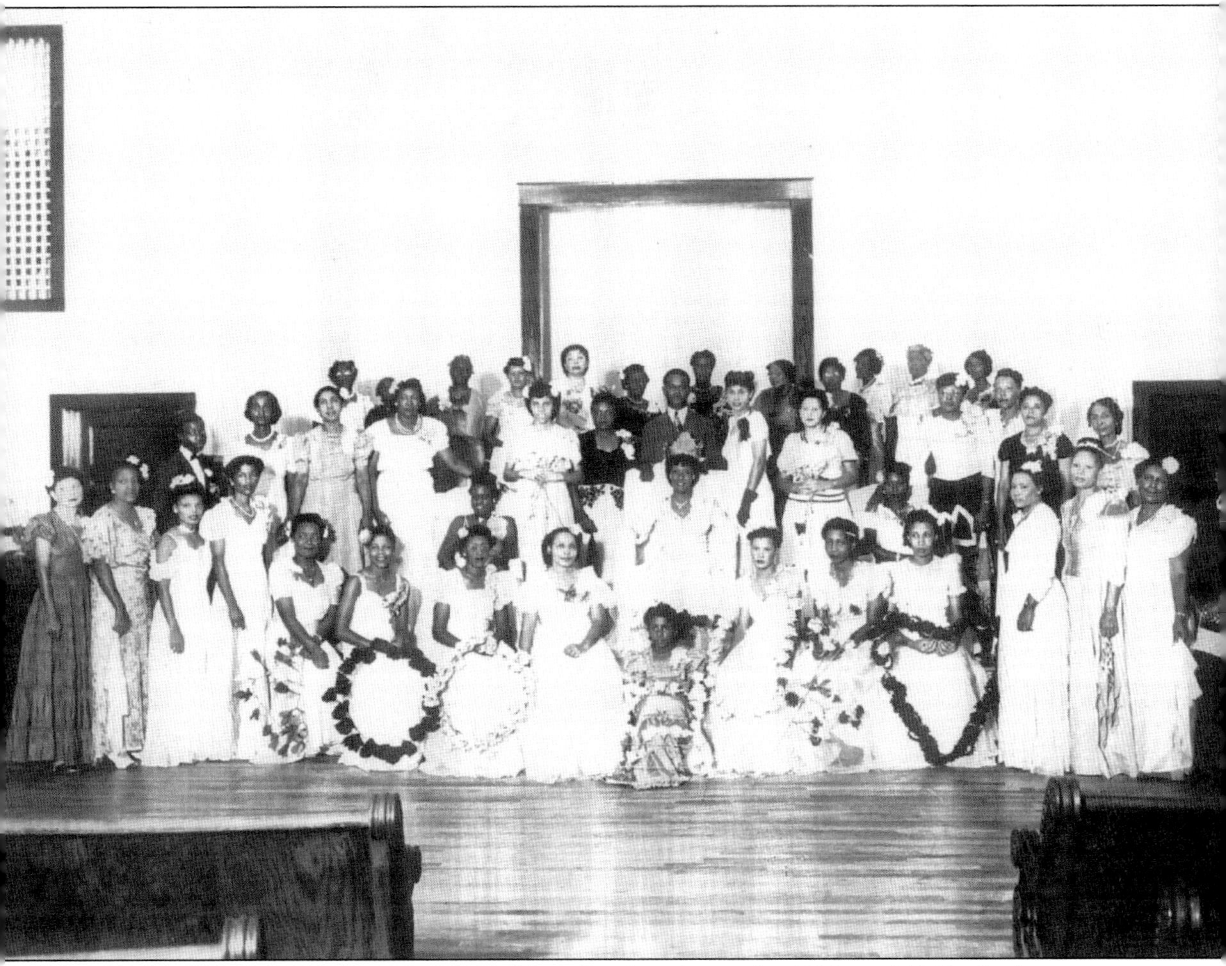

Many community social events were held in churches during the 1930s and 1940s. In this image of the inside of Little Zion Baptist Church, a young lady has just been crowned church queen of 1945. She received this honor because of the amount of money she raised on behalf of the annual fund-raising event. Rev. N.C. Chappell, who stands behind her in the center of the picture, helps crown the queen. (Courtesy of Little Zion Baptist Church.)

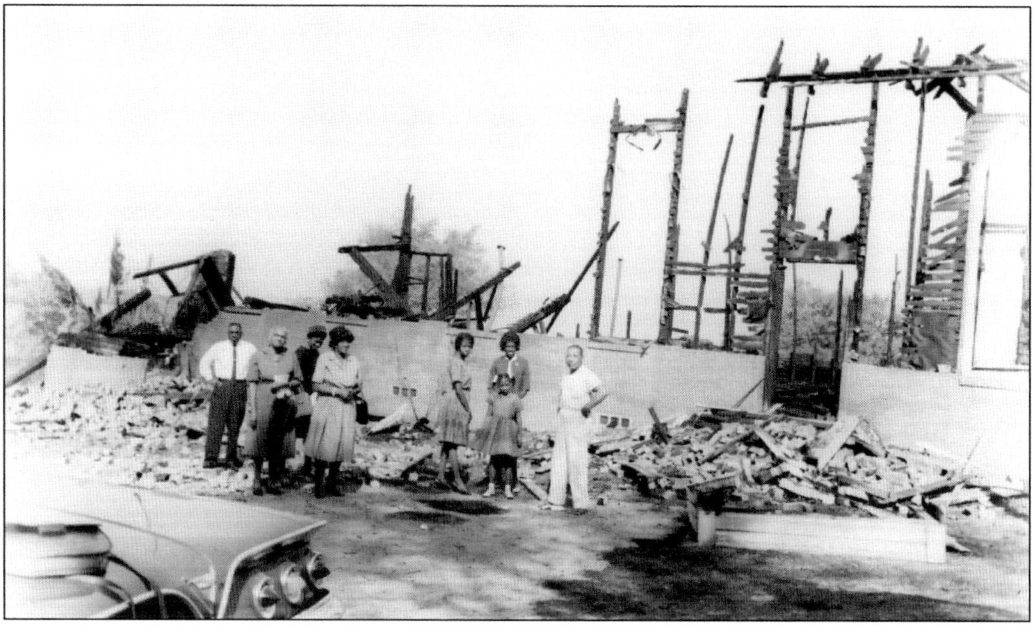

St. Paul Christian Methodist Episcopal Church was erected in 1875. This image shows the church, which was destroyed by fire in 1959 or 1960. It is not known how the fire began, but strong community support and combined efforts led to the completed rebuilding of the church in two years. St. Paul Christian Methodist Episcopal Church is the oldest black Methodist church in the city. (Mertie Mims Collection.)

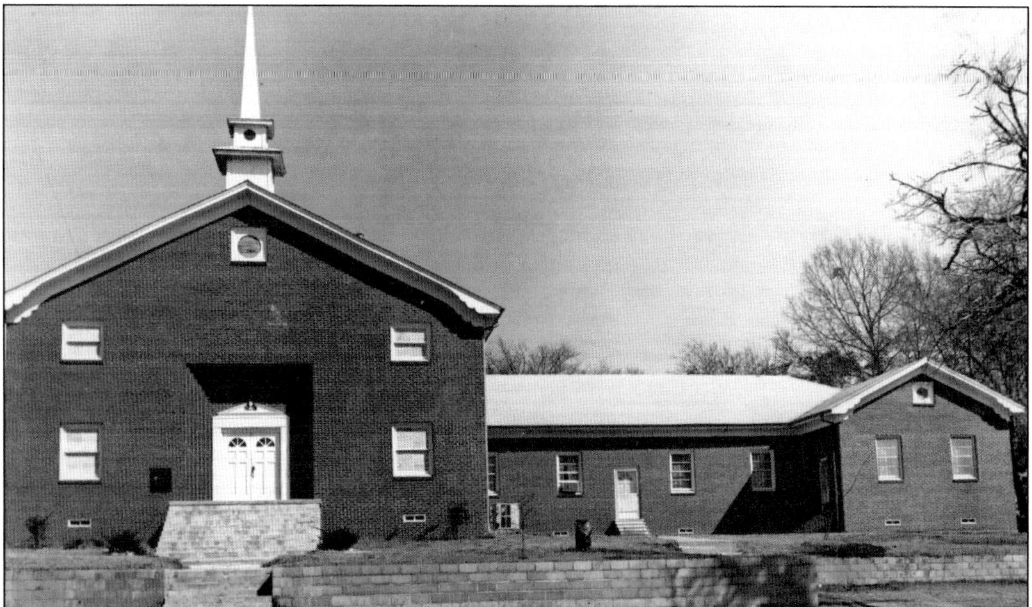

In 1875, a small group of Christians met with Rev. Lawson Reed and formed the Union Church, which was initially supported by three denominations—Baptists, Methodists, and Presbyterians. The Methodist congregation formed a separate church in 1875 and named it St. Paul Methodist Episcopal Church. In 1900, the church moved to its present location on the corner of Greer and Moore Streets. (Mertie Mims Collection.)

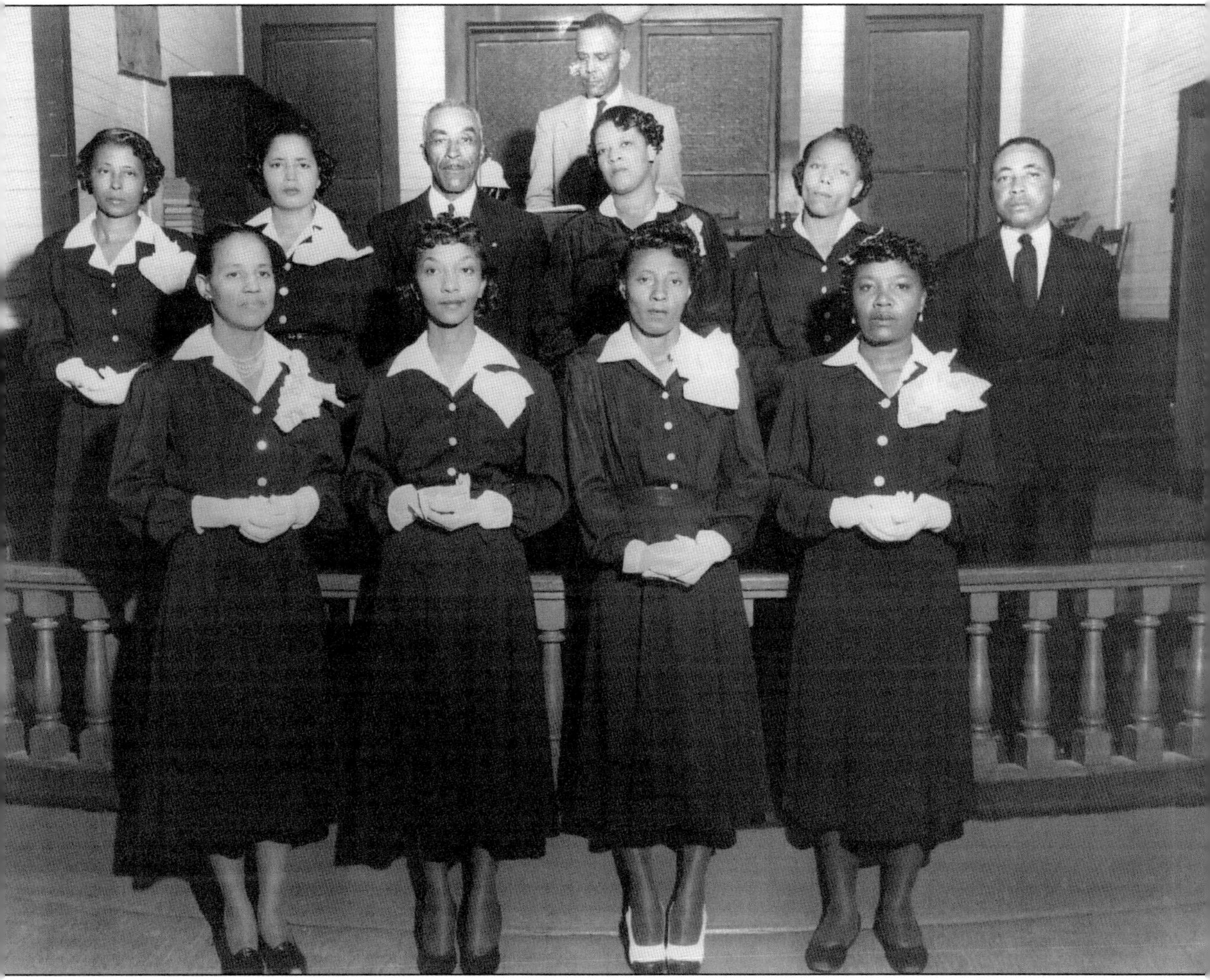

The role of the usher board is considered one of the most important roles in an African American church. They meet and greet people with smiling faces and make them feel comfortable at the church service. In this image at St. Paul Methodist Episcopal Church, it appears the ushers have completed their training to learn church order, precision, and obedience. (Mertie Mims Collection.)

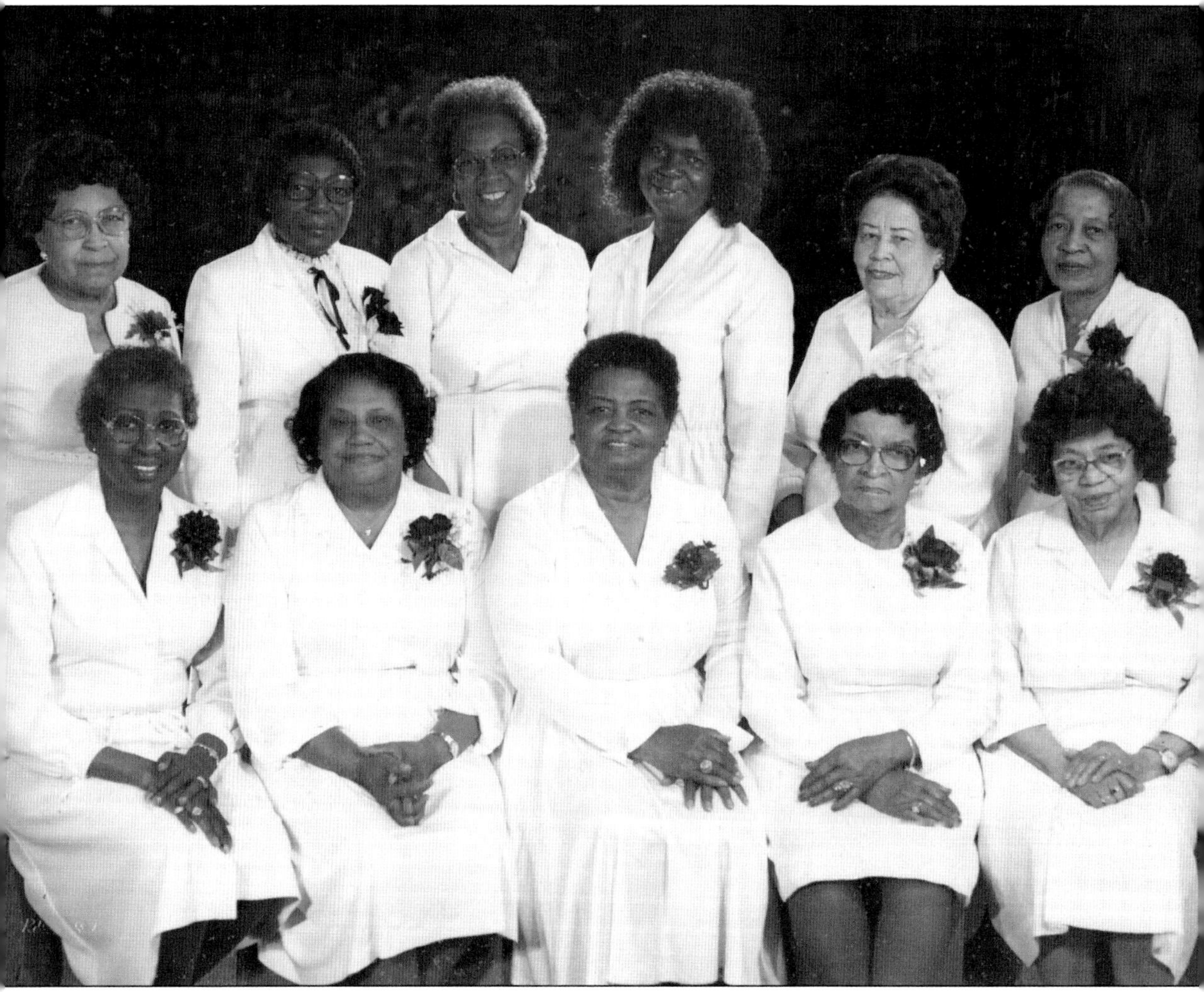

In most black churches, the mission groups looked forward to wearing white because they believed being dressed alike showed unity. In this image, members of St. Paul Methodist Episcopal Church pose for a formal photograph, most likely before or after a church event. Most mission groups are committed to supporting all church activities and willing to help one another. The black church and mission societies have been intertwined since slavery. (Mertie Mims Collection.)

Three

Reading, Writing, and Arithmetic

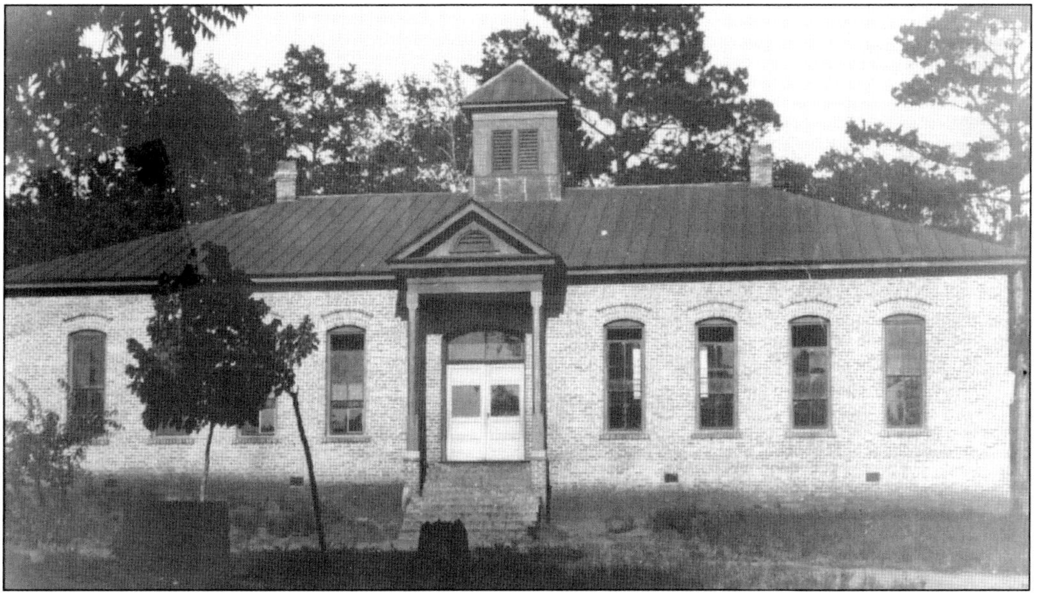

Before 1903, colored children were educated at two different locations by teachers Will Sanders, Peyton Walton Sanders, and T.C. Ayers. The two schools eventually combined to form one. The new school became a four-room brick building that was moved to Shawnee Street. There, it was known as the colored school. Will Sanders became the first principal. E.J. Campbell became the second principal in 1904, and it was because of his success that the colored school was renamed the E.J. Campbell High School in 1937 after his death. (Courtesy of Carolyn Ericson.)

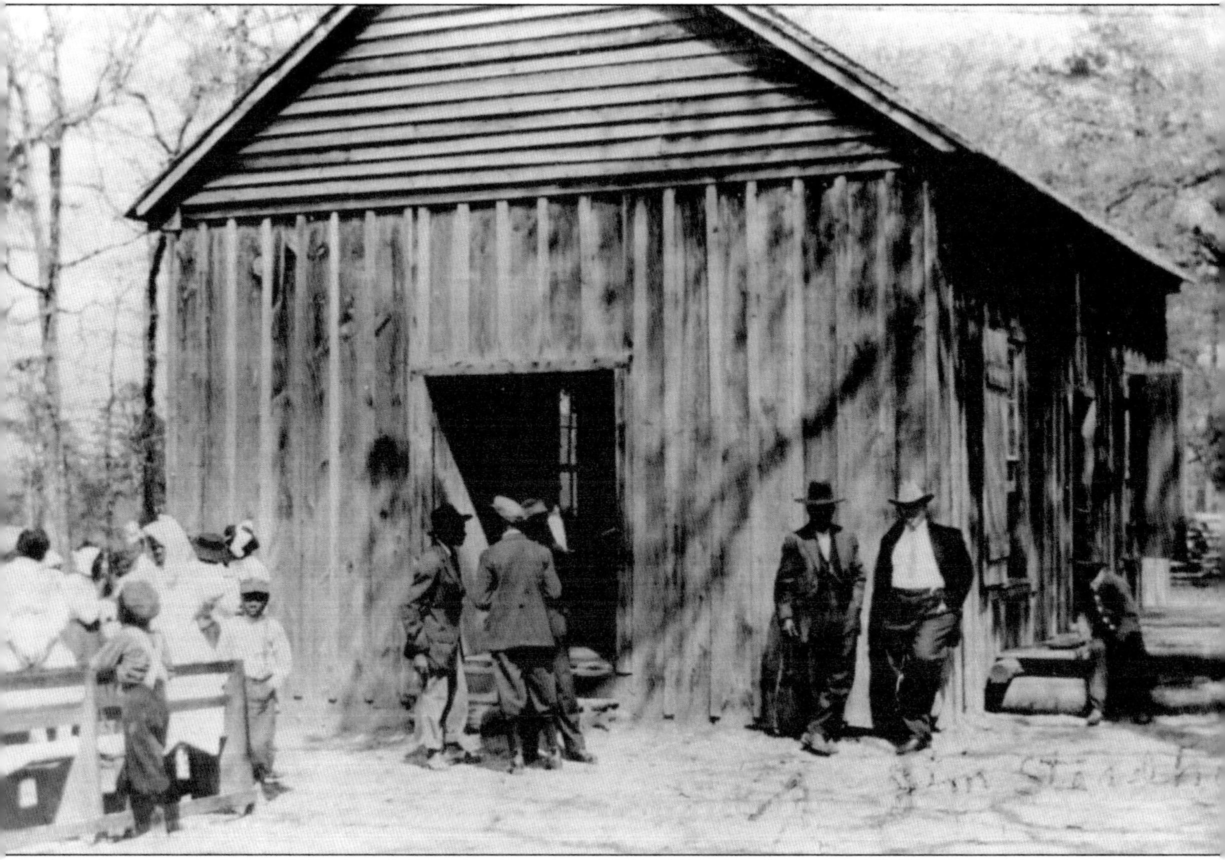

This building, constructed in the late 1800s or early 1900s, was the first church in the Grayland community. During this period in history, the school and church were often housed in the same building. Prior to the 1930s, Negro or colored school buildings were often unpainted shacks with tiny windows. Inside the building were few, if any, desks; no blackboards; and limited school supplies. These bare conditions prompted the creation of Rosenwald Schools. (Courtesy of Robbie Lee Johnson.)

Annie Bell Russaw is pictured with students in the Winters Hill–Grayland community around 1920. She started her teaching career in this one-room school building, teaching first- through 10th-grade students. She retired after 47 years as a teacher and principal. (Courtesy of Robbie Lee Johnson.)

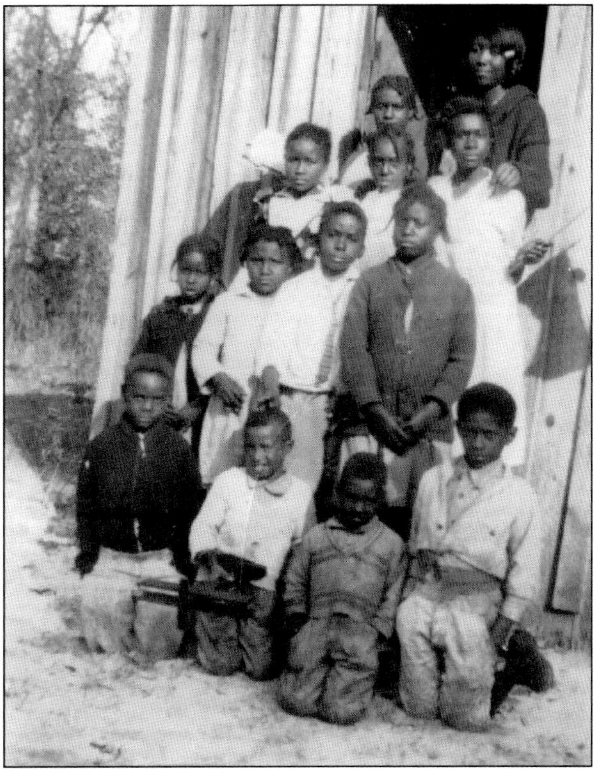

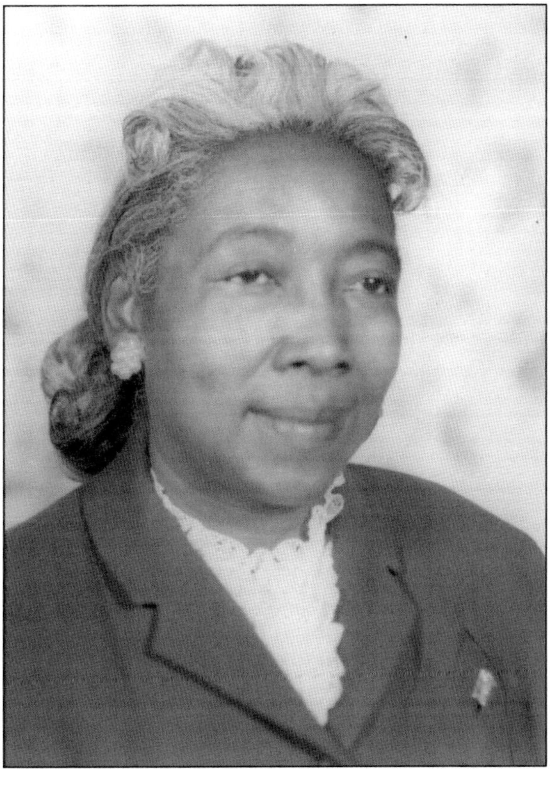

Early black teachers did not get the same level of training as white teachers and were not allowed to teach ideas about equality and freedom. Annie Belle Russaw, however, was an exceptional educator who taught her students to be proud of who they were. According to her former students, she never compromised excellence, always requiring the best from her students. (Mertie Mims Collection.)

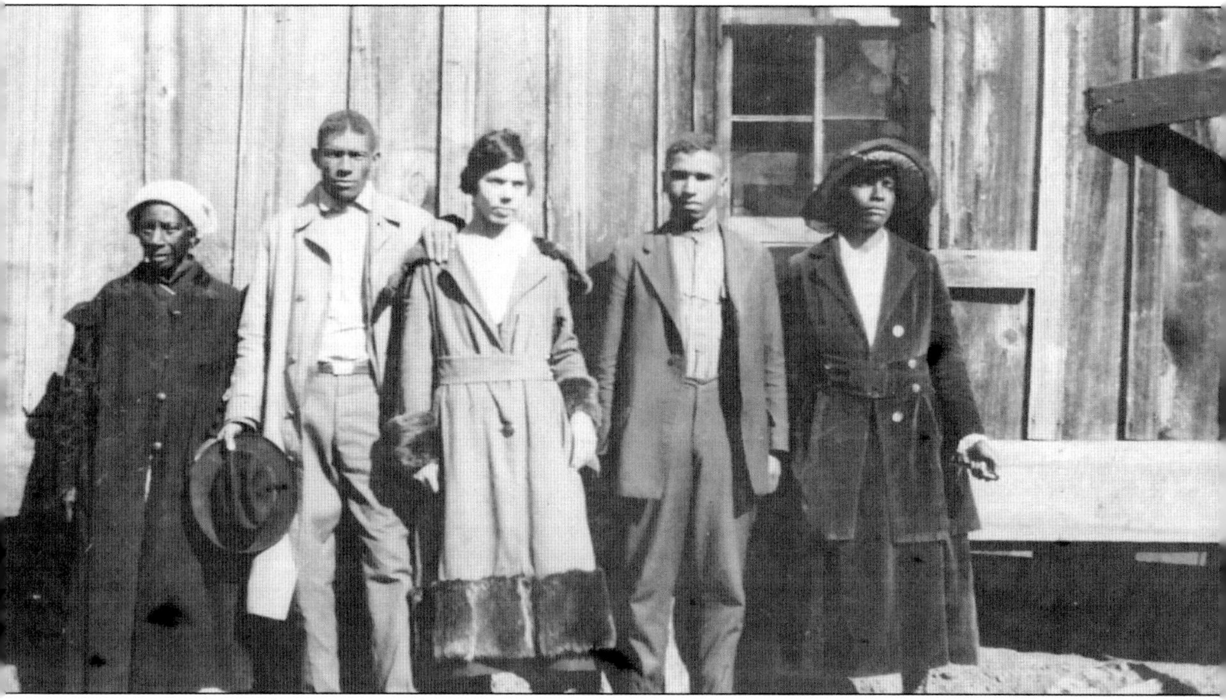

During the early 1900s, rural teachers were paid less money to teach than teachers in towns. They were often paid by services like cutting their wood and providing eggs and vegetables. Many of the educators shown in this image were volunteers and not certified teachers. They taught students what they knew based on life experience and limited formal education. (Mertie Mims Collection.)

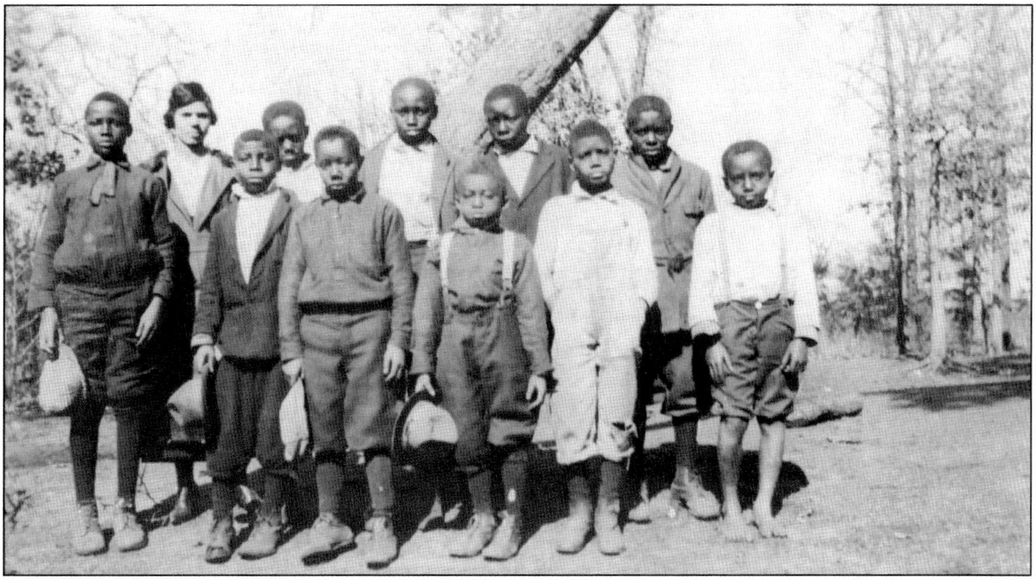

Boys from Sand Hill School pose for this picture. There was a strict rule about separating the genders as much as possible when not in the classroom. Boys were often tasked with cutting firewood and starting fires for the woodstove. They were also responsible for drawing water from the schoolyard well. (Mertie Mims Collection.)

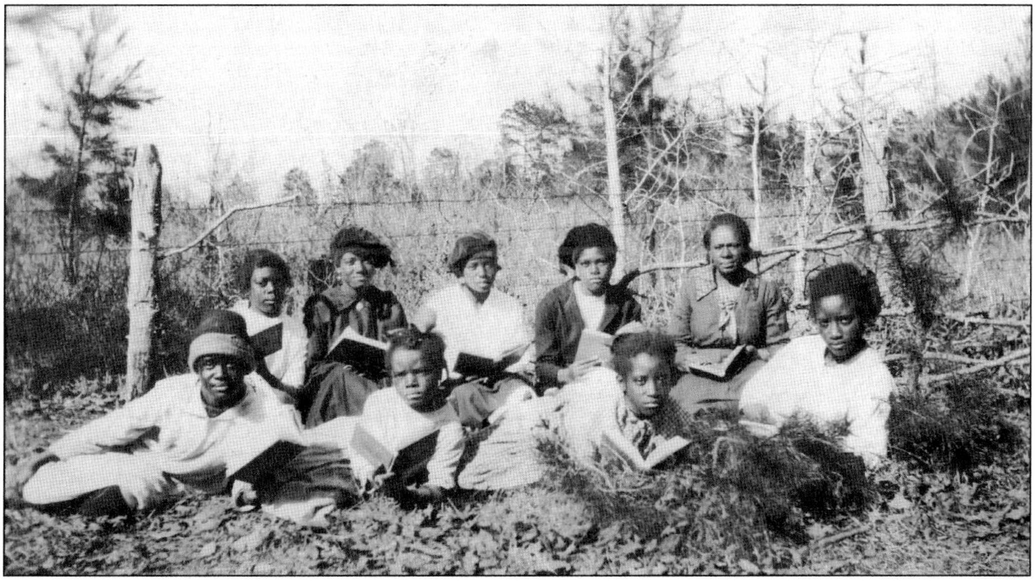

This group of girls, also from Sand Hill School, poses for what was perhaps the yearly class photograph, likely taken during recess or lunchtime. Female students sometimes helped to prepare meals and take care of younger students. Notice that each student has a book, which was quite unusual for that era. (Mertie Mims Collection.)

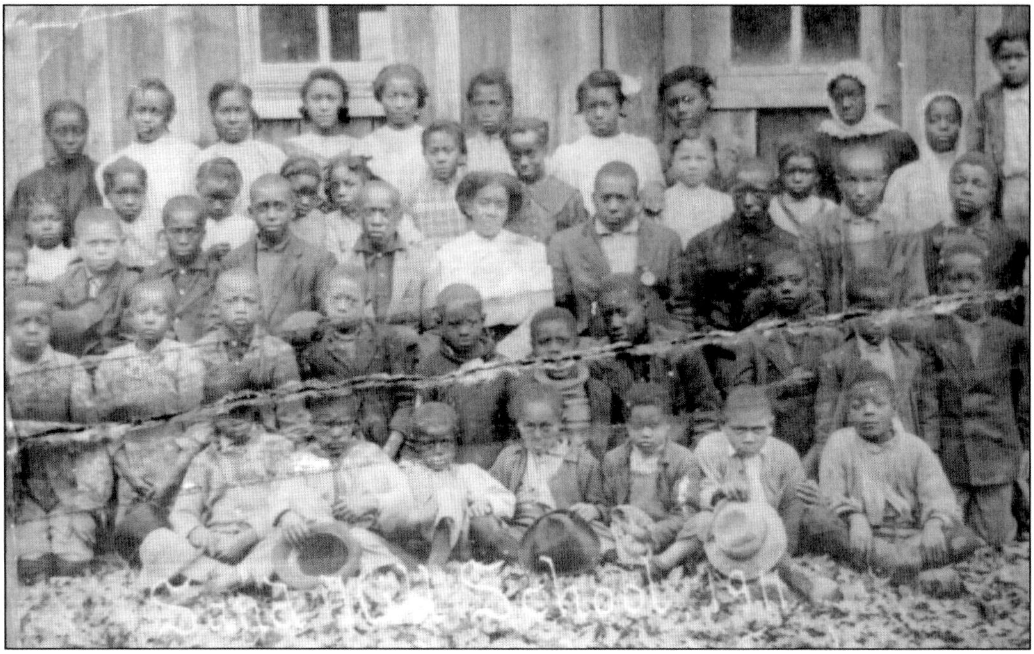

In the early 1900s, few black students were enrolled in school full time because they were needed in the fields to gather crops. Many black families realized the importance of education, so they made sacrifices and sent their children to school anyway. This 1911 image of Sand Hill School shows the parents' commitment to providing a good education versus manual labor. (Courtesy of Mable Ferguson Hall.)

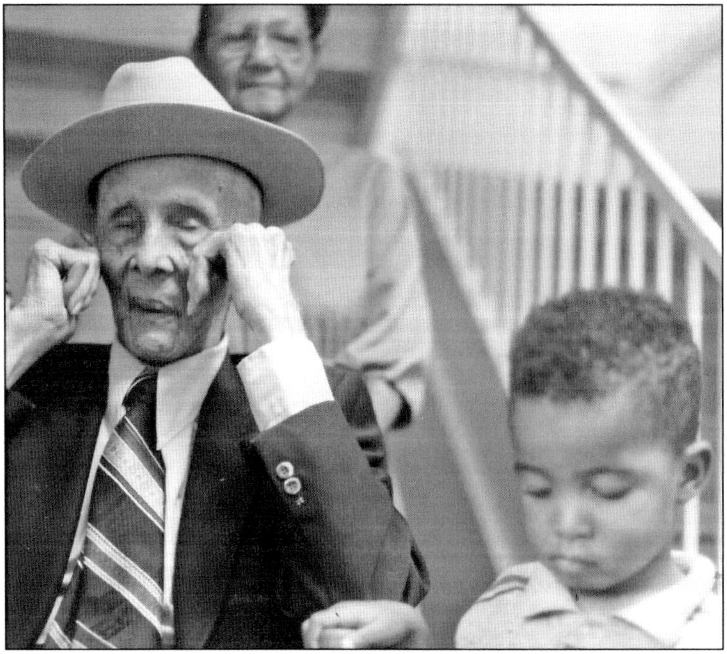

George W. Skillern is shown with great-great-grandson Marcus in front of the Gladys Hampton Building in downtown Nacogdoches being recognized as the oldest citizen living on the El Camino Real Trail in the late 1980s. He lived to be 108 years old. He was well known by all the kids at church because he would thump their heads if they misbehaved. He was a dedicated member of Sand Hill Baptist Church, serving as church clerk about 50 years. (Courtesy of Mable Ferguson Hall.)

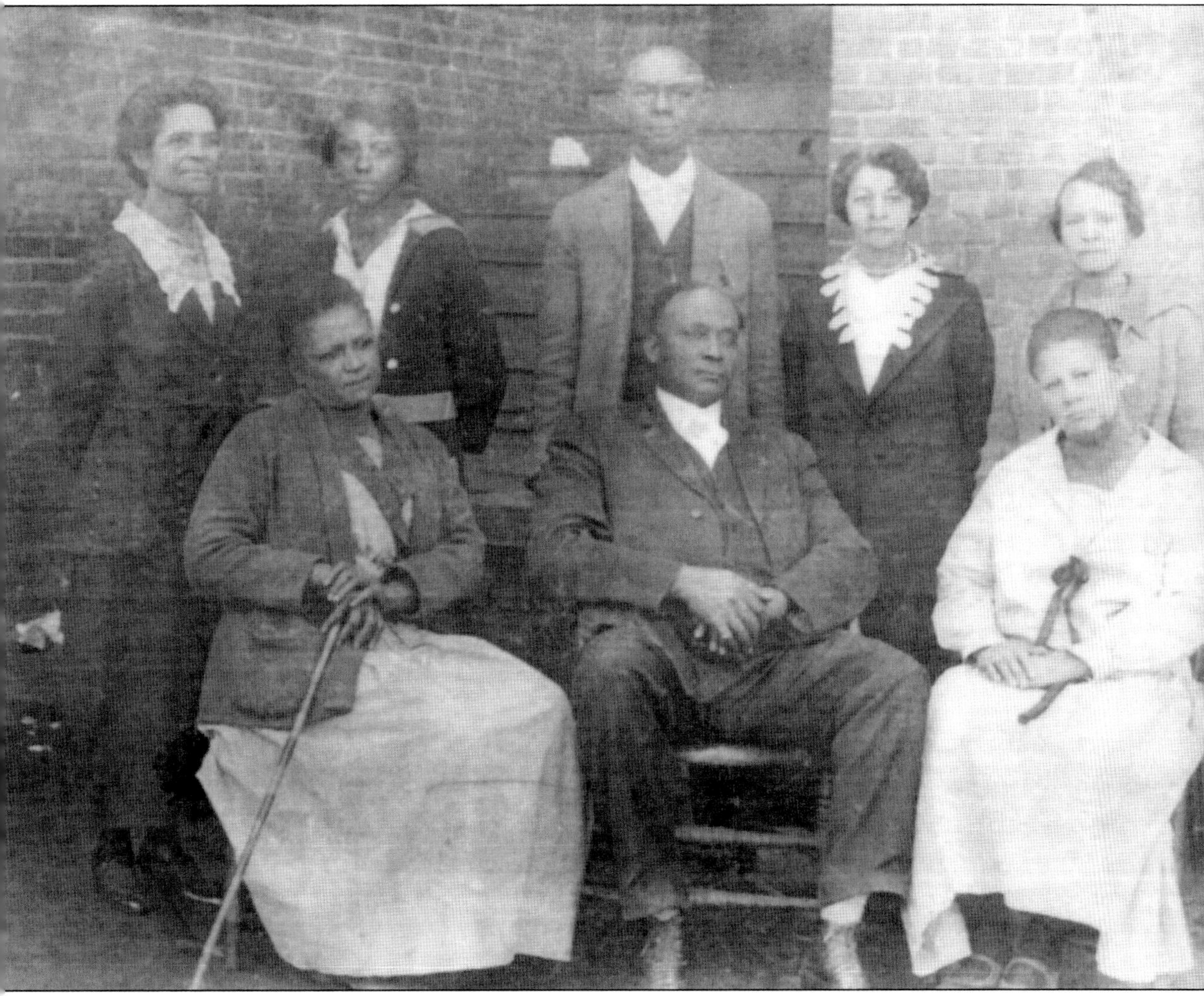

E.J. Campbell became principal of the Nacogdoches Colored School in 1907 and is shown here posing with his first faculty. Standing area, from left to right, Polly Quinn, J.E. "Mama" Brooks, A.A. Hooper, Emeline Carpenter, and an unidentified person. Sitting are, from left to right, Mary G. Campbell, E.J. Campbell, and an unidentified person. (ETRC.)

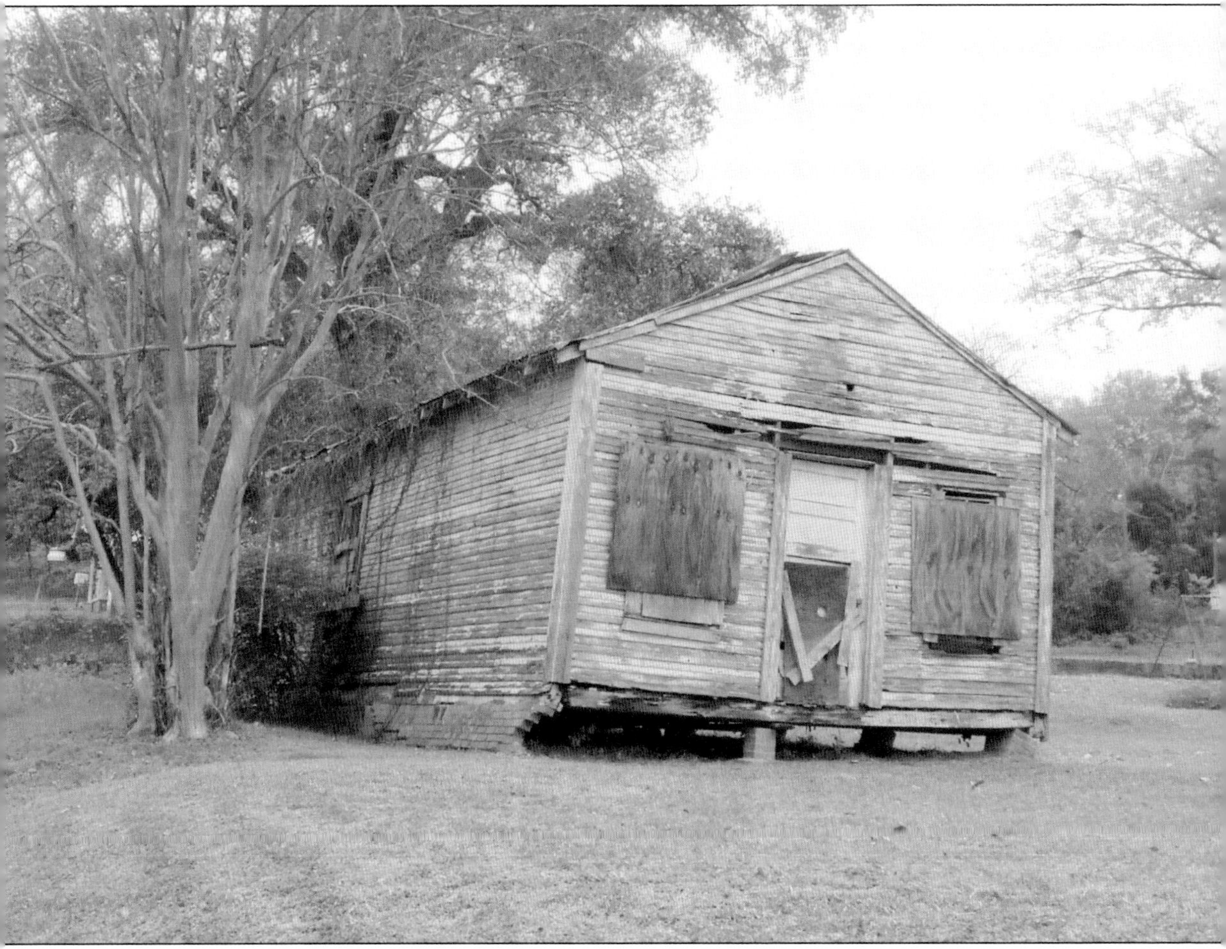

This building still stands on historic Shawnee Street, reminding residents of an era that once was. Dr. R.E. Hanson, an African American medical doctor, once used this building to see patients when they could not access him at the colored hospital down the street. It also temporarily housed schoolchildren after their school building was destroyed by fire. (Courtesy of Adell Mills.)

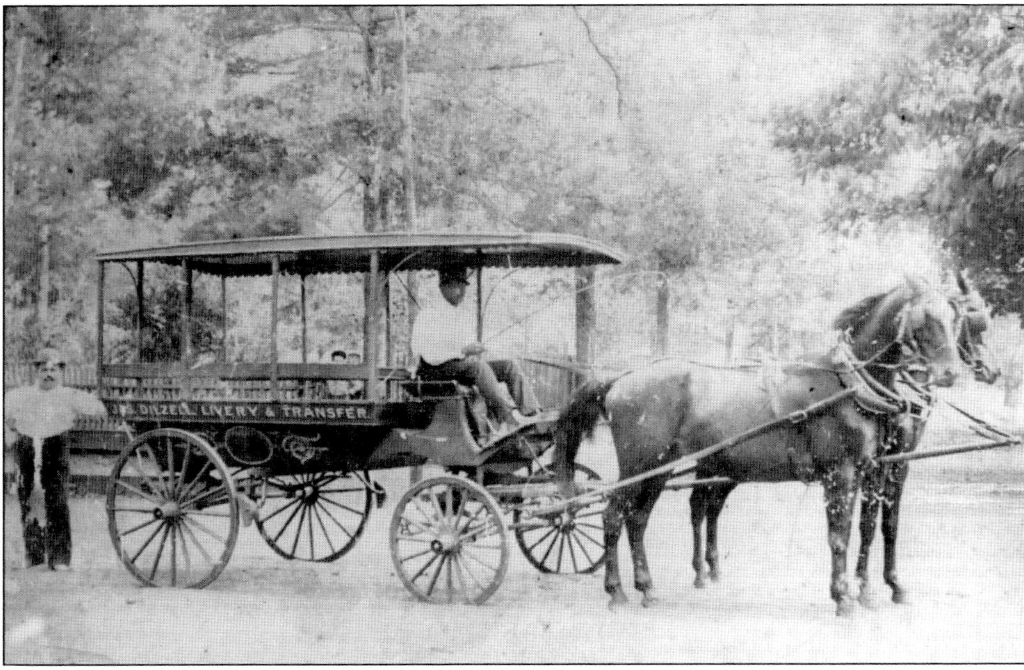

The first-known school bus recorded in American history was in 1827. It was drawn by a horse and capable of transporting 20 to 25 students. This image shows an African American driver with a horse-drawn carriage. It is not likely he was transporting students in this 1920s photograph; however, this carriage ensemble is representative of a typical early school bus. (Courtesy of Carolyn Ericson.)

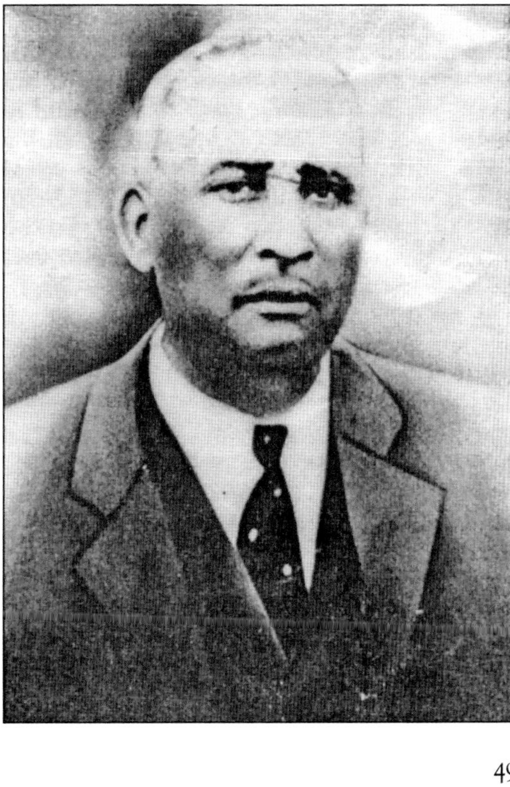

Edward J. Campbell (1877–1937) was an outstanding educator. The following was taken from a monument erected on the campus named after him: "E.J. Campbell inspired the people of a country, a part of the state, a part of the world. He brought hope to his fellowman, from the cornfields of Douglass to the Hall of Justice and Knowledge. His inspiring presence radiated hope and emancipated his people from the shackles of ignorance. From the Riverbanks of Angelina to the Dome of the State Capitol, he added dignity to the land and to the people. He made us proud to be Americans. E.J. Campbell High School was named in his honor in 1937." (Courtesy of the *Nacogdoches Daily Sentinel.*)

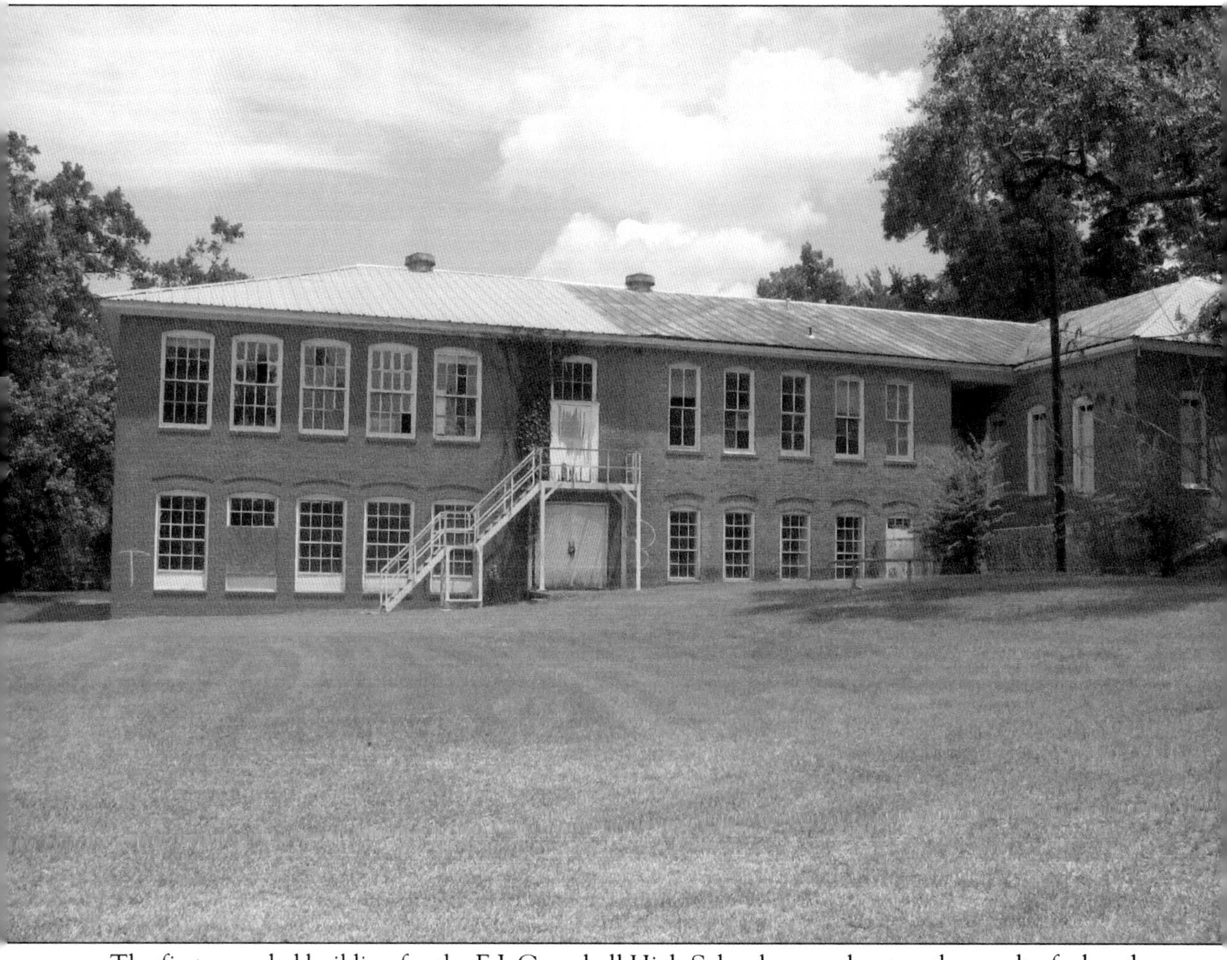

The first recorded building for the E.J. Campbell High School came about as the result of a bond issue passed in 1902. In 1903, the Nacogdoches Colored School consisted of a four-room brick structure located near the site of the current school, shown in this image, which is located on Shawnee Street. (Courtesy of Carolyn Ericson.)

W.E. Jones began his administrative career in Nacogdoches by becoming the principal of the colored high school in 1937 after the death of Principal E.J. Campbell. He was a strong and successful principal, never missing an opportunity to ask the school administration for equipment and supplies for his students. Under his leadership, the academic and sports programs were expanded and extended to other parts of East Texas. (Courtesy of Brooks-Quinn-Jones Elementary School, Nacogdoches Independent School District.)

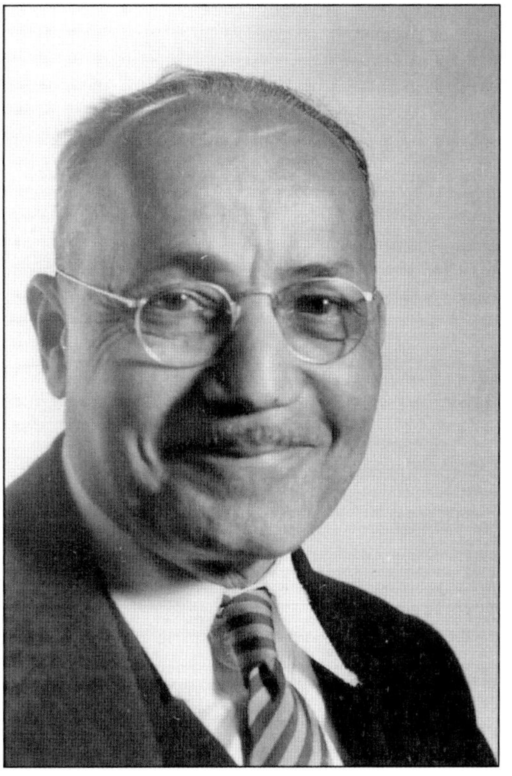

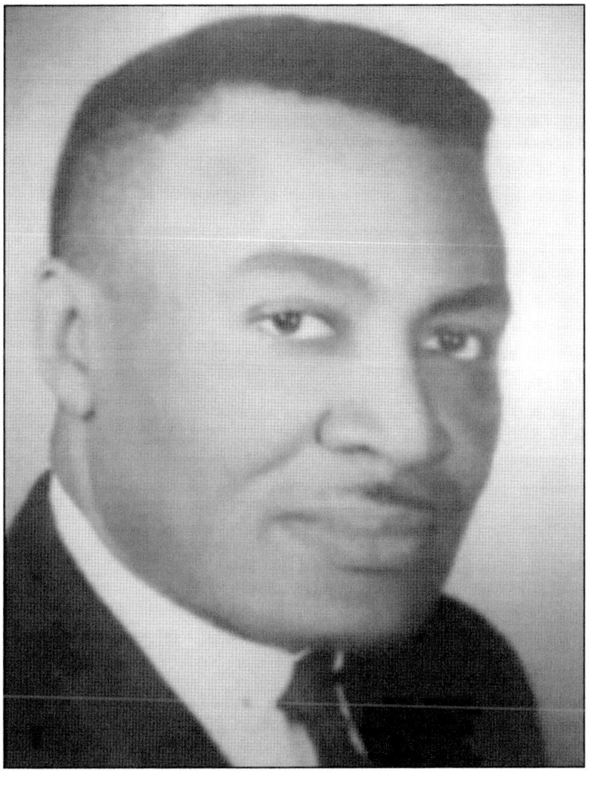

Because of his achievements in education, a school in Cushing, Texas, was named in honor of C.L. Simon. Simon came to E.J. Campbell High School as principal in 1961. After integration in 1970, he was named coprincipal of Nacogdoches High School until he moved into an administrative position as a personnel director, where he remained until he retired in 1990. Because of his civic achievements, the Nacogdoches Recreation Center's gymnasium was named in Simon's honor. (Photograph by Rolonda Teal; courtesy of the City of Nacogdoches.)

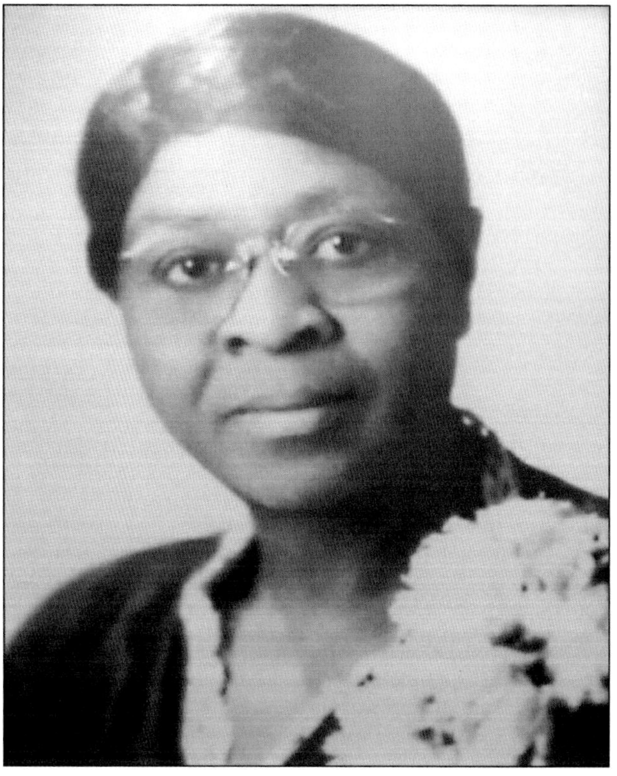

One former student described Ms. J.E. Brooks as a "quiet and humble person who was always willing to help people in the community." She was a "firm but fair teacher" according to another former student. Brooks began her teaching career in 1930. Serving as owner and manager, she established a hotel-rooming house for blacks on Shawnee Street. Many people still referred to her as "Mama Brooks." A local school is partially named in her honor and is known as the Brooks-Quinn-Jones Elementary School. (Photograph by Rolonda Teal; courtesy of Nacogdoches County School District.)

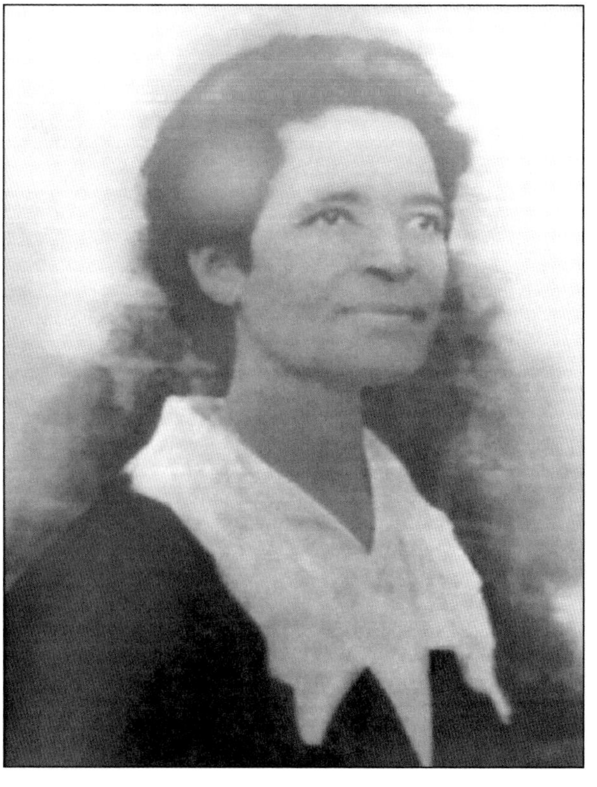

Molly Quinn began her career in the early 1900s. She was described as a very dignified and highly respected woman of high morals. A former student said Quinn was her inspiration for becoming a teacher. As with Ms. Brooks, a local school shares the honor of being named after her. (Photograph by Rolonda Teal; courtesy of Nacogdoches County School District.)

Emeline Carpenter, born in 1880, taught in Nacogdoches schools for over 50 years. She was admired and respected as a dedicated and committed teacher. Her teaching style and service to the community influenced many young scholars to become teachers. According to a Nacogdoches veteran educator, Joyce Mills, "I became a teacher because Mrs. Carpenter influenced me as a child." Emeline Carpenter Elementary School is named in her honor. (ETRC.)

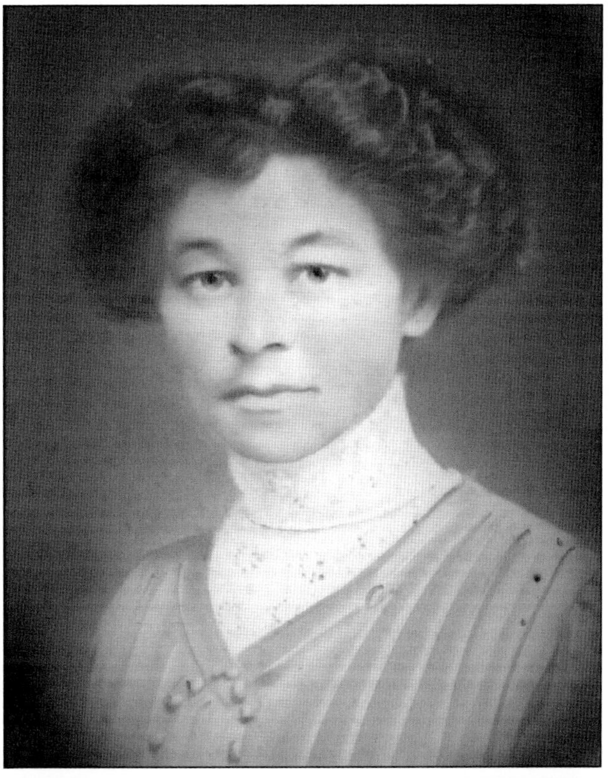

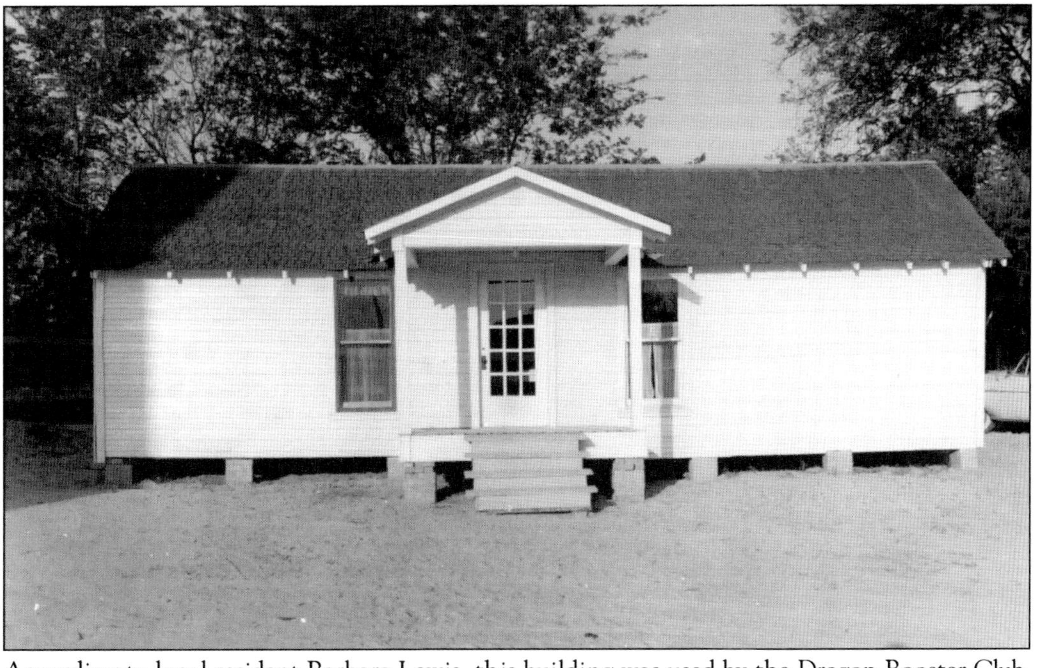

According to local resident Barbara Lewis, this building was used by the Dragon Booster Club, which was part of E.J. Campbell High School. Located on Orton Street, this facility, like several others, is where many community events were held during the 1950s and 1960s. Later, the building served as a church cafeteria. (Mertie Mims Collection.)

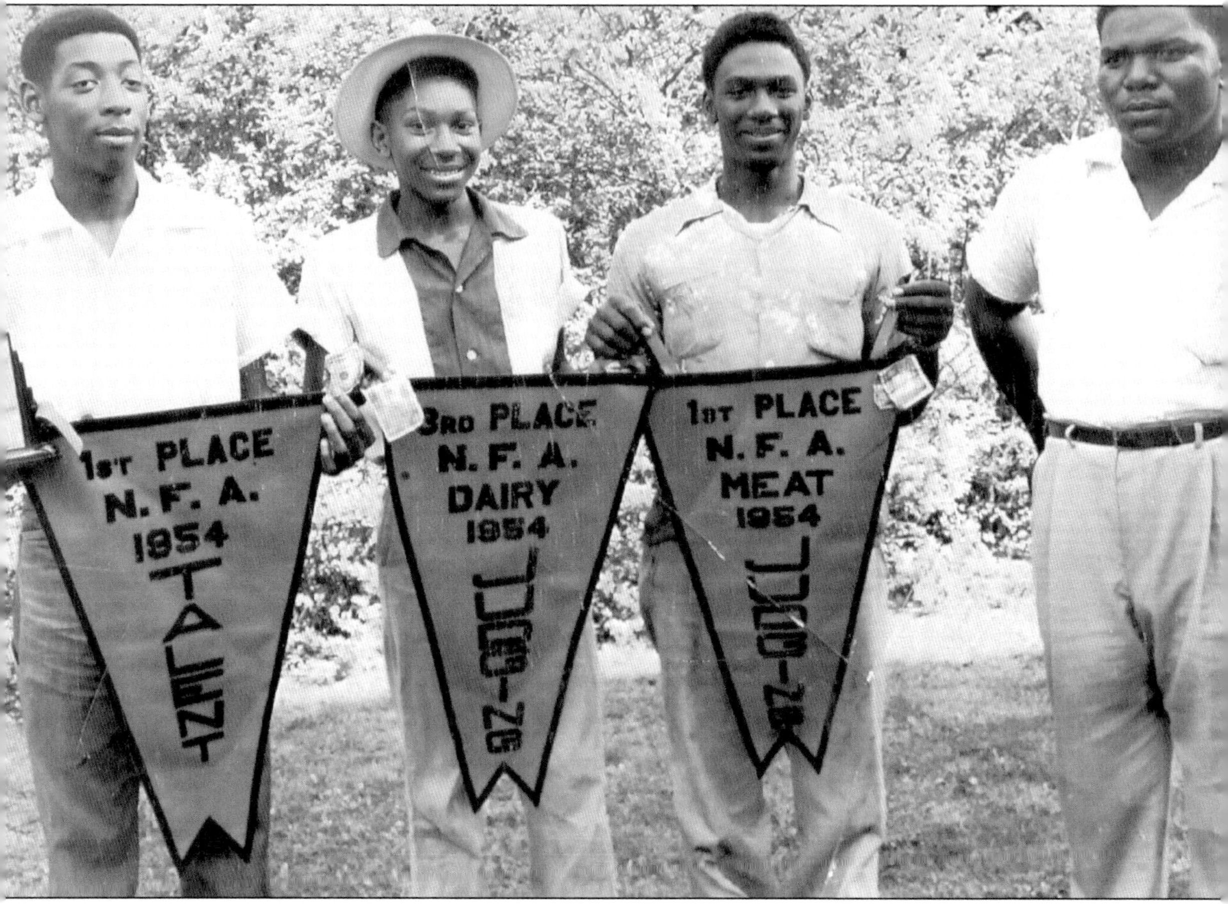

The New Farmers of America (NFA) group proudly shows off its first- and third-place banners after competing in state competition. Pictured on the far right is Fred Burrell, a loved and respected educator who taught agriculture in the Nacogdoches Independent School District for over 25 years. (Courtesy of Almeda Burrell.)

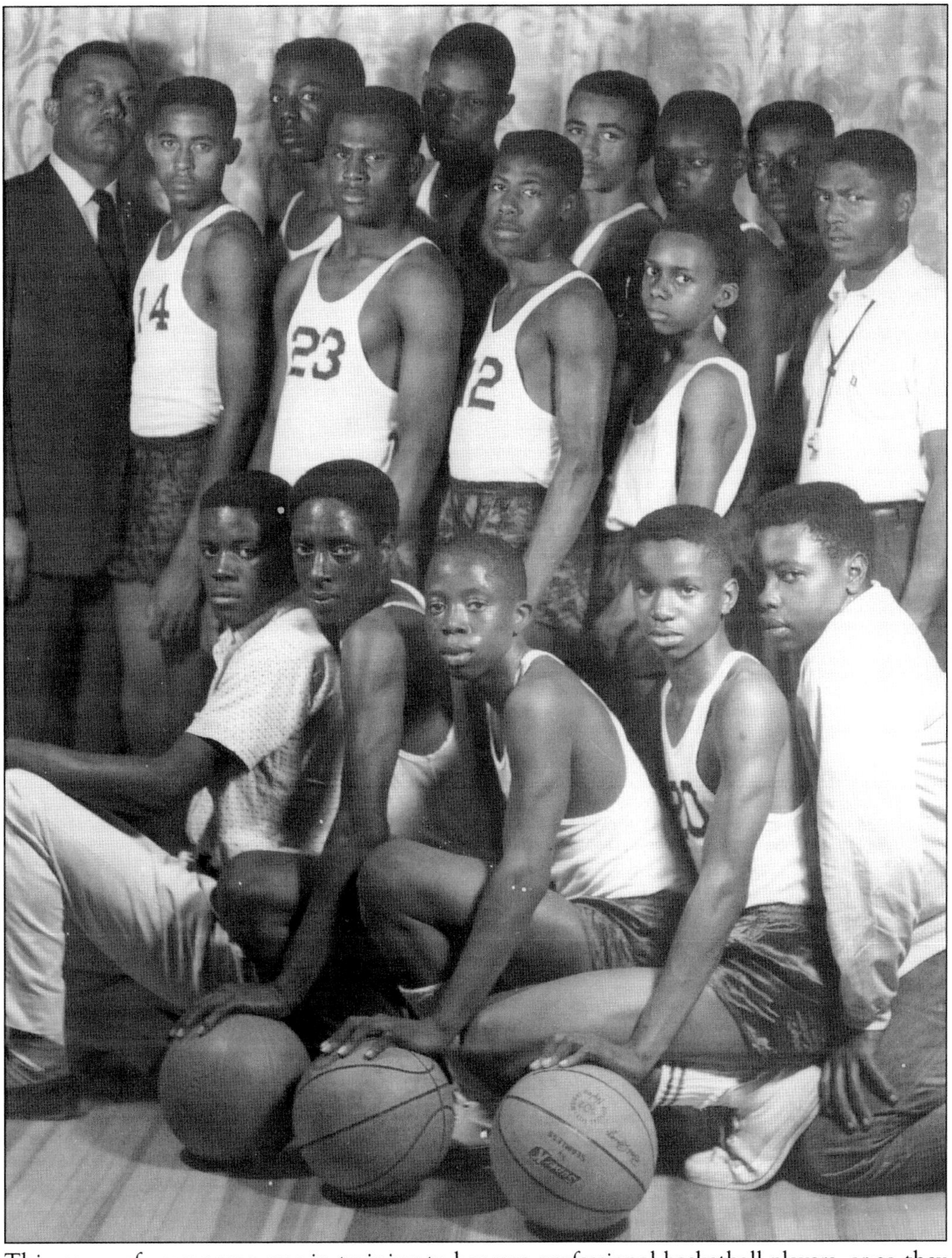

This group of young men was in training to become professional basketball players, or so they thought. They were part of Brooks-Quinn-Jones Junior High School before it became an elementary school in the early 1960s. Basketball, football, and track offered black males a chance to make money besides the usual occupations of farming. (Mertie Mims Collection.)

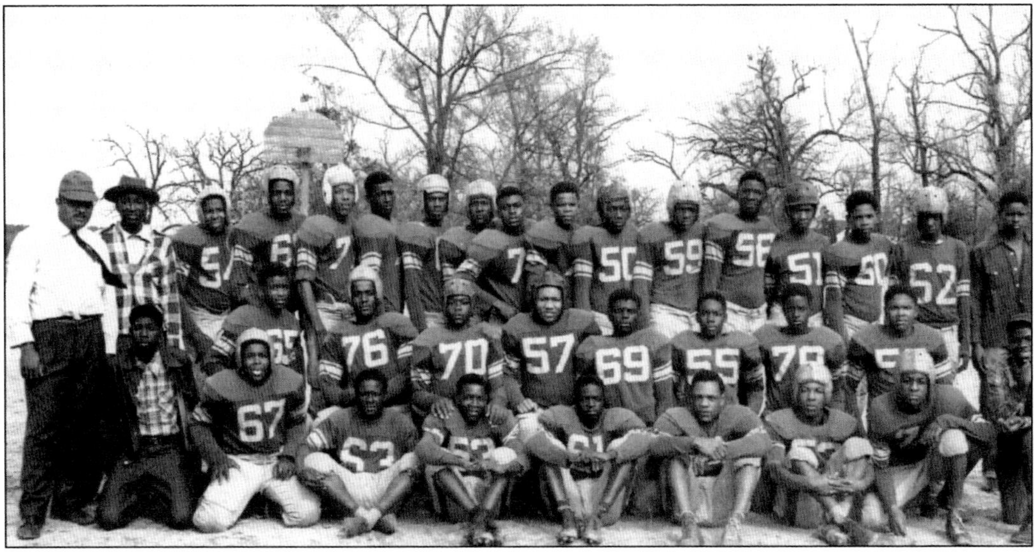

The 1949 E.J. Campbell football team, led by legendary coach Bo McMichael, sits for an annual photograph. Pictured wearing the hat and tie, McMichael, in addition to coaching and teaching, also washed football uniforms and delivered children safely home after practice. In the summer, McMichael operated the segregated swimming pool for black citizens. (ETRC.)

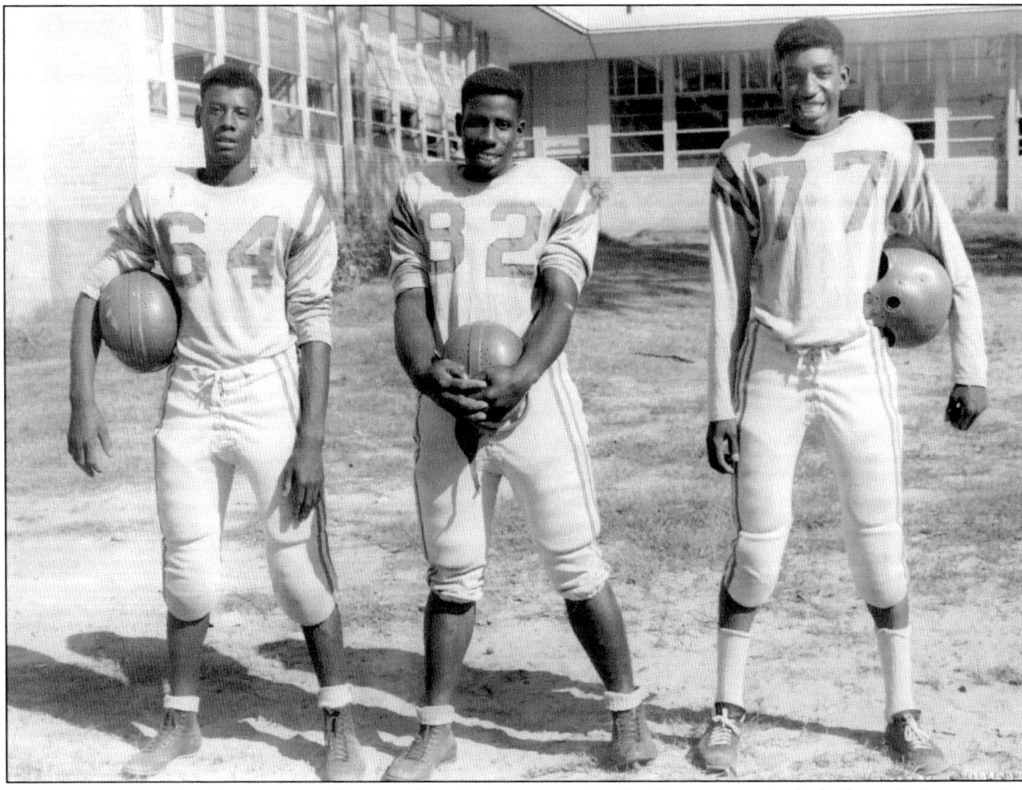

During the 1950s, the starting lineup for the Dragon football team included, form left to right, Wilford Barrett, M.J. Forney, and Doris Resino. Another starter, Adell Mills, is not pictured. Some players received college scholarships, which were arranged by coach Bo McMichael. (ETRC.)

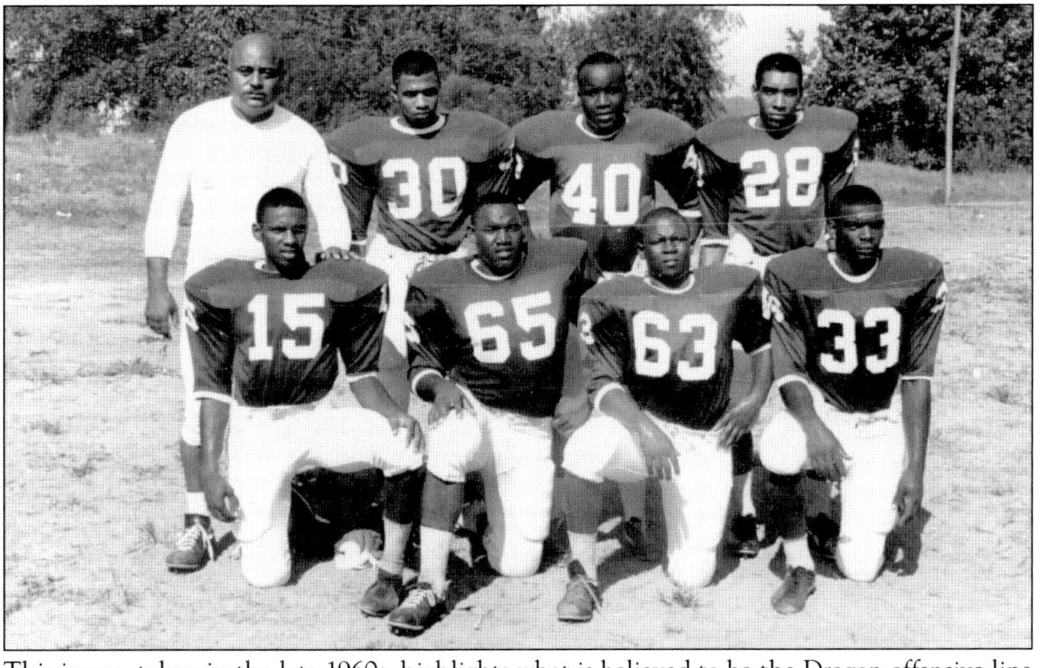

This image, taken in the late 1960s, highlights what is believed to be the Dragon offensive line just before practice time in an area affectionately known as "the hill." These players would climb an incline to a smooth area of flat land located behind the school to practice. The hill was mostly used for scrimmage games. (ETRC.)

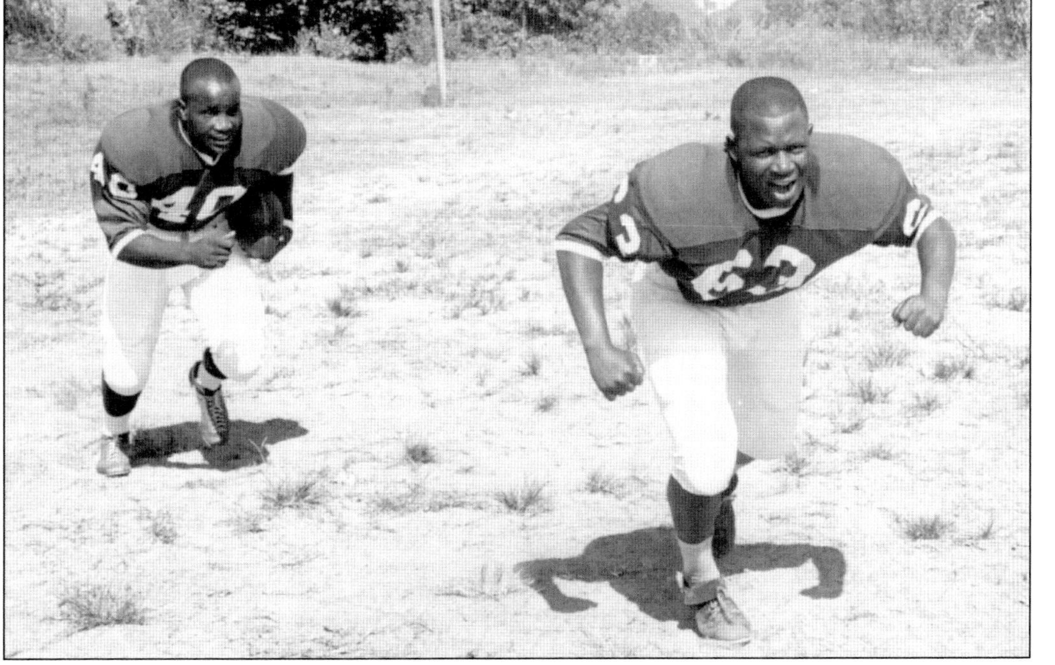

Two unidentified football players are preparing for practice on the hill. It was customary for their coach to yell, "Boys, hit the hill." It was also on the hill that other recreational events took place for community youth during the summer months. (ETRC.)

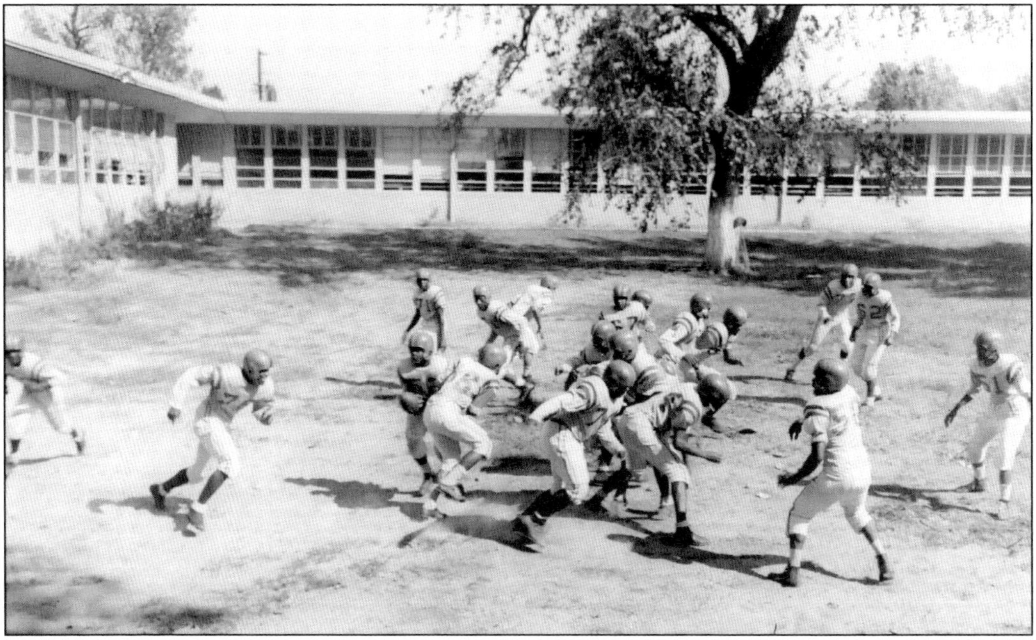

Scrimmage games were an important component of school activities. Sometimes people would gather to watch as long as they did not interfere with the events by heckling the boys. Other coaches of the 1950s and 1960s era were Ralph Allen and Cottrell McGowan. (ETRC.)

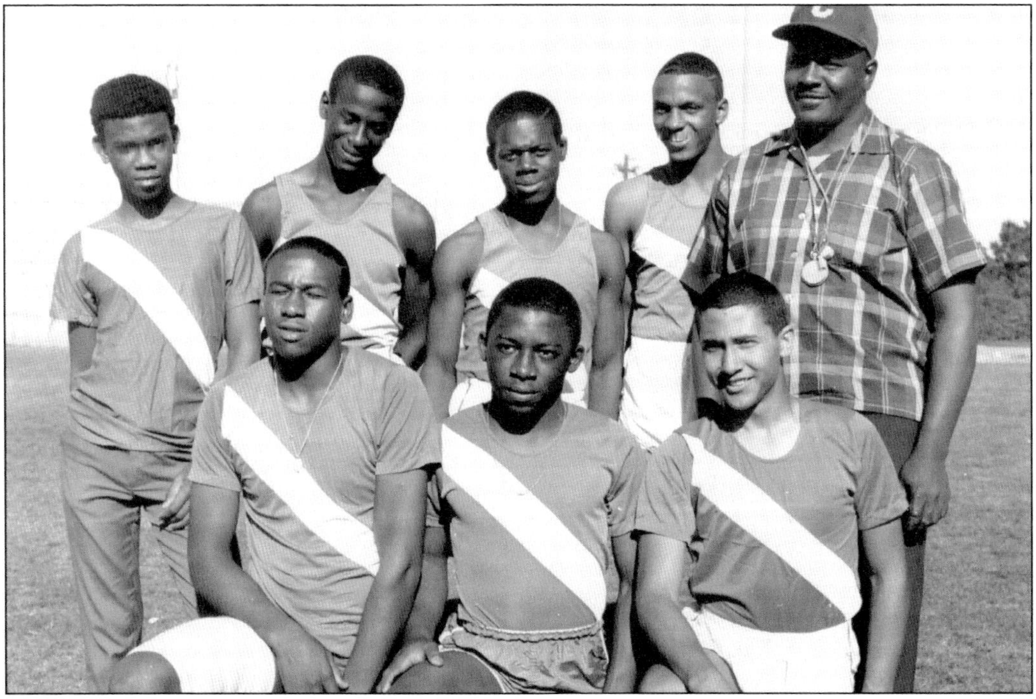

Pictured in the 1950s, coach Eddie Powers's (top right) track team had just won state honors. It appears that the entire team is smiling. Although not as popular a sport as football, these individuals brought pride and distinction back to Nacogdoches when they arrived home with their trophy. (ETRC.)

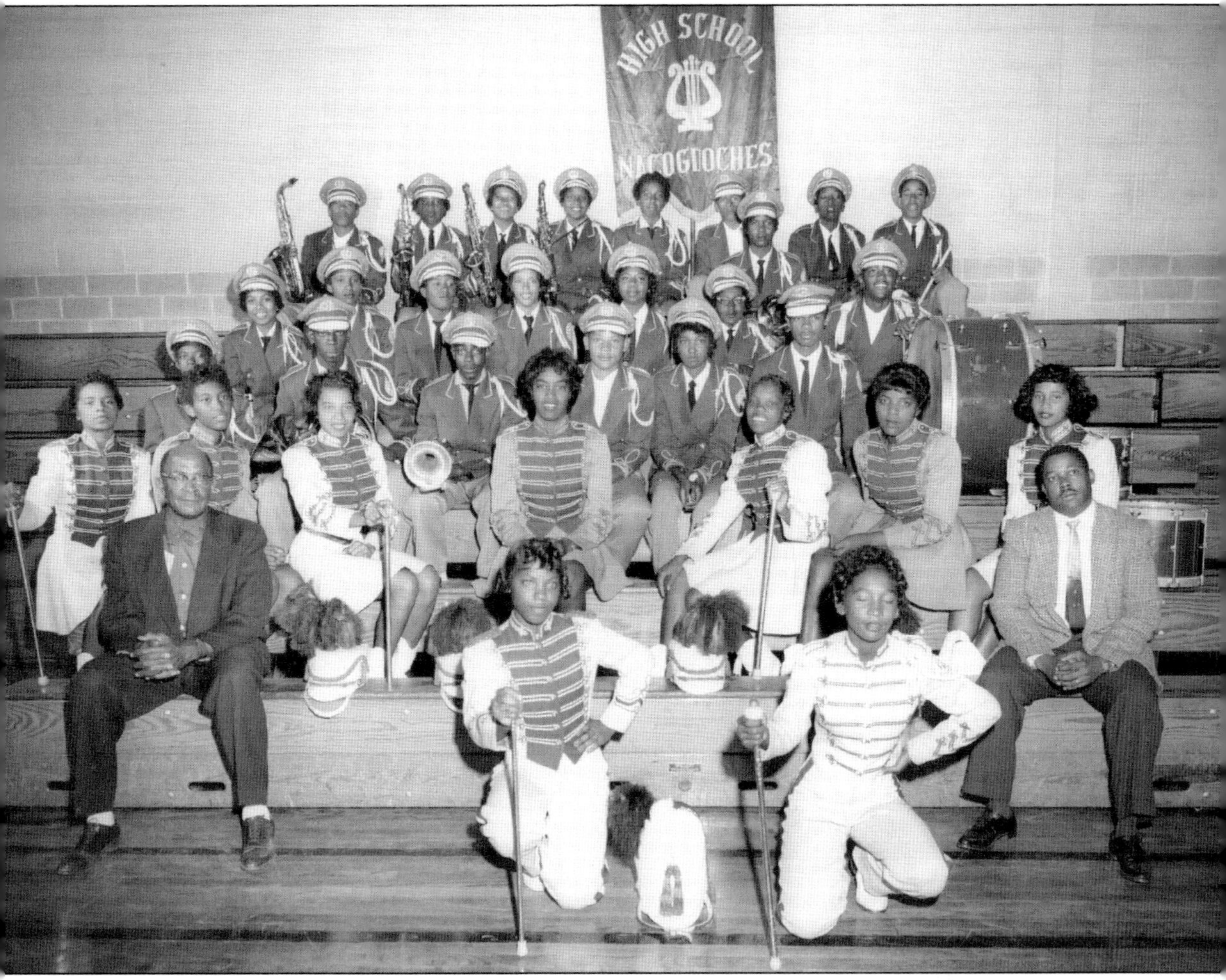

The Nacogdoches black community looked forward to seeing the marching band perform downtown for homecoming parades. E.J. Campbell's marching band received many awards and recognition under the leadership of band director Thomas Jesse Cleaver from 1947 to 1958. As in this image, the band was dressed in full uniform often and travelled to give halftime performances during football games. The band members, with the drill team and flag bearers, loved traveling on buses for out-of-town games. (ETRC.)

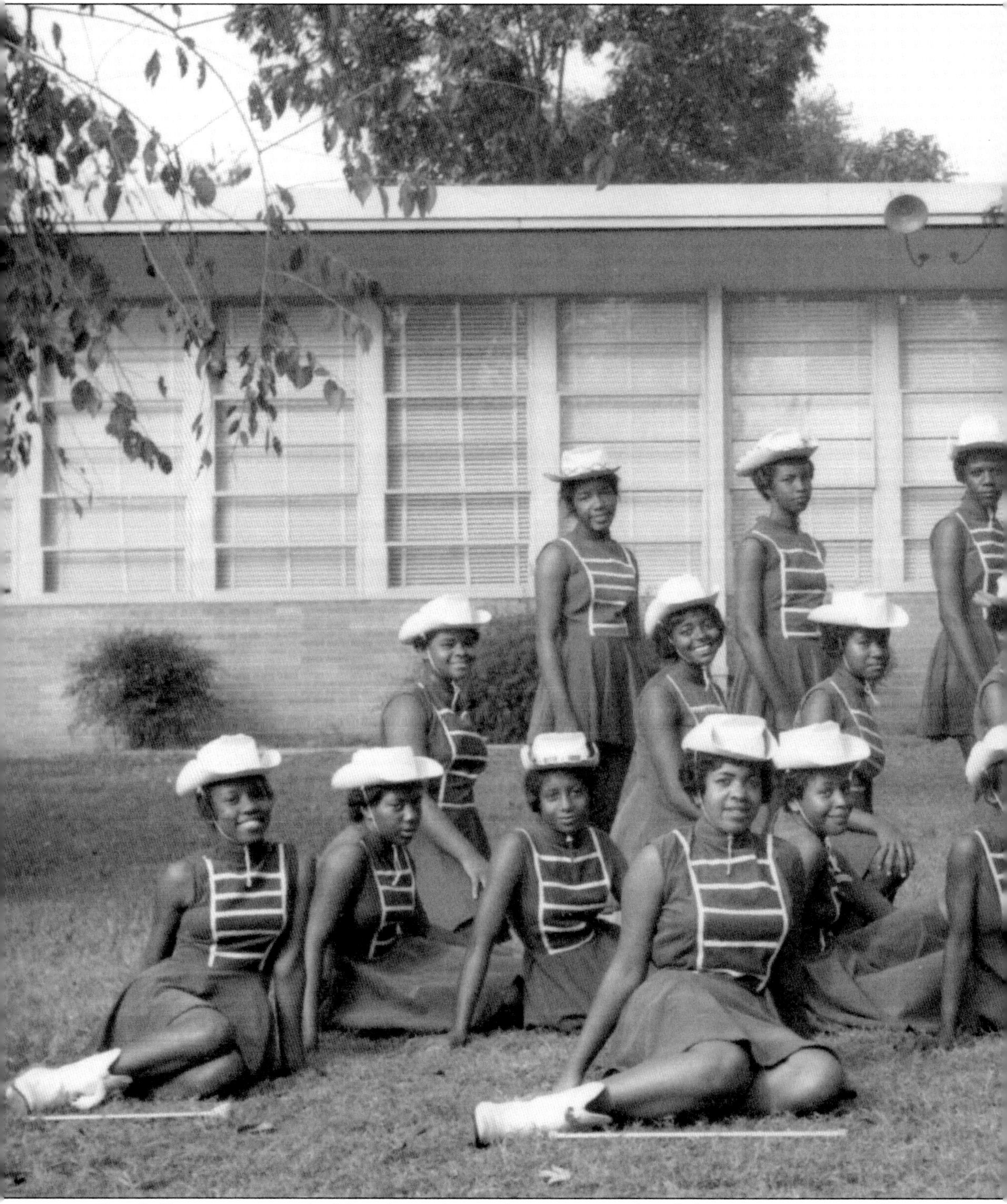

The drill team consisted of female students who were considered the main attraction during halftime at football games. These girls practiced rigorously several times a week for precision and accuracy. Most girls considered it an honor to be part of such a prestigious campus group. In

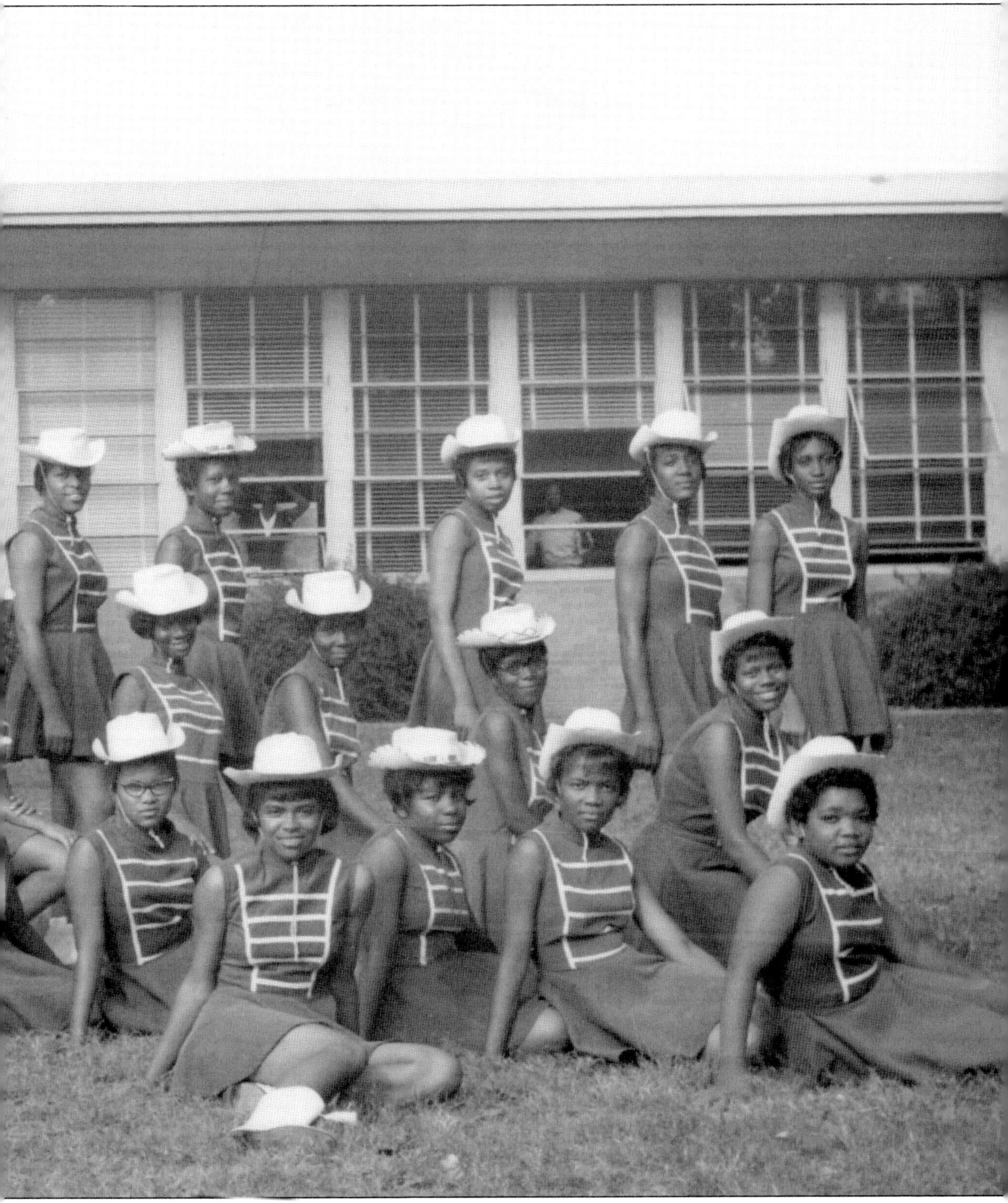

addition to participation in school and community parades, they also offered their services for fund-raising activities. (ETRC.)

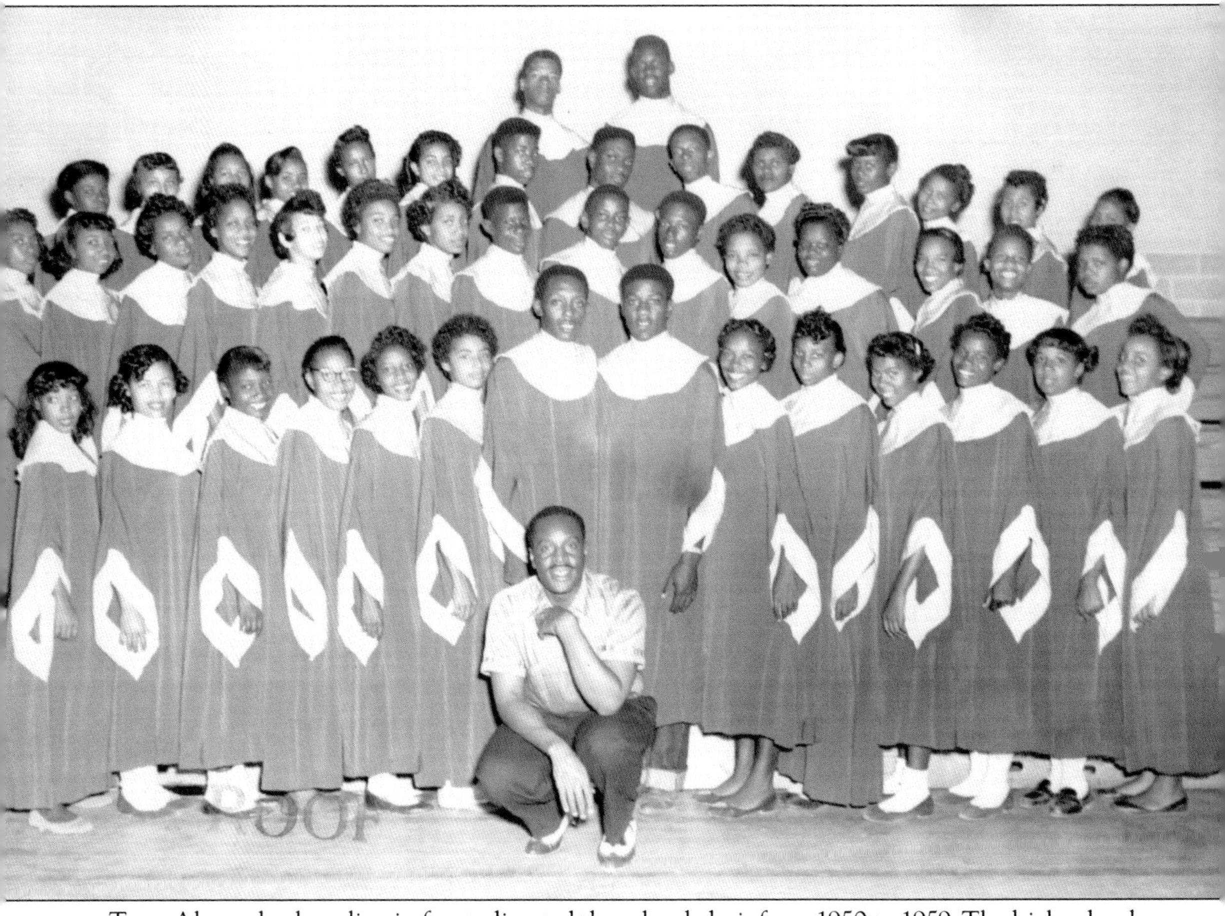

Terry Alexander, kneeling in front, directed the school choir from 1950 to 1959. The high school chorus experience often helped students find their own voice in terms of personal identity. The E.J. Campbell choir often competed with area schools and won musical competitions. Inspired by Terry Alexander, who had the ability to motivate students, a few choir members took their skills and participated in musical performances throughout the region. (ETRC.)

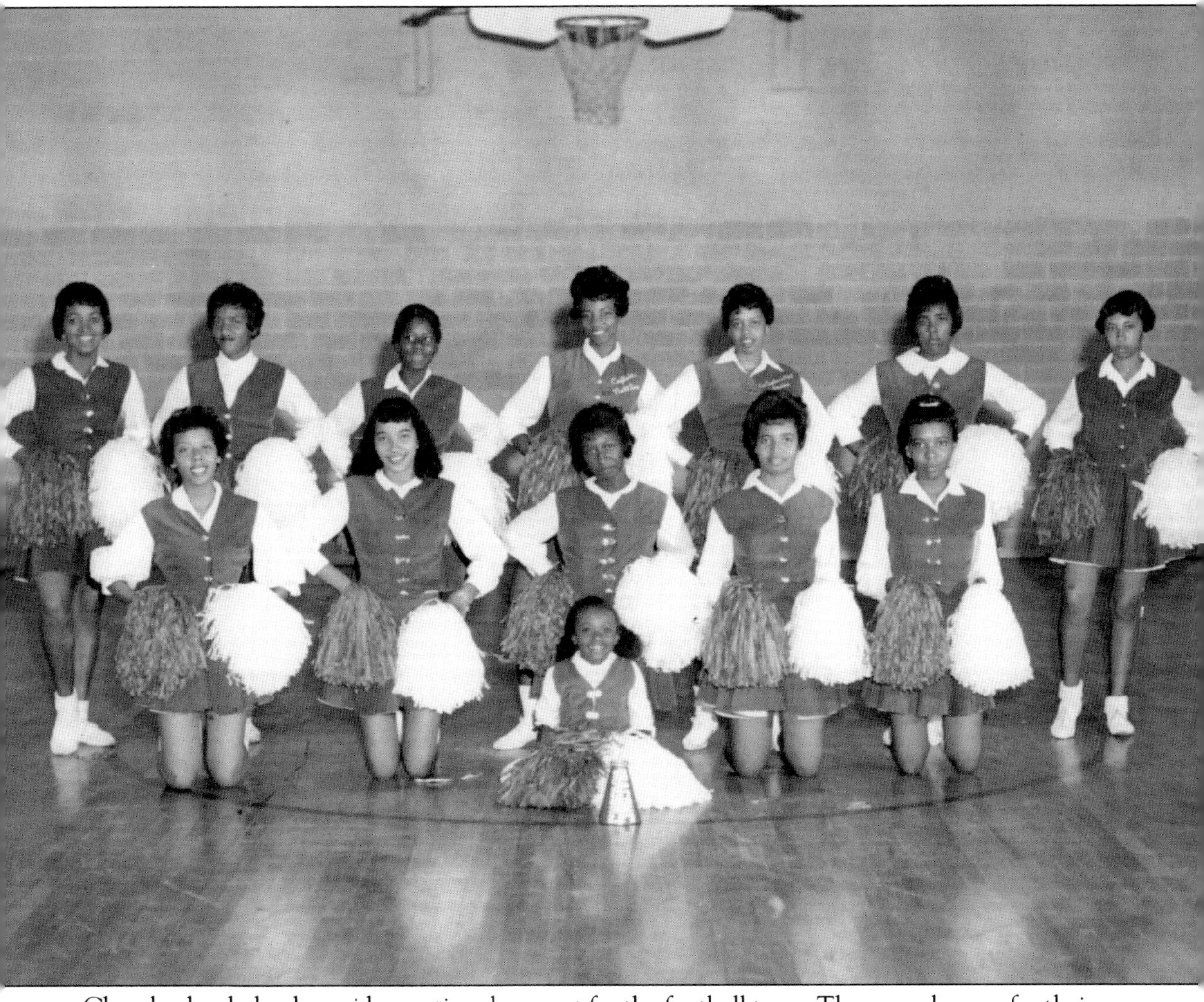

Cheerleaders helped provide emotional support for the football team. They were known for their over-the-top energy and school spirit. They often traveled with the football team as they played other schools from the surrounding area. It was not unusual to see the cheerleading squad at homecoming festivities and local parades. (ETRC.)

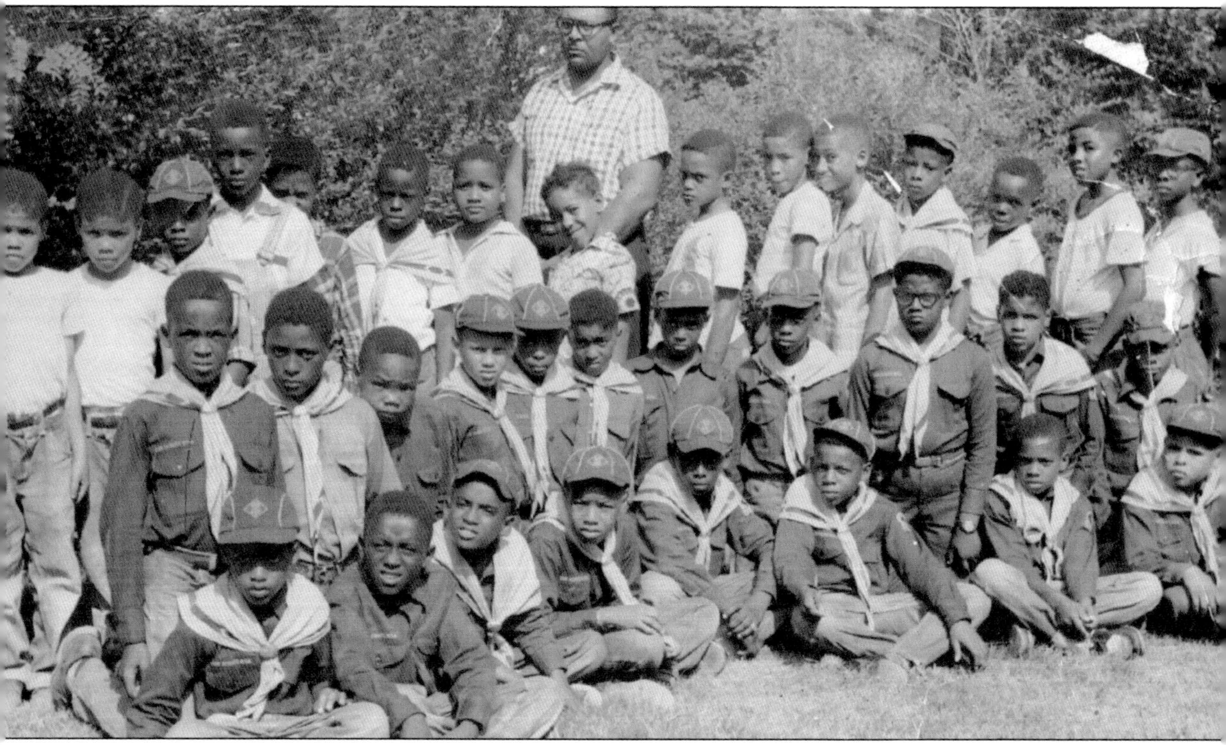

This photograph shows one of the earlier Cub Scout groups organized through several of the local churches. Established in 1930, the national Cub Scouts were intended to develop leadership skills for young males in the first through third grades. This was a segregated group, as were most organizations in the early 1950s, when this image was taken. (Courtesy of Helen Gallon.)

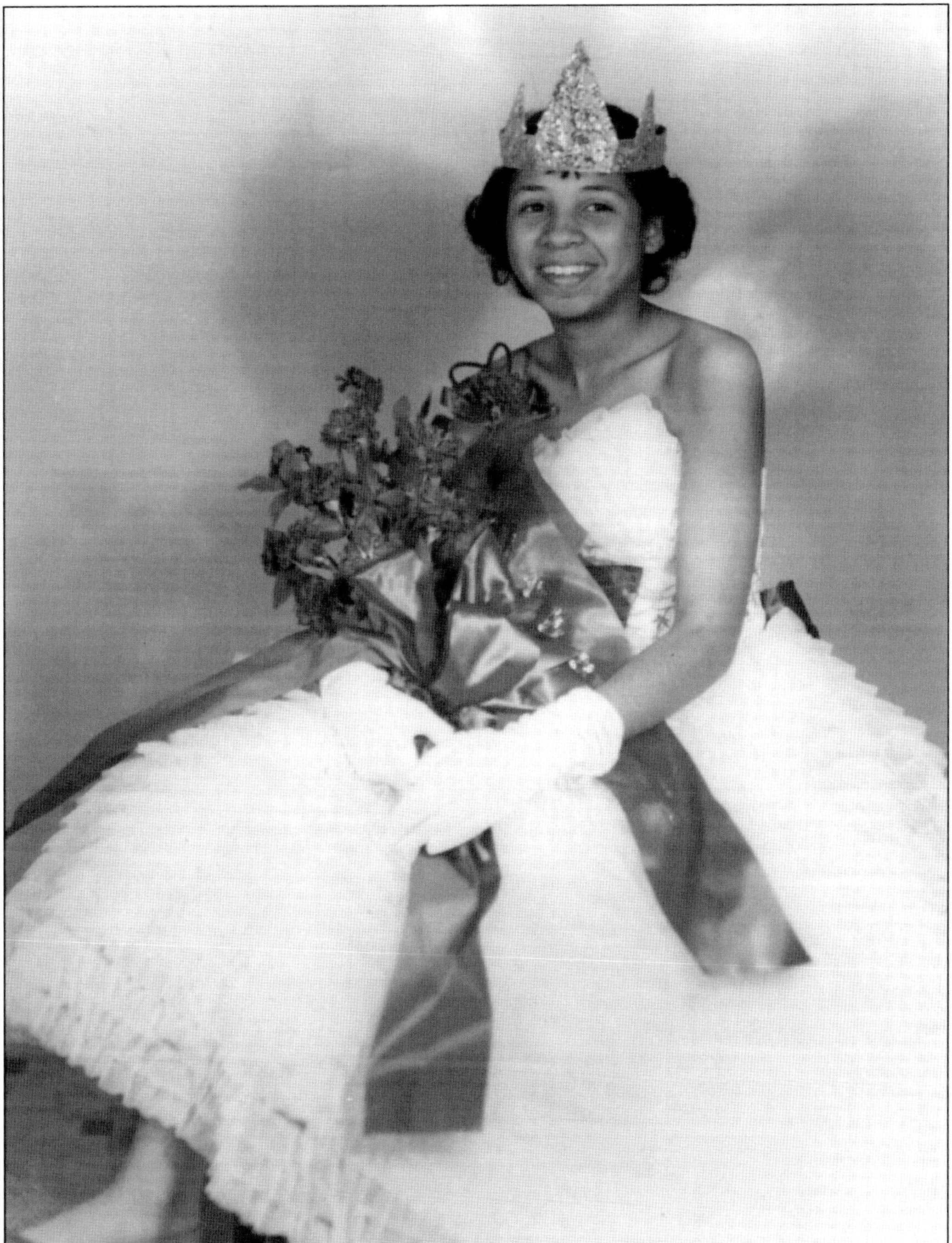

Wearing a formal gown, Yvonne Preston was crowned Miss E.J. Campbell in the 1950s. For a girl to receive this honor, she had to be well liked by other students and be in good academic standing. The crowning ceremony for both males and females brought the community together in a celebratory manner. (ETRC.)

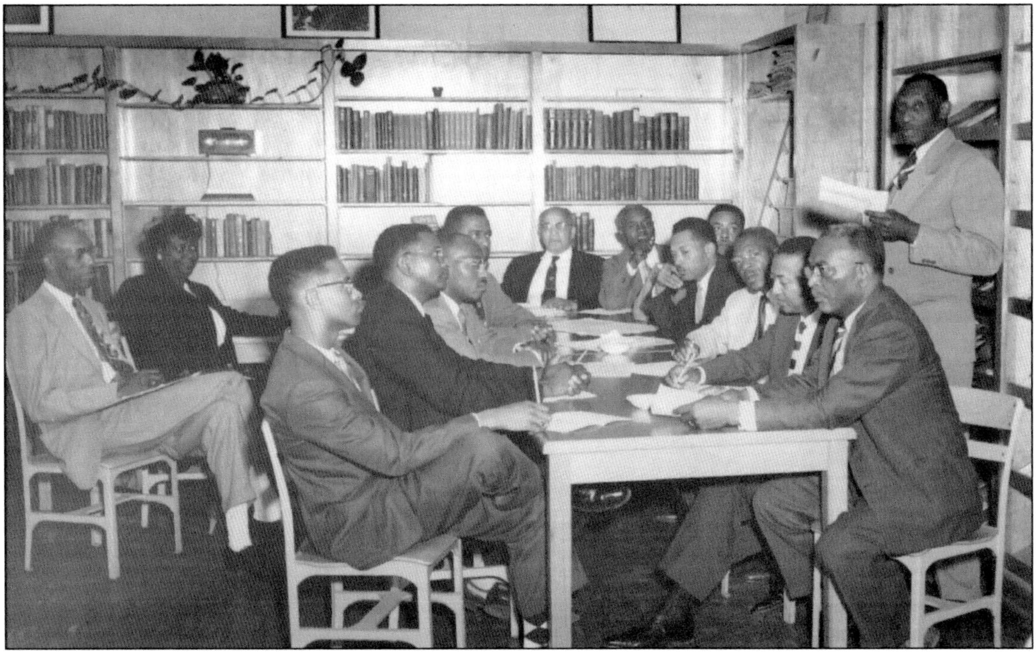

This photograph suggests an in-service meeting involving school and community leaders. It was common for such leaders to gather and discuss salaries and duties of educators as well as community concerns, such as transportation for students. No doubt held in the school library, the seriousness of the event is reflected by the attire of the gentlemen present. (Mertie Mims Collection.)

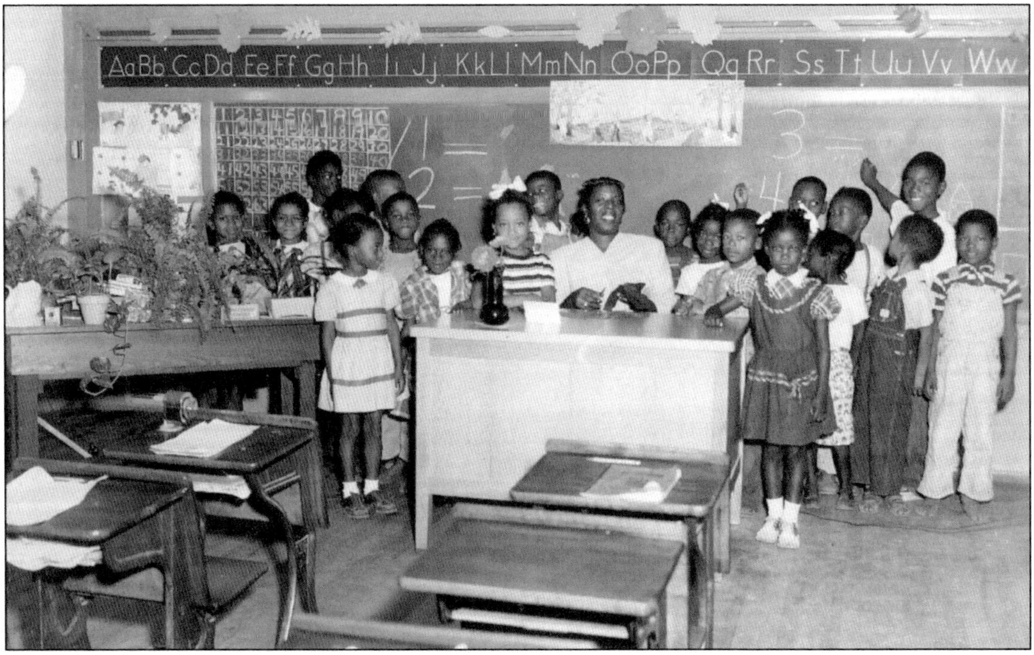

This unidentified teacher and her students pose for an official classroom photograph. The plants on the left side of the photograph suggest that she is teaching elementary biological science. Each classroom had a different focus, and subjects offered ranged from art to math. (Mertie Mims Collection.)

Four

They Lived Quite Well Considering

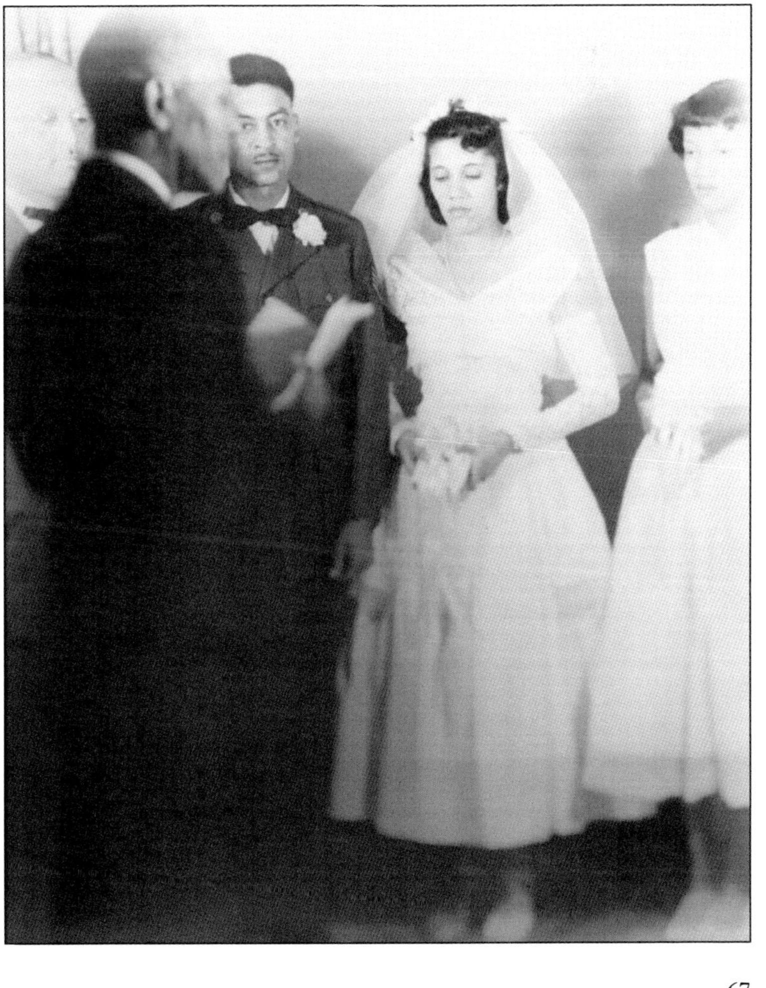

Here, a bride and groom say their vows. Earlier in the ceremony, the bride, Wordna Brown, was given away in marriage by her father, Lorenzo Brown. Wordna's sister Amelia Brown Johnson was a bridesmaid. The groom was McGill Blount. This wedding took place in the late 1940s. (Mertie Mims Collection.)

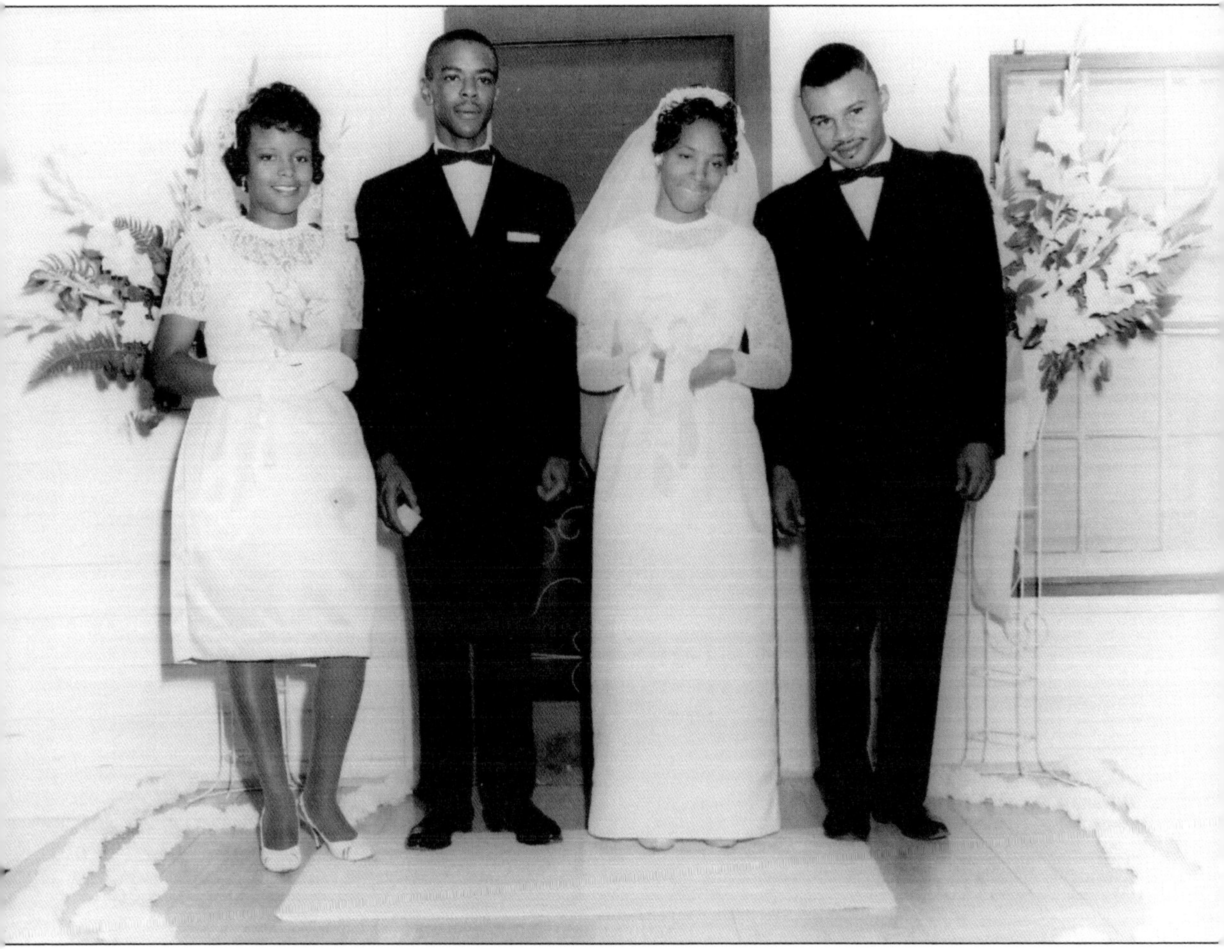

Middle-class African American families often held their daughter's wedding in their homes. There appears to be a double wedding happening in this image. The arrangement of fresh flowers in baskets and floral arrangements on the porch floor represent a family who could afford some luxuries. (Mertie Mims Collection.)

Anera Randle Martin is shown in the late 1930s with her brother Clifton Randle when they were students at E.J. Campbell High School. After graduation, Clifton joined the military and reached the rank of private before being killed in Germany in 1942. He was buried at Sand Hill Cemetery. (Courtesy of Peggy Jasso.)

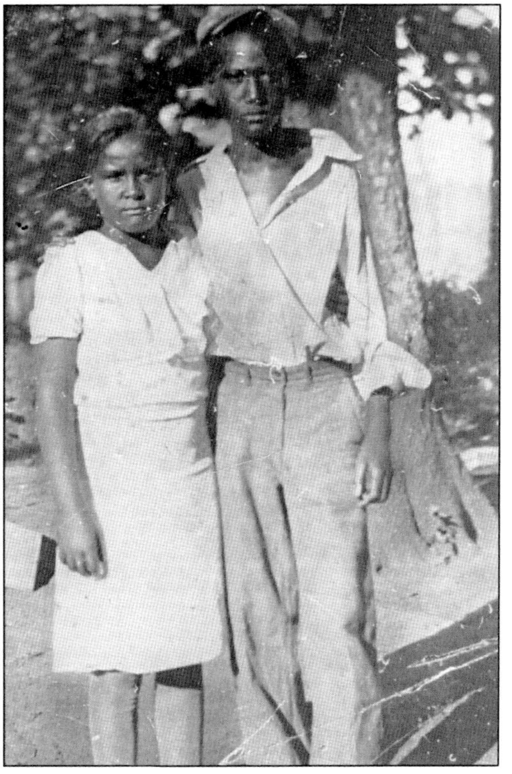

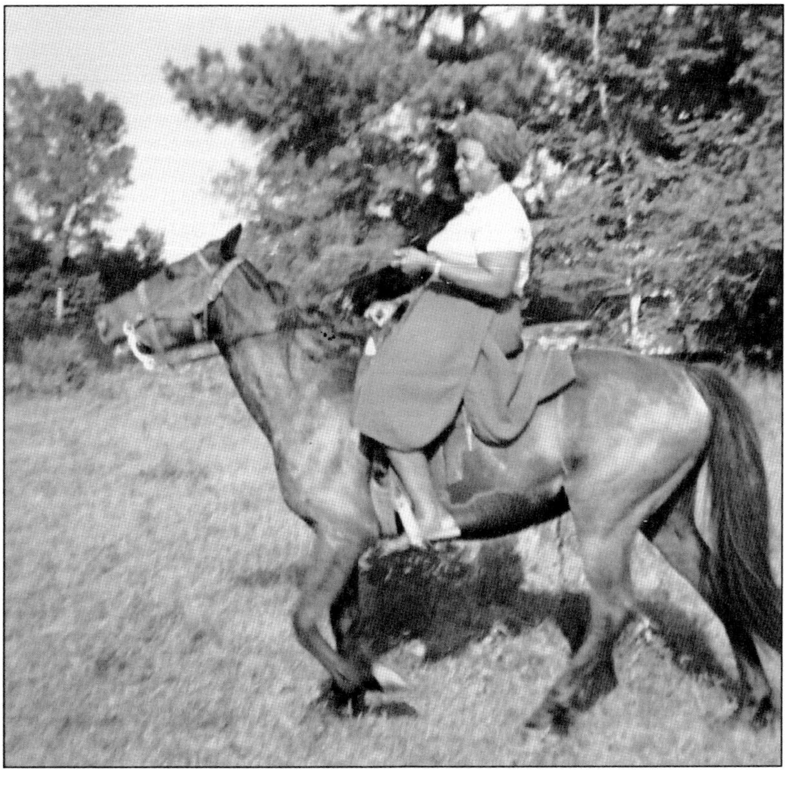

Here, Anera is seen riding a horse, as was common during her day. In some cases, women owned their own horses, which meant they did not have to depend on men to transport them to work, church, or social gatherings. Anera married her high school sweetheart, Oran Martin, in 1941. After completion of service, Oran returned to Nacogdoches and worked at Lone Star Feed Co. for 35 years. (Courtesy of Peggy Jasso.)

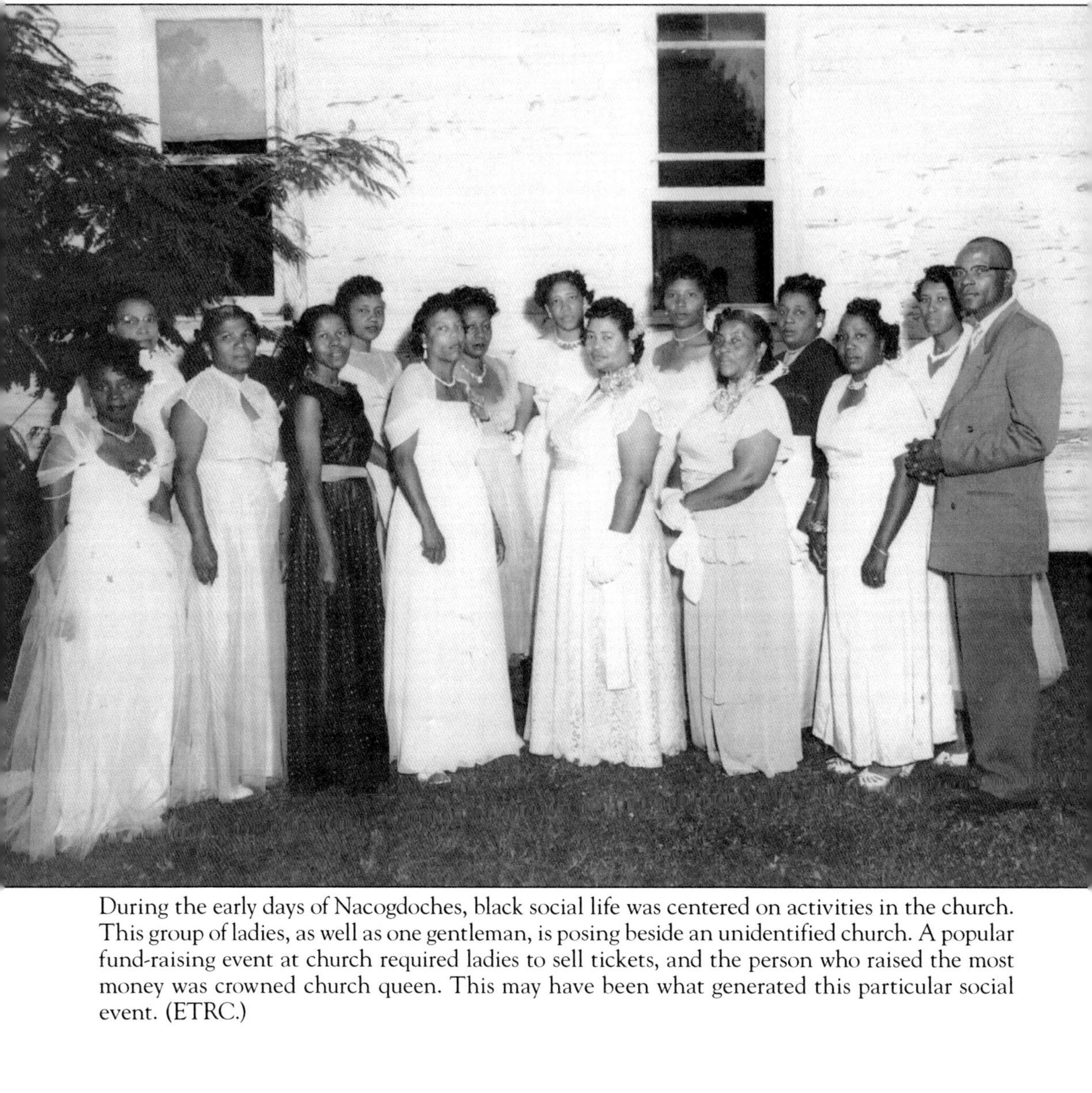

During the early days of Nacogdoches, black social life was centered on activities in the church. This group of ladies, as well as one gentleman, is posing beside an unidentified church. A popular fund-raising event at church required ladies to sell tickets, and the person who raised the most money was crowned church queen. This may have been what generated this particular social event. (ETRC.)

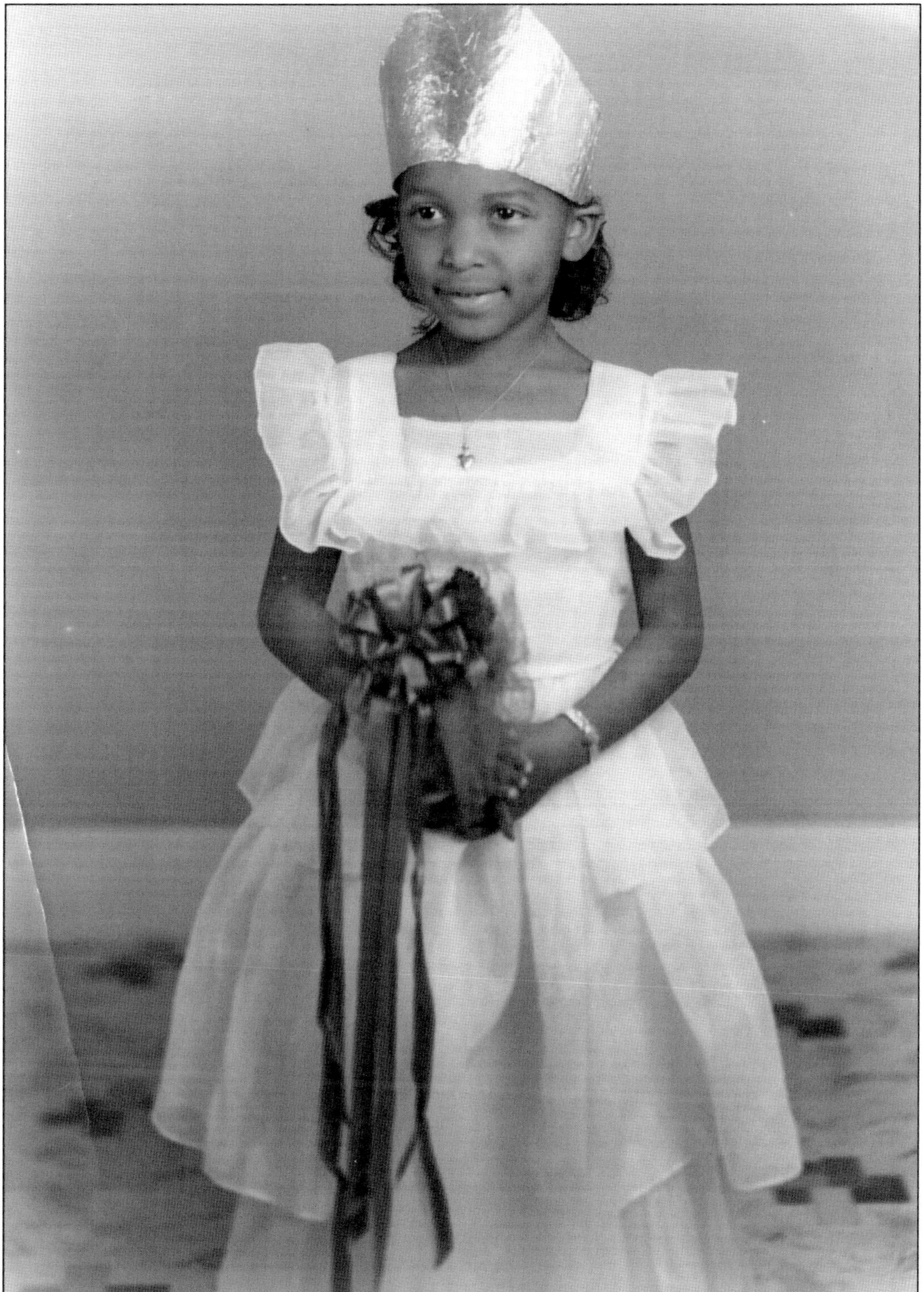

Tom Thumb church weddings were also a popular fund-raising event for churches. It involved young children participating in a mock wedding. A girl and boy were selected as the bride and groom while other children made up the wedding party. Another popular fund-raising event was a box supper auction, where men would bid on decorated box suppers made by single young women. (Mertie Mims Collection.)

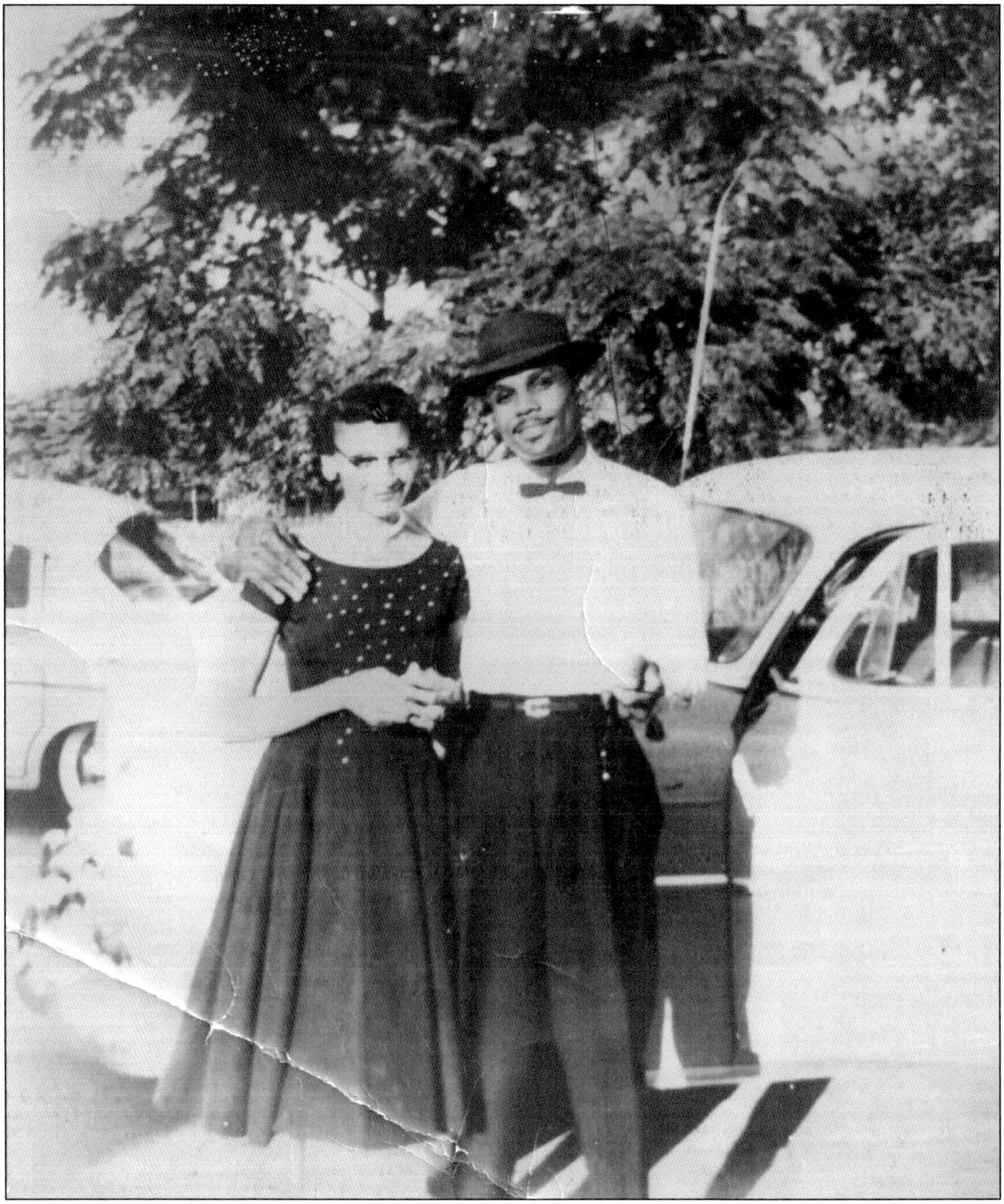

A young Robbie Johnson is shown with her husband, Nahala Johnson, on their wedding day in the 1950s. Robbie and Nahala were typical of young African Americans who were in love and married right out of high school. This Nacogdoches couple raised a family and stayed married until his recent death. Some of their descendants remain in the area. (Courtesy of Robbie Johnson.)

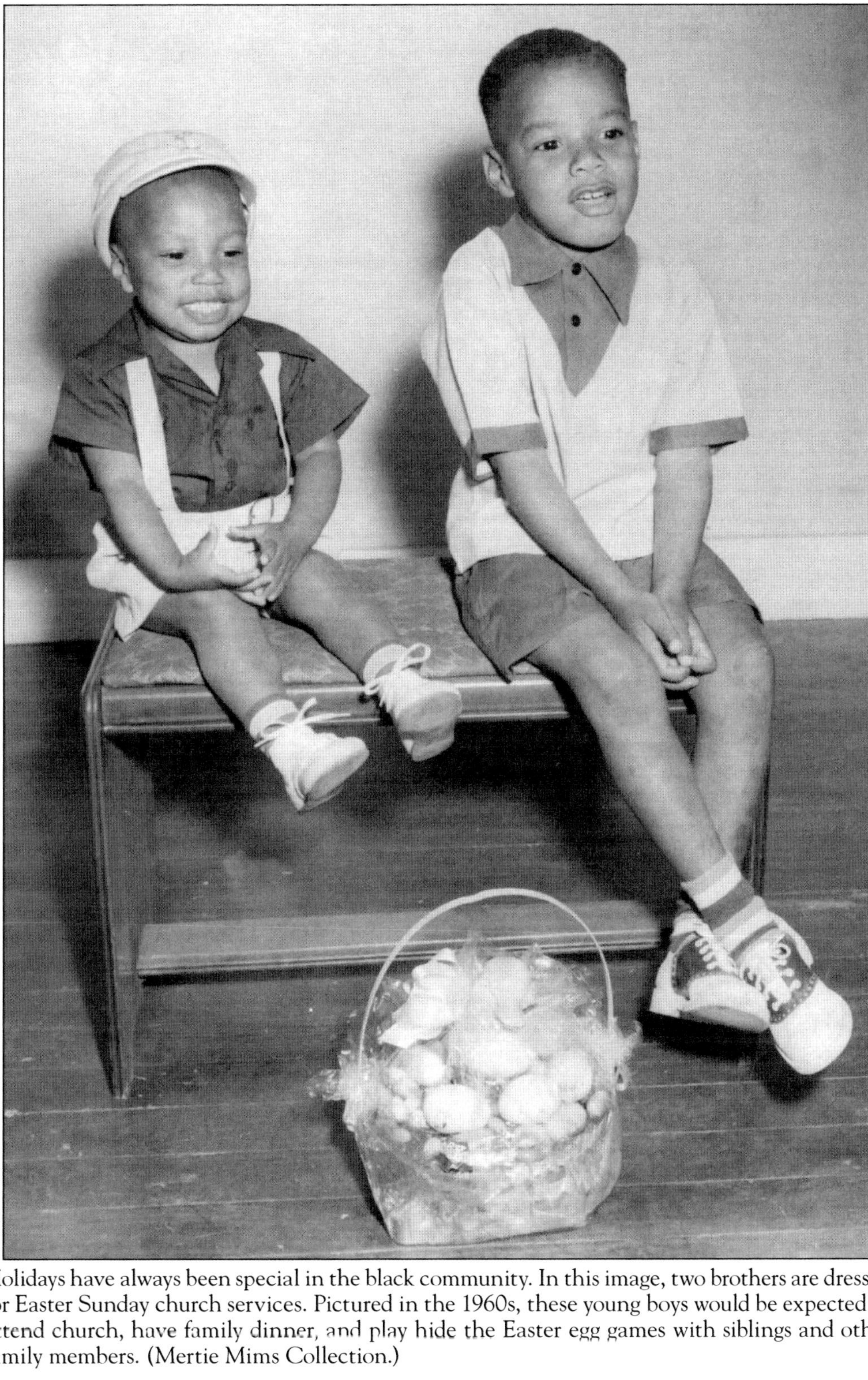

Holidays have always been special in the black community. In this image, two brothers are dressed for Easter Sunday church services. Pictured in the 1960s, these young boys would be expected to attend church, have family dinner, and play hide the Easter egg games with siblings and other family members. (Mertie Mims Collection.)

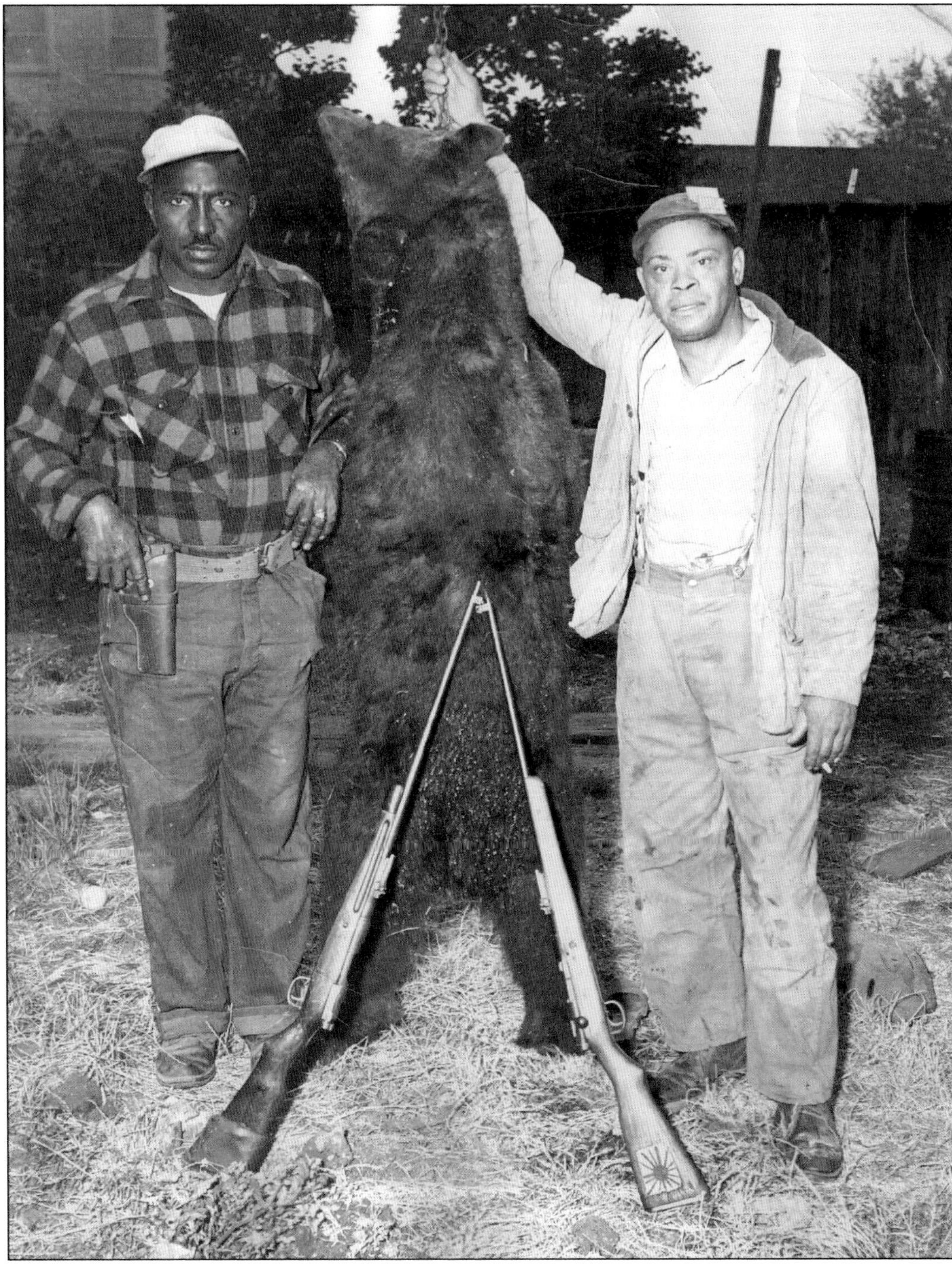

Louisiana black bears inhabited the Nacogdoches region for decades. Their meat and fur provided food for hunters and a source for income for trappers. By the 1920s, however, excessive hunting nearly depleted the population. This image, taken in the 1940s, shows at least one successful hunt. (Mertie Mims Collection.)

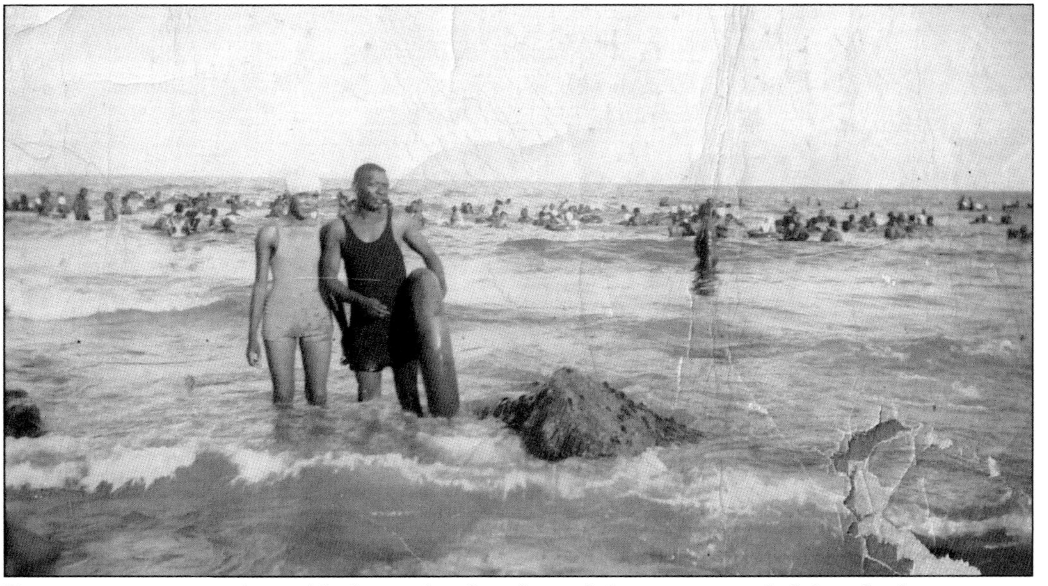

Due to segregation policies, black people often formed their own social clubs, which sometimes included meeting in different people's homes for fun activities. This couple belonged to a social group that planned an annual trip to Galveston, Texas. As depicted in this 1936 photograph, the beach was segregated into areas for blacks only. (Courtesy of Pascal Brown.)

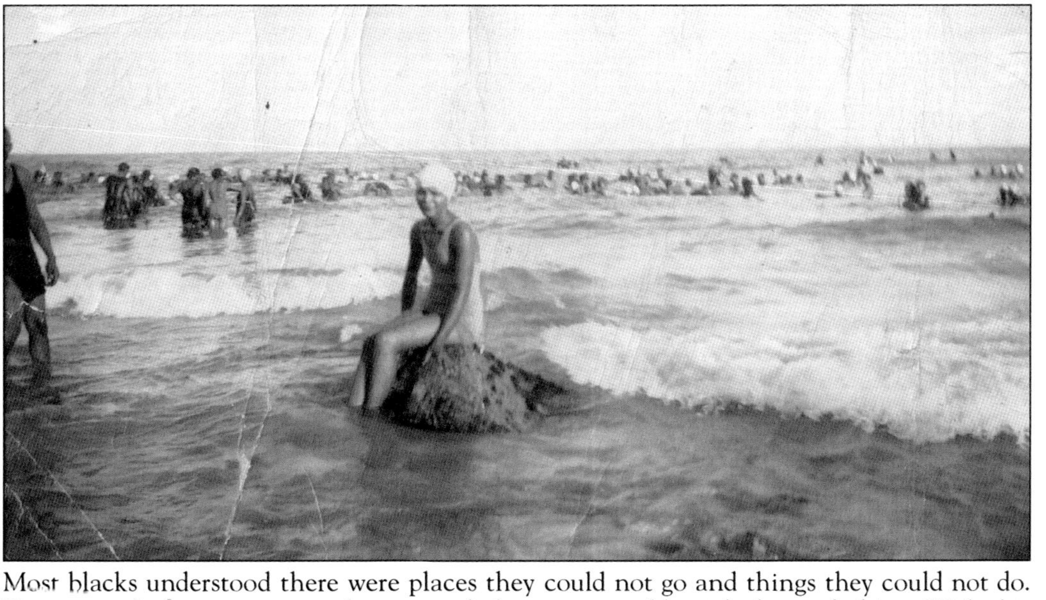

Most blacks understood there were places they could not go and things they could not do. To cope with the restrictions, they created places comparable with those of whites. With this acceptance, blacks were able to enjoy the beauty and waves of the Gulf of Mexico. (Courtesy of Pascal Brown.)

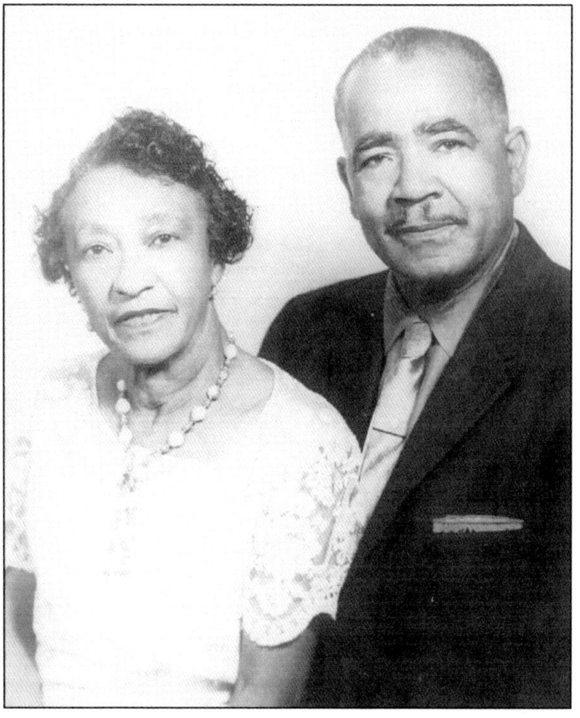

I.D. "Teacher" and Annie Garrett were considered one of the most influential black families in the city. Both husband and wife worked at the post office with more than 80 years of combined service. Known for their eccentric lifestyles, the Garretts often held lavish parties and planned expensive vacation trips with other African Americans in East Texas. (ETRC.)

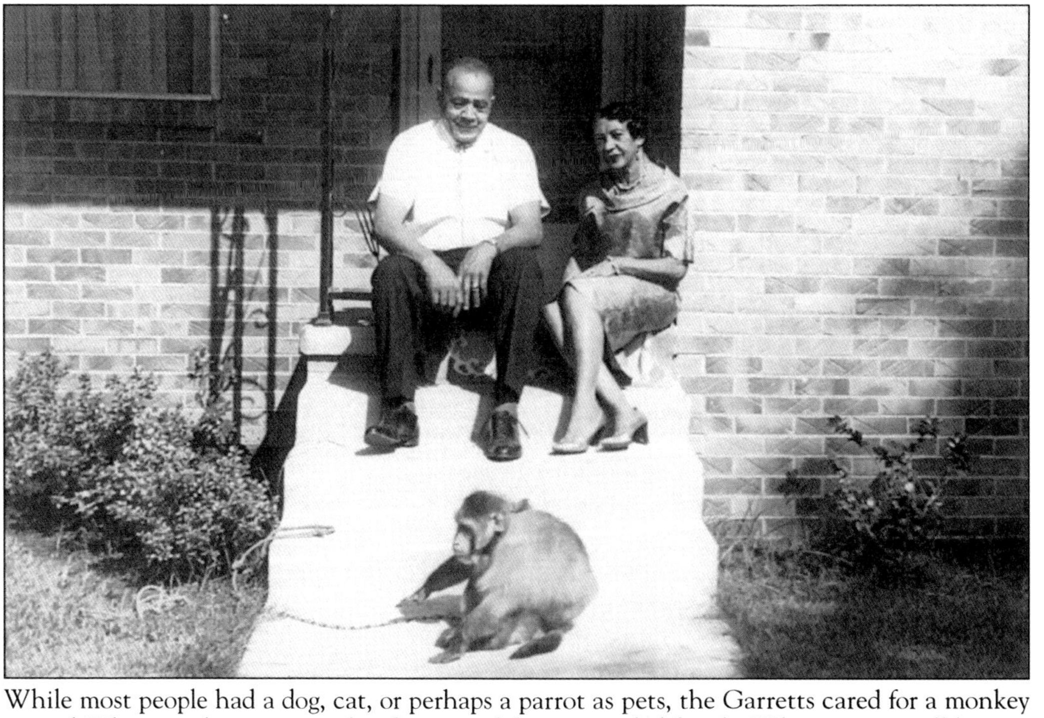

While most people had a dog, cat, or perhaps a parrot as pets, the Garretts cared for a monkey named Whimpy who was considered a part of their extended family. Whimpy was well known in the community, participating in local parades and community events. At his death, a formal funeral was arranged with Whimpy being buried in a tuxedo in the Garretts' backyard. (Courtesy of the Garrett family.)

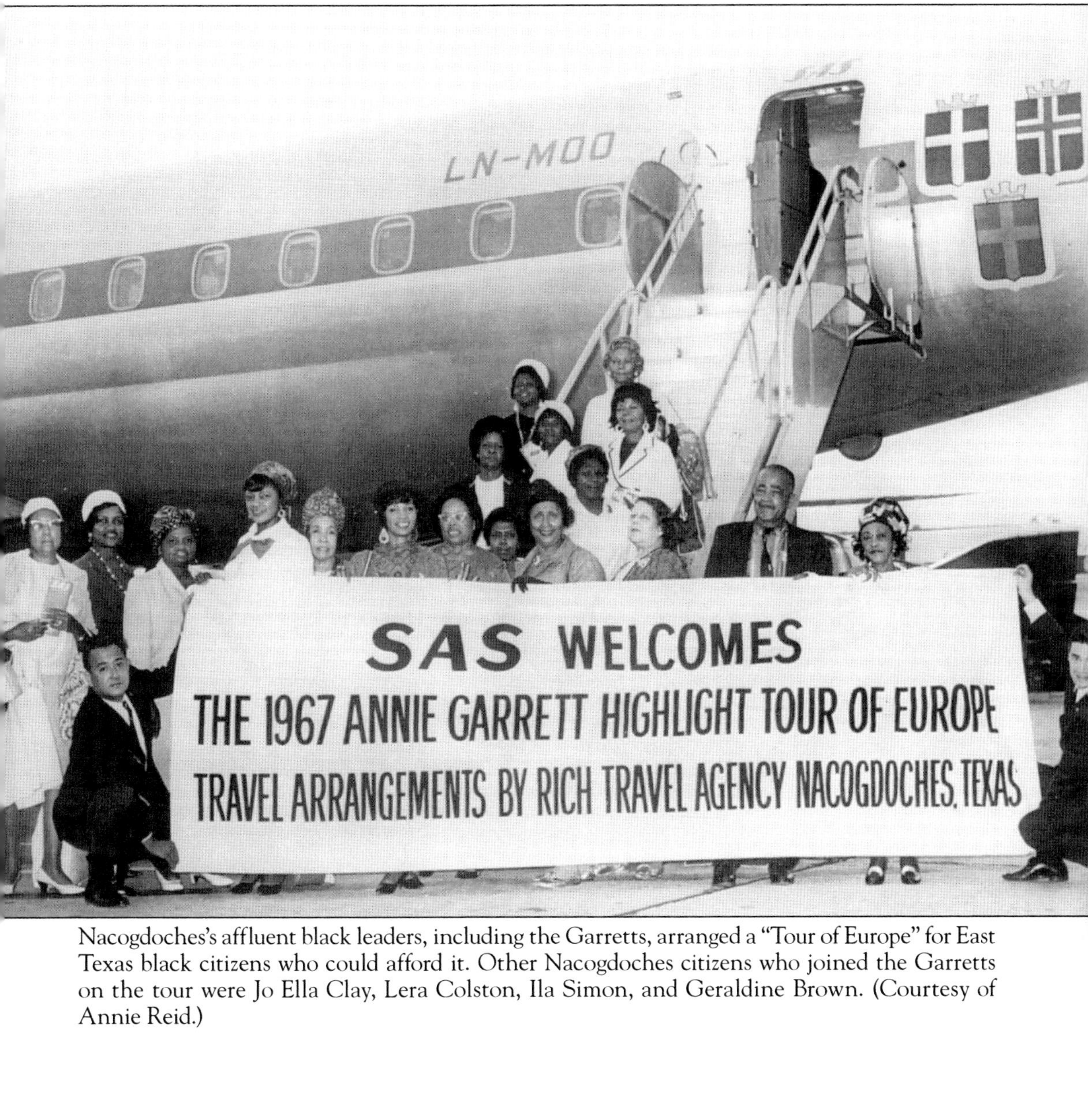

Nacogdoches's affluent black leaders, including the Garretts, arranged a "Tour of Europe" for East Texas black citizens who could afford it. Other Nacogdoches citizens who joined the Garretts on the tour were Jo Ella Clay, Lera Colston, Ila Simon, and Geraldine Brown. (Courtesy of Annie Reid.)

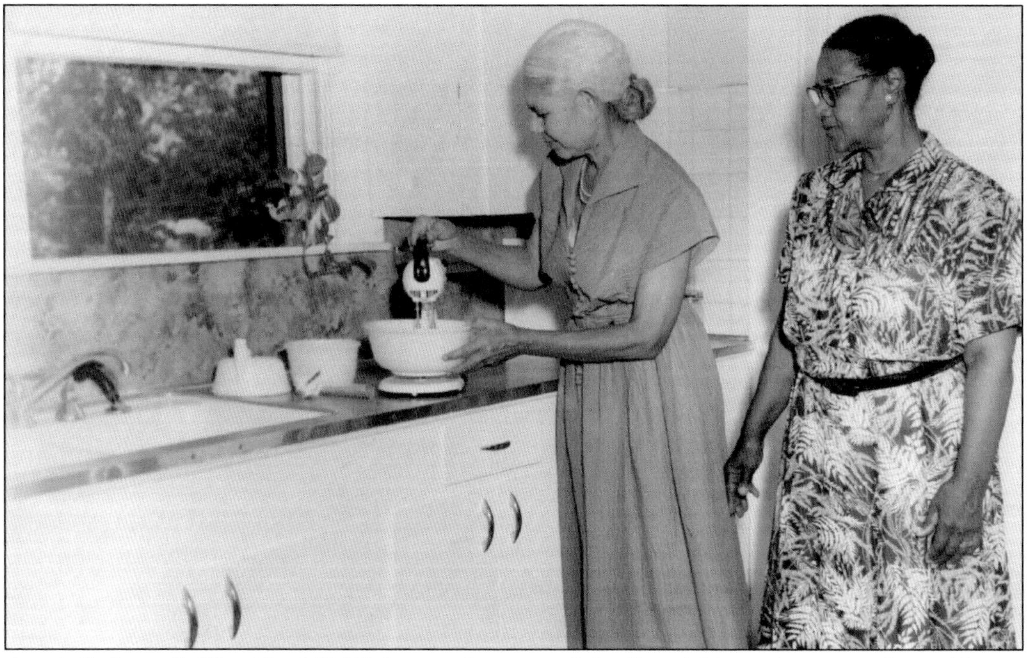

Annie Roberts (left), wife of Sid Roberts, who opened the first African American funeral home in Nacogdoches, shows her friend how to use one of her new appliances. The success of the Royal Funeral Home and similar businesses led to the beginning of the black middle class in the city. (Mertie Mims Collection.)

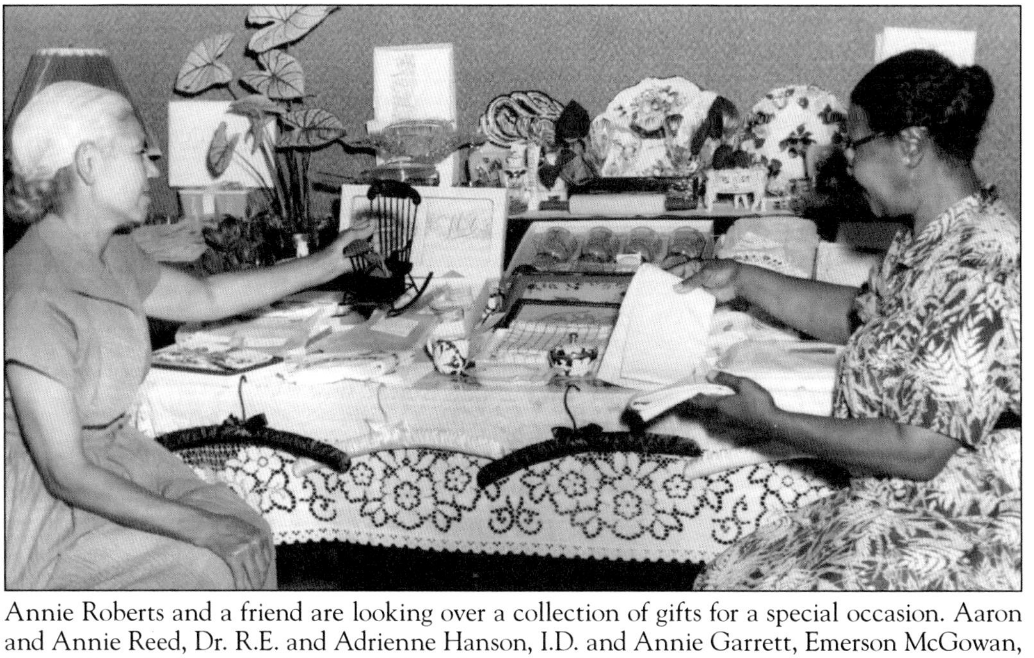

Annie Roberts and a friend are looking over a collection of gifts for a special occasion. Aaron and Annie Reed, Dr. R.E. and Adrienne Hanson, I.D. and Annie Garrett, Emerson McGowan, Ira and Lera Colston, Dr. M.L. and Torry Harris, and Sid and Annie Roberts were among the African American affluent and prominent. In addition to having lavish parties in their homes, this group formed a square dancing team that, on occasion, was permitted to join the local university team. (Mertie Mims Collection.)

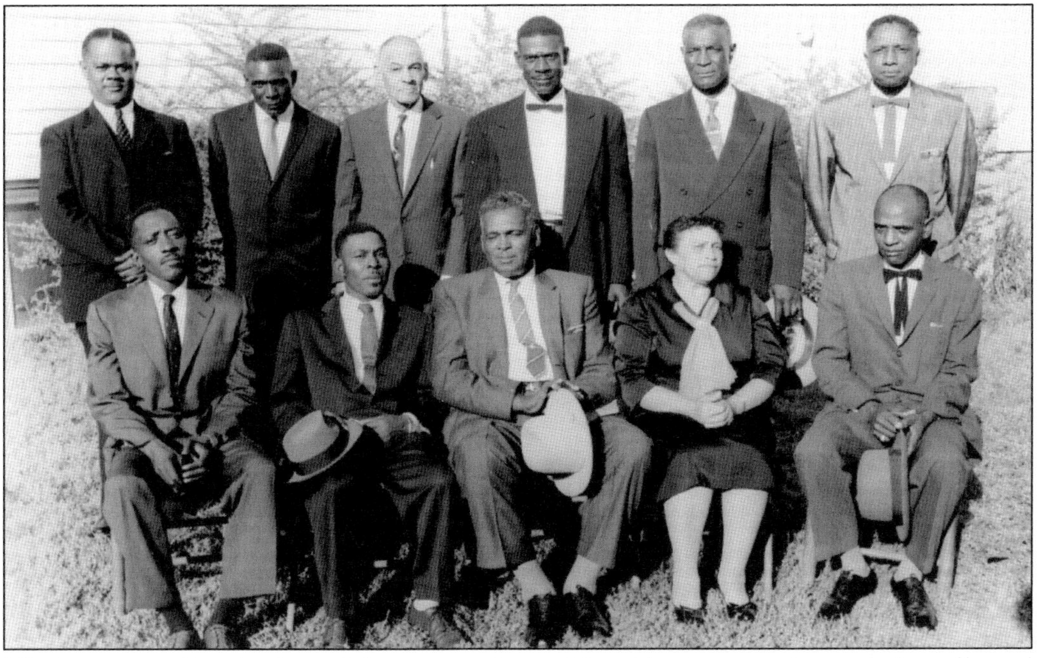

Ministers, as well as leaders of the community and local businesses, often met formally and informally to discuss issues in their neighborhoods. This image suggests the group met after a church service and could have discussed the church building fund, choir, or fund-raising activities. (Mertie Mims Collection.)

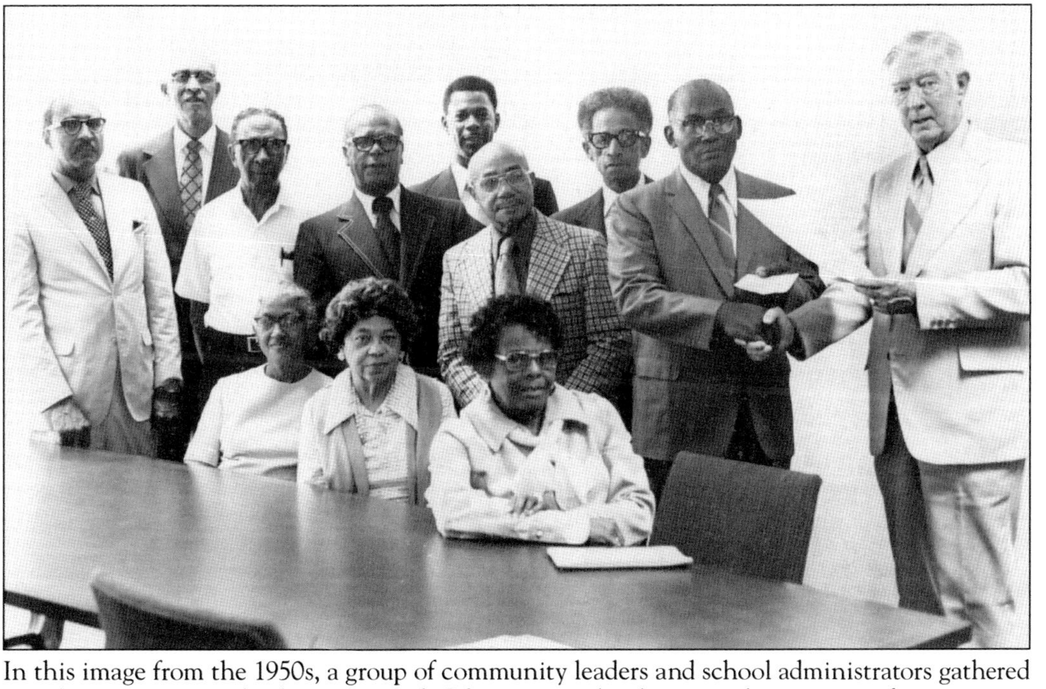

In this image from the 1950s, a group of community leaders and school administrators gathered together to receive a check or an award. Oftentimes, schools received recognition for a sports or academic achievement. W.E. Jones, who was the principal of E.J. Campbell High School, stands in the background. (Mertie Mims Collection.)

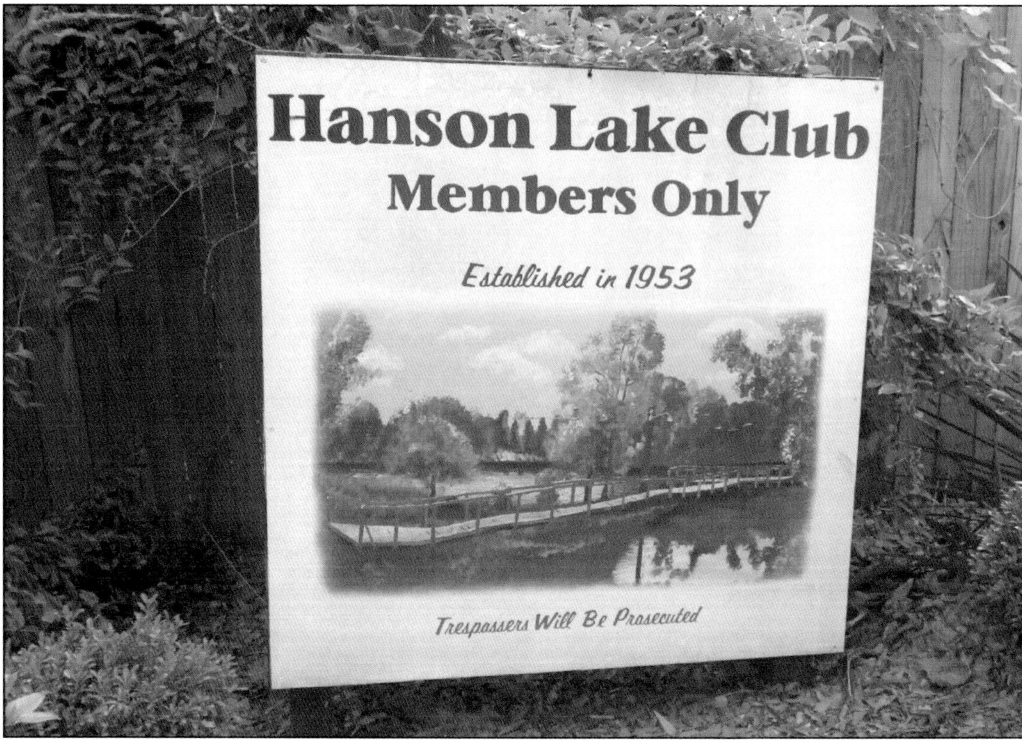

Jim Crow laws restricted blacks from all public facilities, limiting their access to various activities. In some communities, blacks had to be off the streets by nightfall. In response to those restrictions, in 1953, a group of 40 African American men came together and purchased 96.6 acres of land, including a lake. They wanted to create their own place to gather, eat, swim, fish, play, and have fun with family and friends. Known as Hanson Lake, this area is still maintained by private membership and considered the country club for blacks in Nacogdoches. Over the years, a pavilion, boating ramp, fishing pier, and playground equipment for children have been added. (Both, courtesy of Rolonda Teal.)

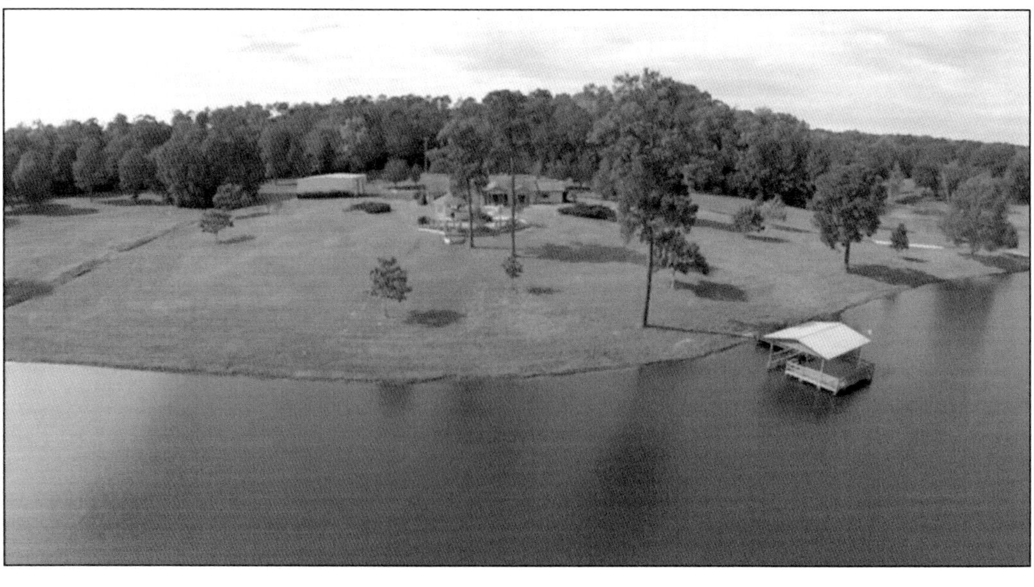

This musician was dressed in his best attire as he posed for this photograph. During the week, he would likely come home and sit on the front porch where he practiced his craft. Musical expression was one way to relax and vent after a hard day's work. (Mertie Mims Collection.)

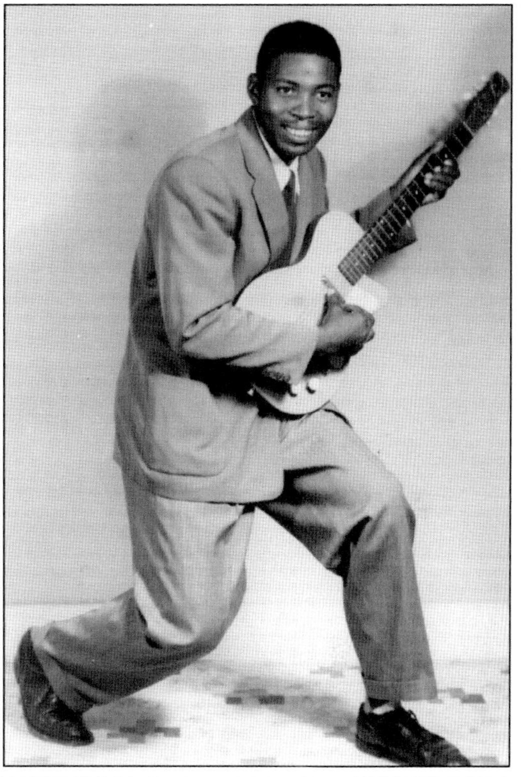

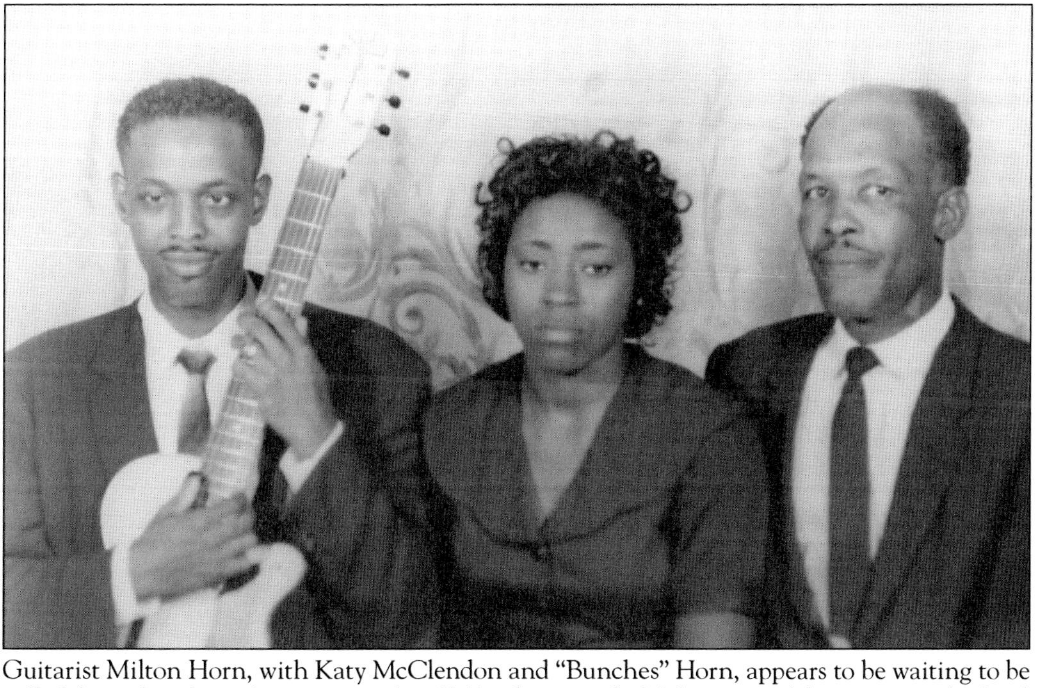

Guitarist Milton Horn, with Katy McClendon and "Bunches" Horn, appears to be waiting to be called for a church performance in this 1960s photograph. Making a joyful noise unto the Lord with guitars, drums, tambourines, pianos, and organs is expected and accepted in many black churches. (Mertie Mims Collection.)

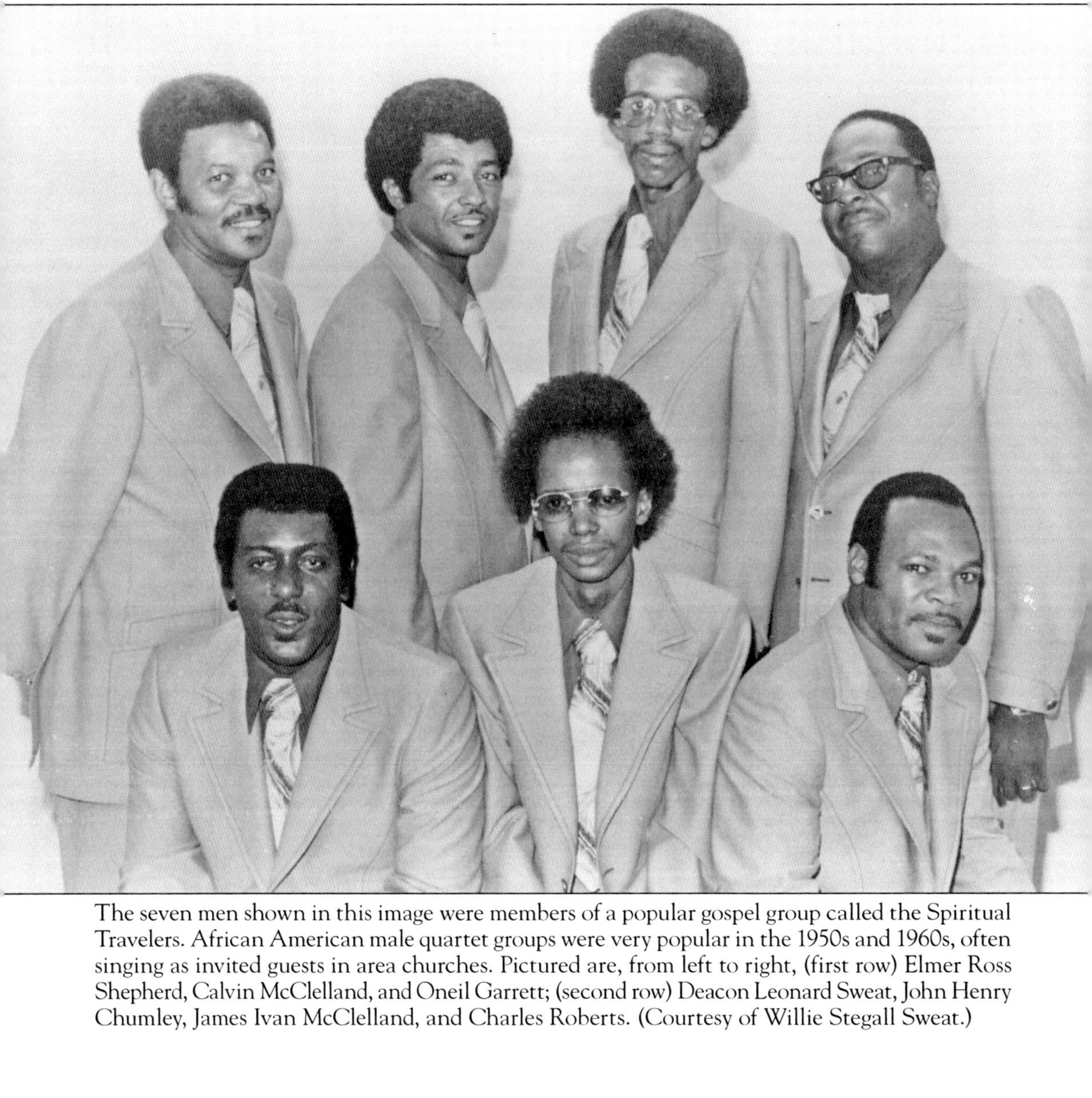

The seven men shown in this image were members of a popular gospel group called the Spiritual Travelers. African American male quartet groups were very popular in the 1950s and 1960s, often singing as invited guests in area churches. Pictured are, from left to right, (first row) Elmer Ross Shepherd, Calvin McClelland, and Oneil Garrett; (second row) Deacon Leonard Sweat, John Henry Chumley, James Ivan McClelland, and Charles Roberts. (Courtesy of Willie Stegall Sweat.)

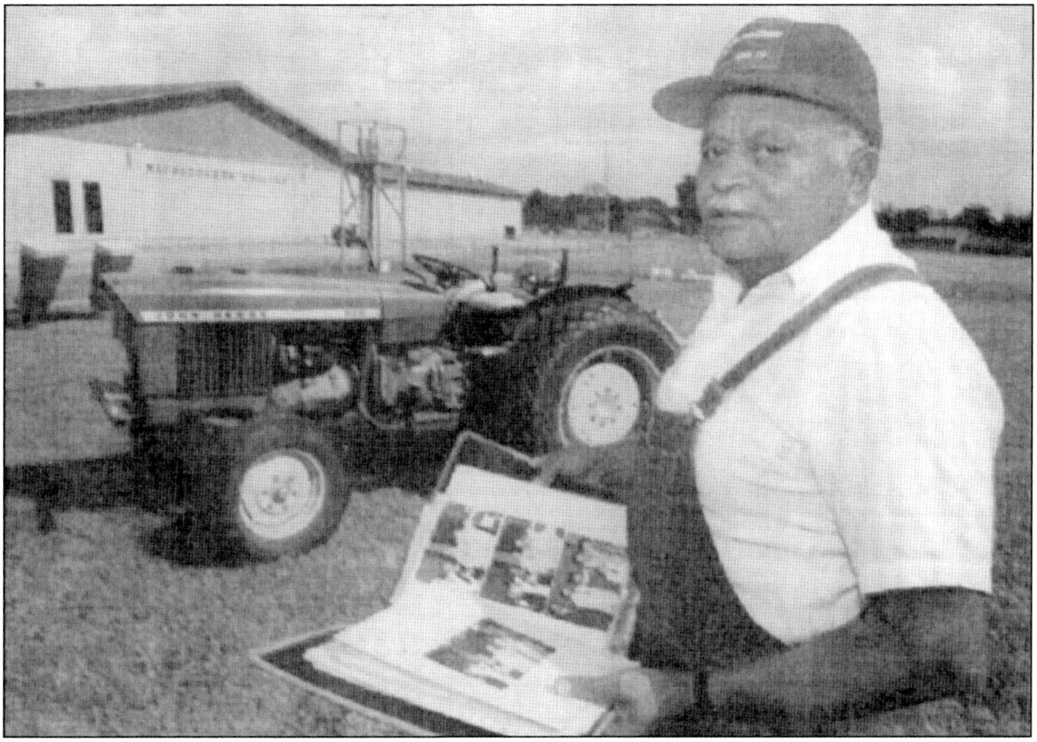

In addition to being an award-winning coach, Bo McMichael was a man who loved to farm. During his retirement years, he was known to raise vegetables and give them away to those in need. McMichael found almost as much joy in farming as he did coaching the high school football team. (Courtesy of the McMichael family.)

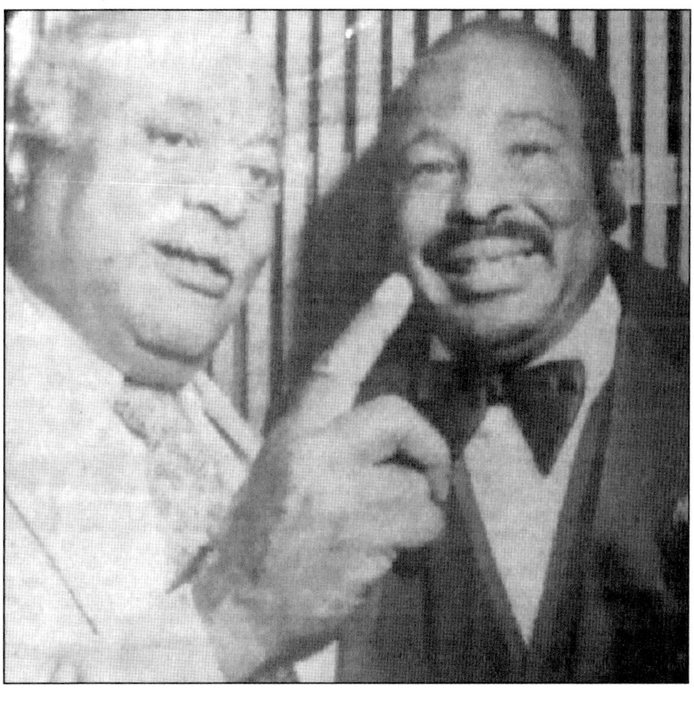

"Crazy Ray," whose real name was Wilford Jones, was the unofficial mascot of the Dallas Cowboys football team. He reportedly missed only three games in 46 seasons; Crazy Ray, on the right in this image, stands next to local coach Bo McMichael. (Courtesy of the McMichael family.)

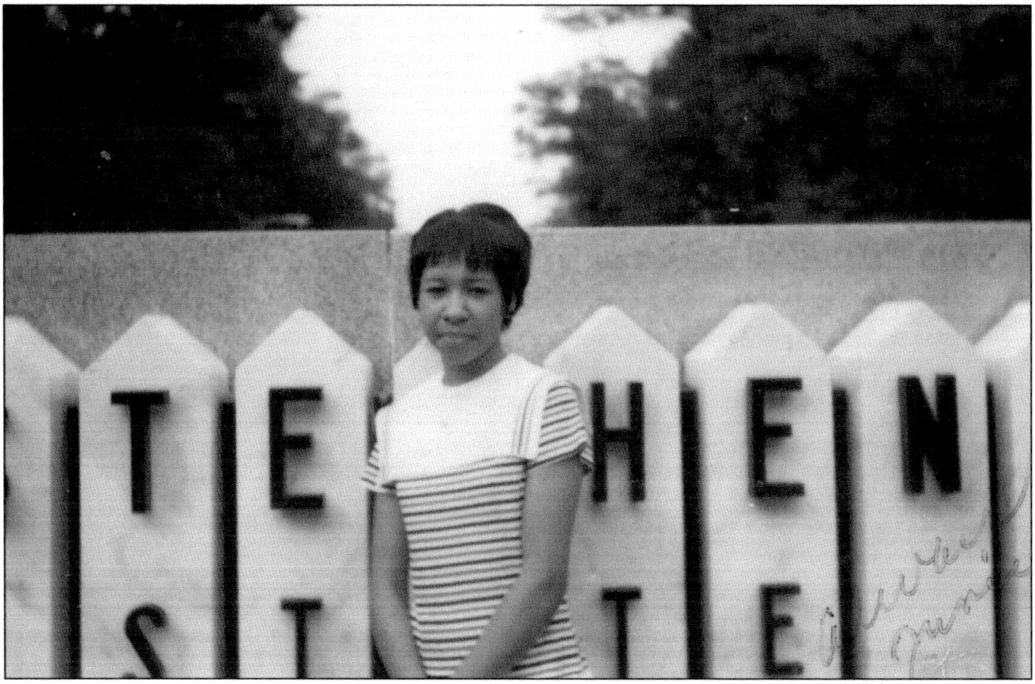

Local citizens said very little was printed in the newspapers or shown on television about the civil rights struggle in Nacogdoches. Like many American blacks, Nacogdoches blacks had their own concerns about inequality and injustices and took to the streets with their protest. Helena Patton, a Nacogdoches native and student at Stephen F. Austin State University, was one of many protestors. (Courtesy of Helena Patton Abdullah.)

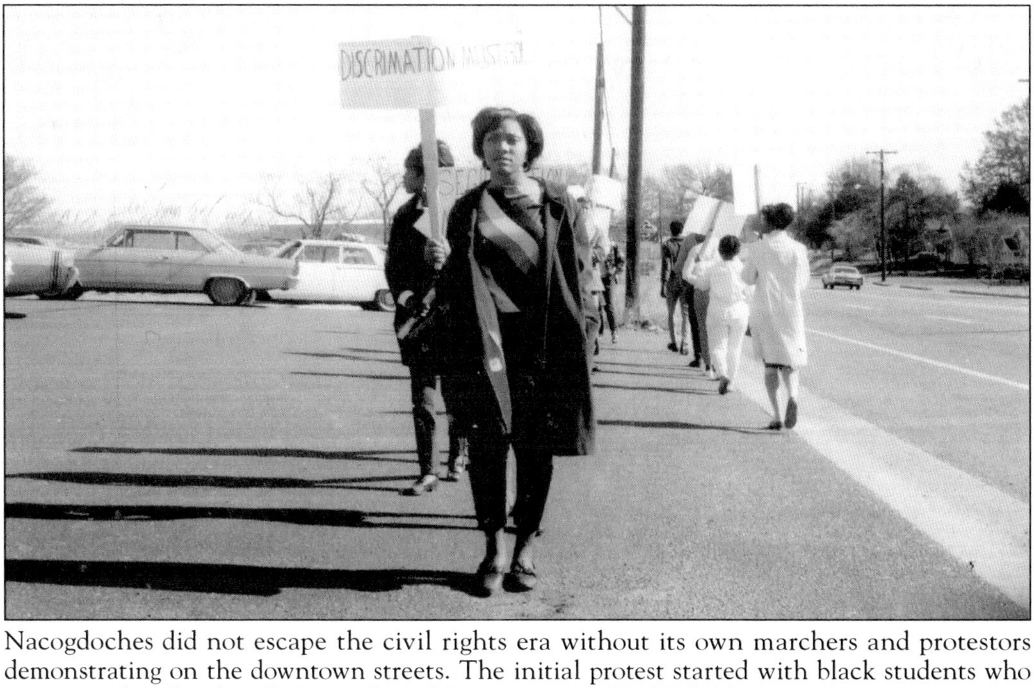

Nacogdoches did not escape the civil rights era without its own marchers and protestors demonstrating on the downtown streets. The initial protest started with black students who were attending Stephen F. Austin State University in 1970. (ETRC.)

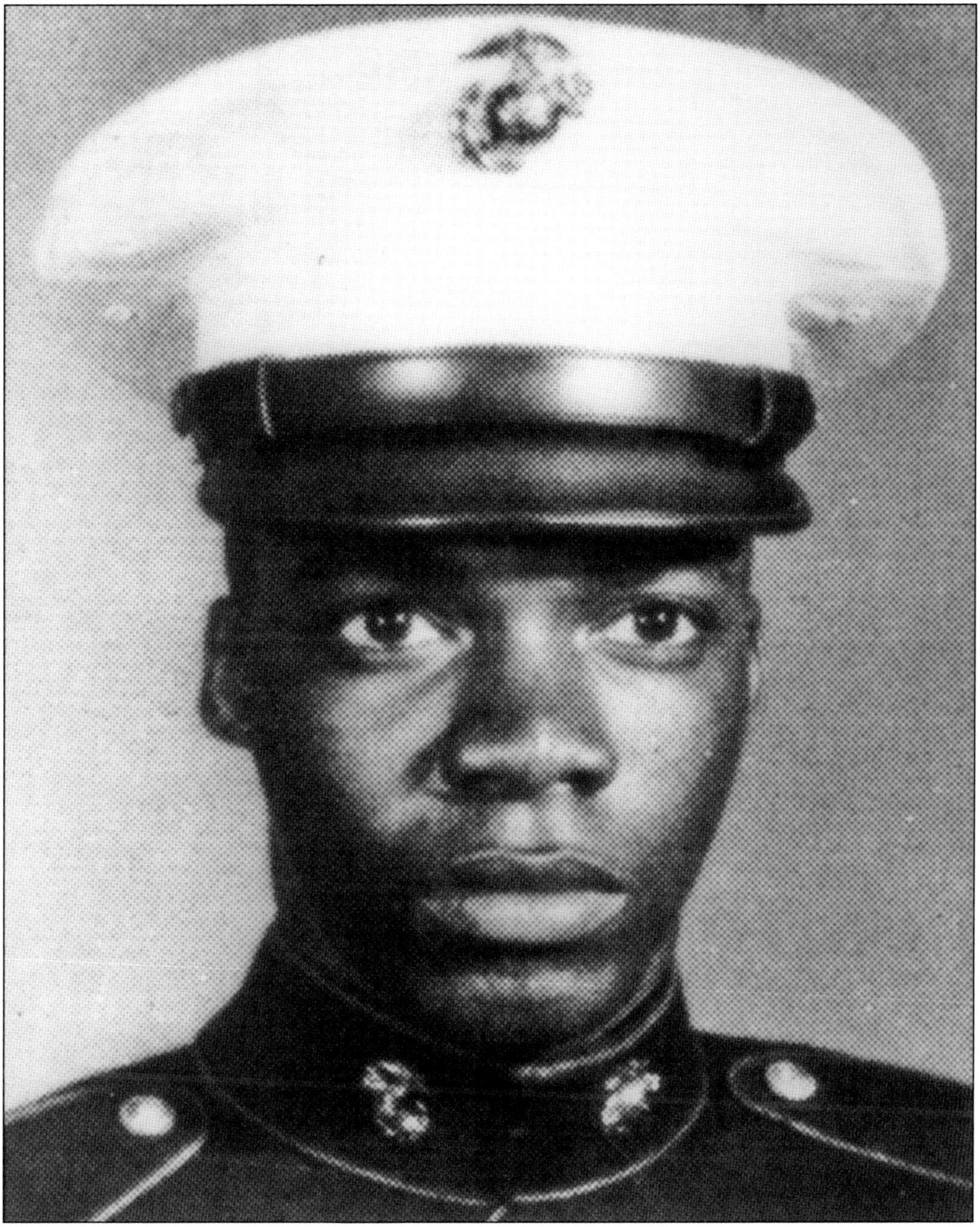

A memorial for Oscar P. Austin sits at the entrance of Nacogdoches Memorial Hospital. PFC Oscar P. Austin was born in Nacogdoches. He was inducted into the US Marine Corps in 1968. This brave soldier was killed by enemy fire in February 1969 when he ignored his own safety to protect an injured fellow Marine. For this heroic deed, PFC Oscar P. Austin, USMC, was a recipient of the Medal of Honor, Purple Heart, National Defense Service Medal, Vietnam Service Medal and the Republic of Vietnam Campaign Medal. A US Navy destroyer was named Oscar Austin in his honor. (Courtesy of the US Marine Corps.)

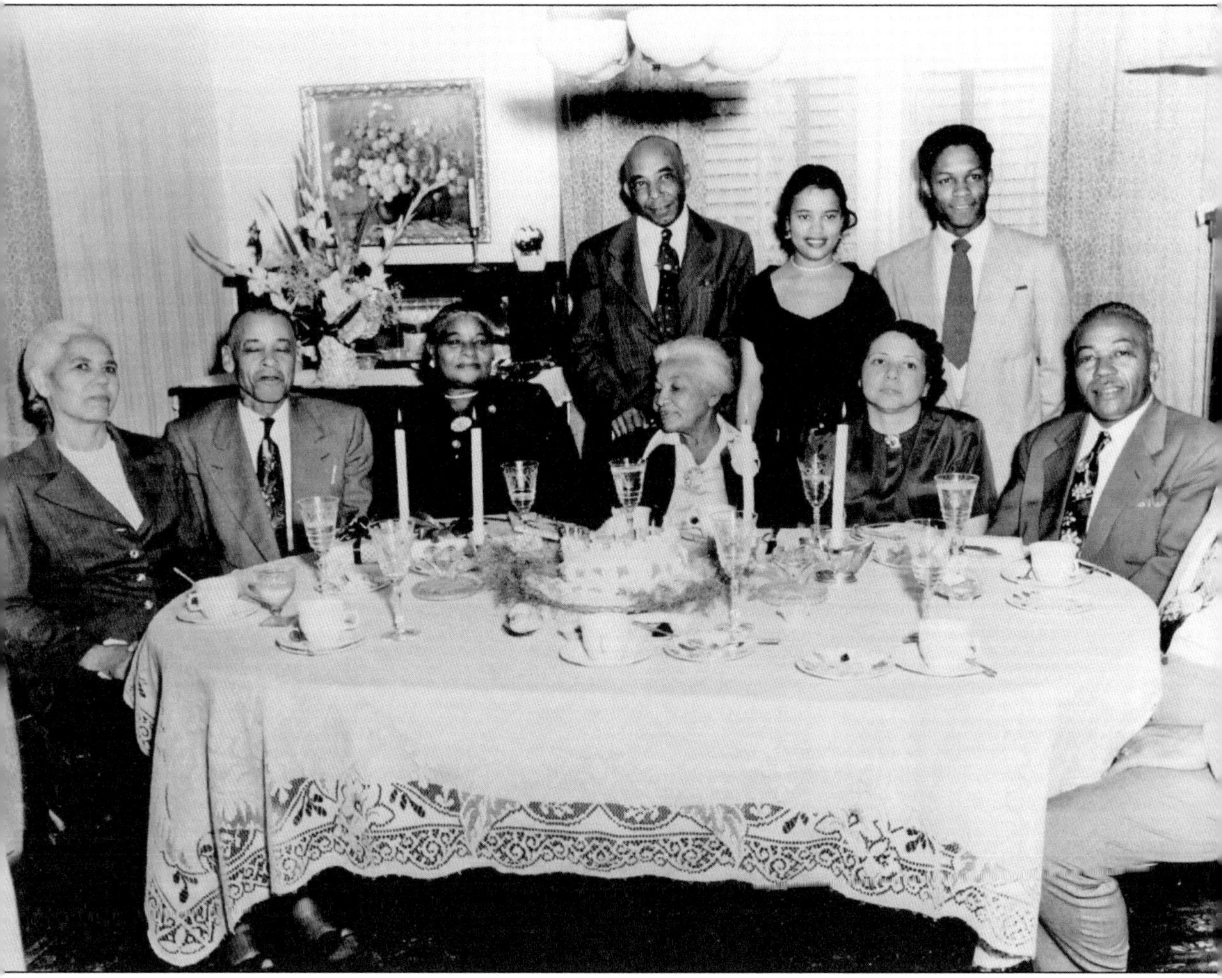

This image shows a dinner party hosted by Sid and Annie Roberts (far left) in their spacious home. Dr. M.L. Harris, a local dentist, and his wife, Tory, were in attendance along with other members of Nacogdoches's black affluent middle class. (Mertie Mims Collection.)

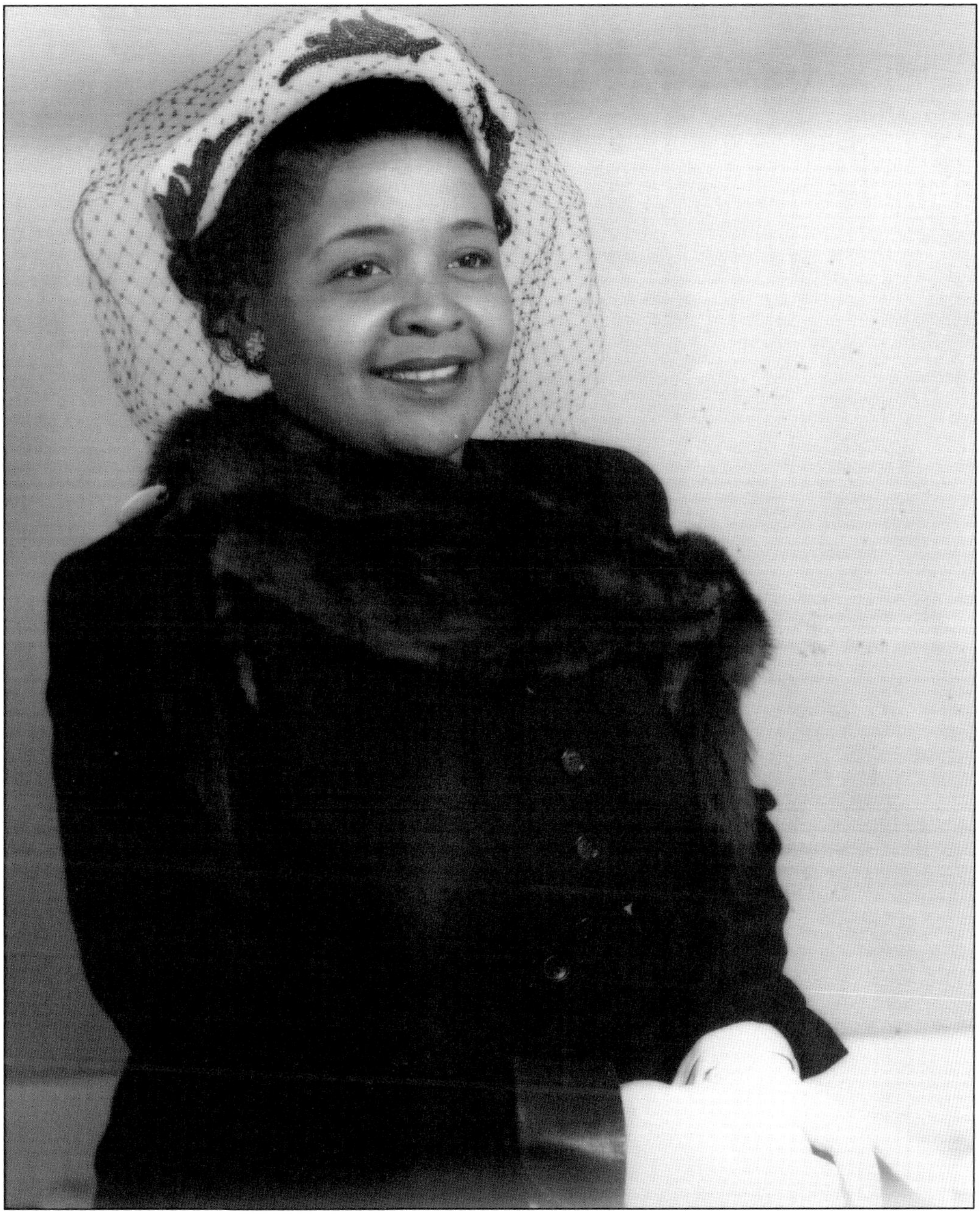

Popular teacher Odessa Preston Terry had the respect and attention of many students. She and her brother coach Ralph C. Allen worked for E.J. Campbell High School and were reportedly devoted to their students. (Mertie Mims Collection.)

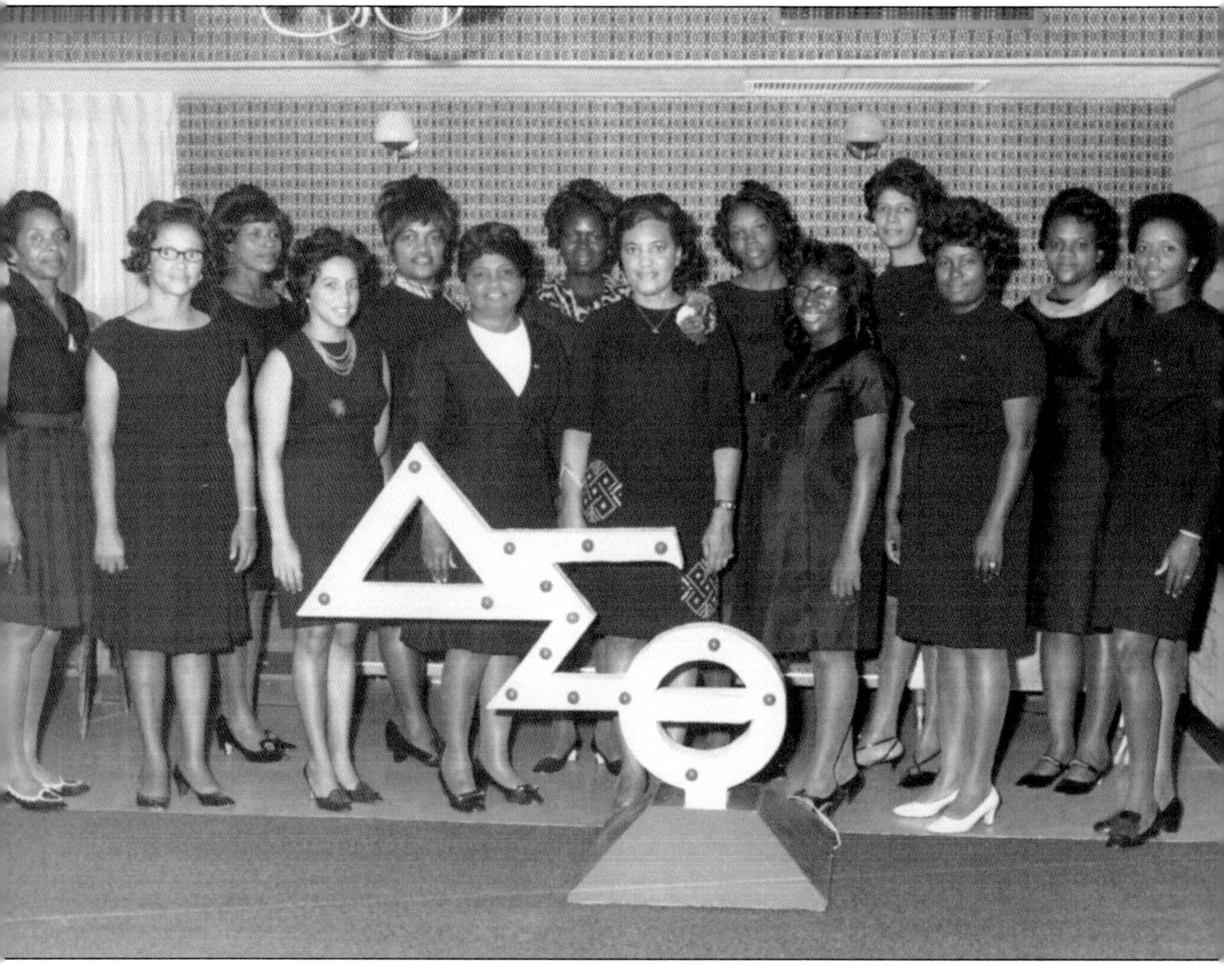

Black sororities and fraternities play a major role in the black community, often providing educational, social, and cultural activities. The national Delta Sigma Theta Sorority, Inc., was established in 1913 in Washington, DC. Lufkin-Nacogdoches alumnae chapter of Delta Sigma Theta Sorority, Inc., charter members are shown here in 1969. (Courtesy of Dorothy Warren.)

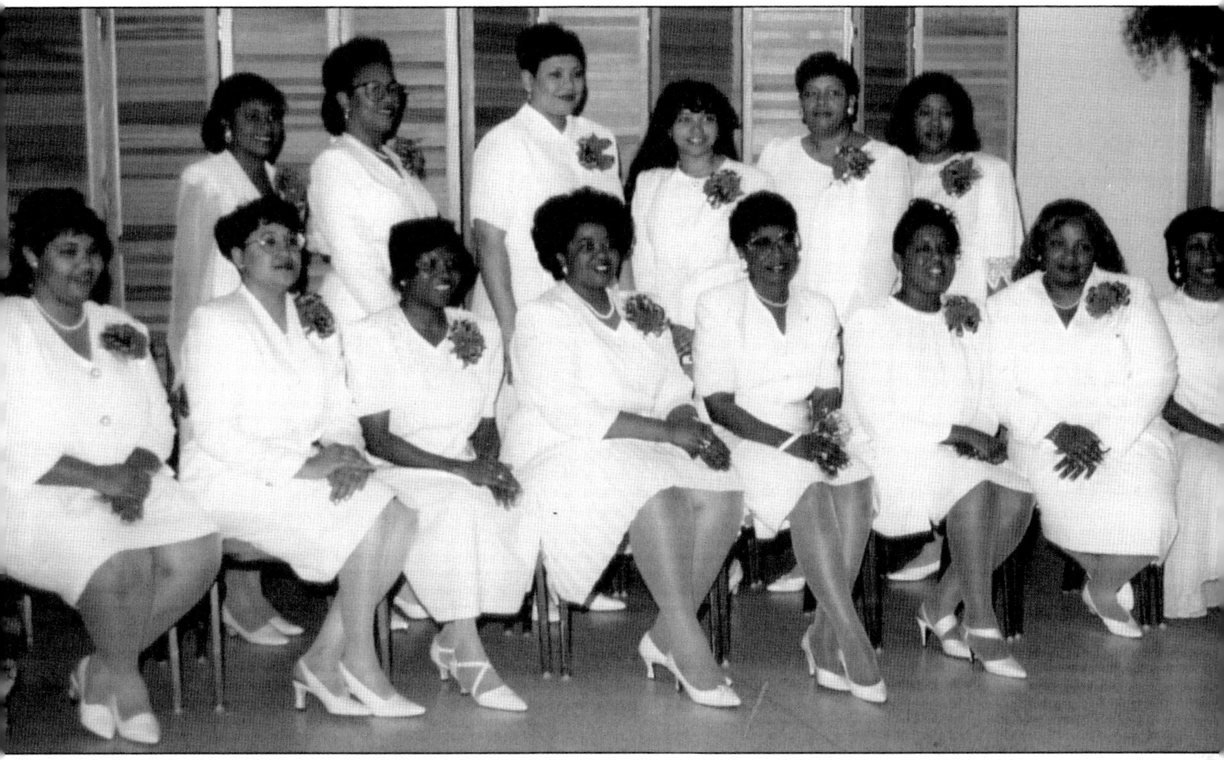

Nacogdoches alumnae members of Alpha Kappa Alpha Sorority, Inc., are shown in this image. The national organization was established at Howard University, in Washington, DC, in 1908. Black sororities and fraternities have contributed to the Nacogdoches community since the early 1950s by working with various ethnic groups. (Courtesy of Maylene Neal.)

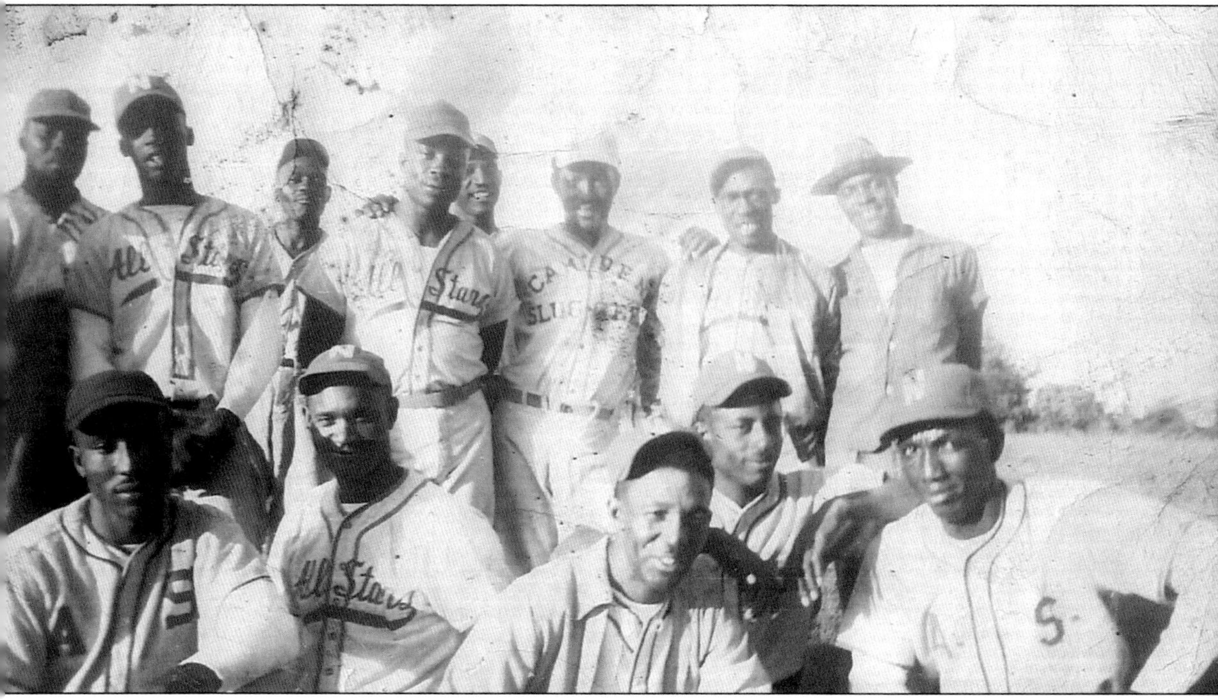

The Nacogdoches All Stars, formed by Archie Rison Sr., originated in the early 1950s in a cow pasture about 13 miles east of the city in the community of Sand Hill. Later, the team moved to a large field where the present-day Walmart is located. Since baseball was a popular way to spend a Sunday afternoon during the warm months, folks came from miles around to see the action. Often the All Stars traveled within a 100-mile radius to play in nearby cities of Marshall, Longview, Kilgore, Lufkin, Crockett, and Jasper. (Courtesy of Archie Rison Jr.)

Five

Bits and Pieces of History

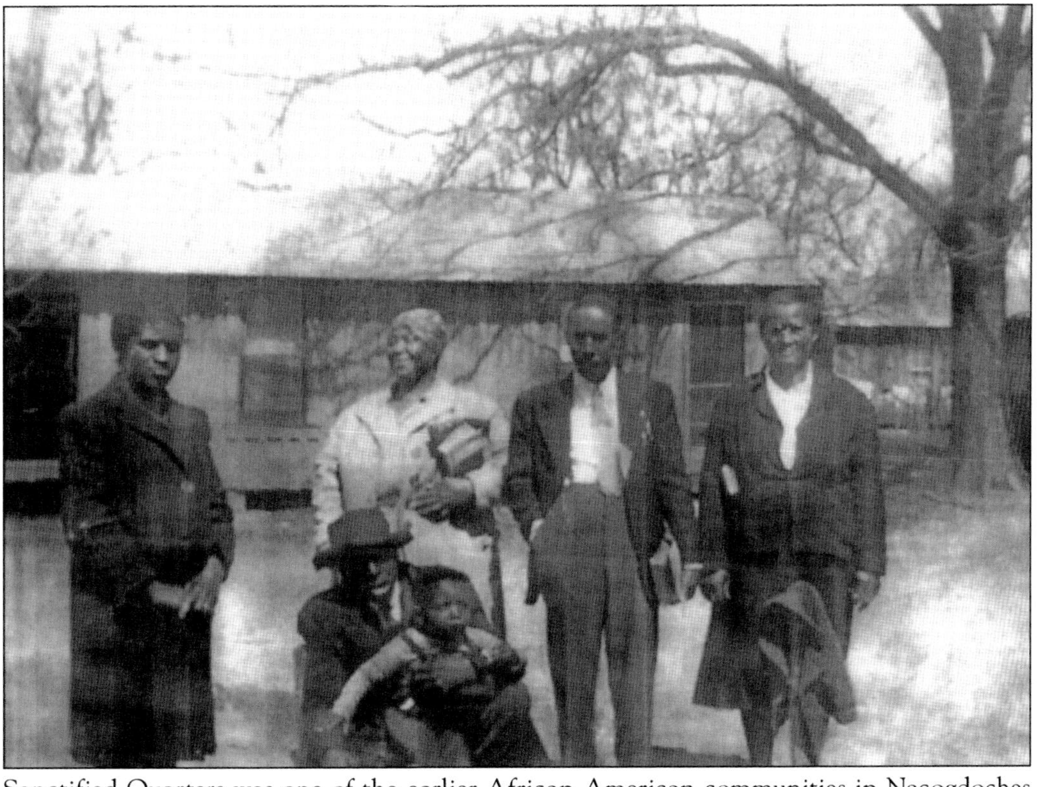

Sanctified Quarters was one of the earlier African American communities in Nacogdoches County. Its name stems from the many community residents that attended the Bethel Temple Church of God in Christ. Gathered after a service are Stegall family members and friends. From left to right are (first row) James Edward Stegall, holding infant son, Delton Stegall; (second row) Arlena Menefee Stegall, Hattie Johnson, William Mergerson, and unidentified. (Courtesy of the Stegall family.)

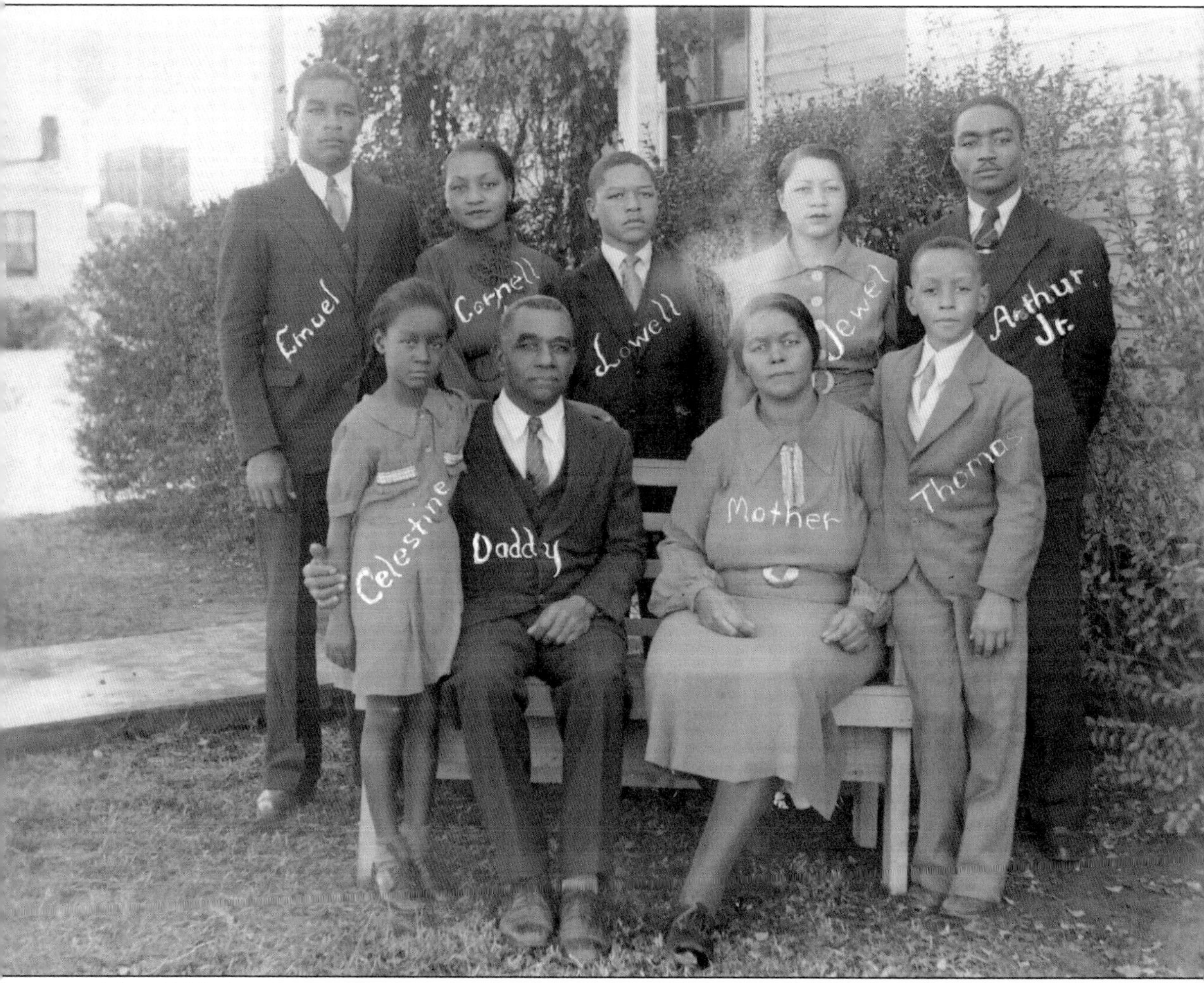

This 1936 photograph shows the family of Arthur G. and Maude Cleaver. Arthur G. is the son of educator Horney Cleaver, who was cited as the richest black man in Nacogdoches and the state of Texas. All seven of Arthur G. Cleaver's children graduated from Prairie View A&M College, and they all received a master's degree, too. One son earned his doctorate and served as vice president of Prairie View A&M College. (ETRC.)

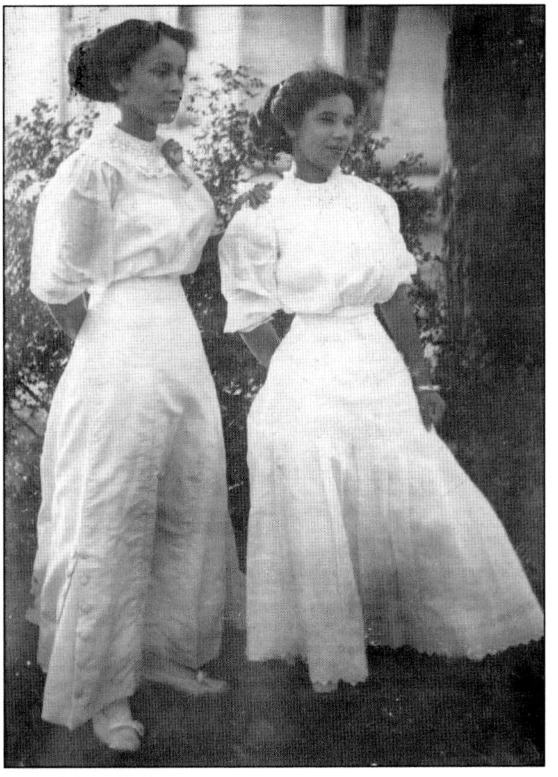

The young ladies in white are descendants of Horney C. Cleaver; the photographs were taken 64 years apart, at right in 1908 and below in 1972. Cornell G. Cleaver Hatchett describes his grandfather Horney C. Cleaver as an early educator, early religious founder, and an astute businessman with strong family values. (Right, courtesy of ETRC; below, courtesy of the Cleaver family.)

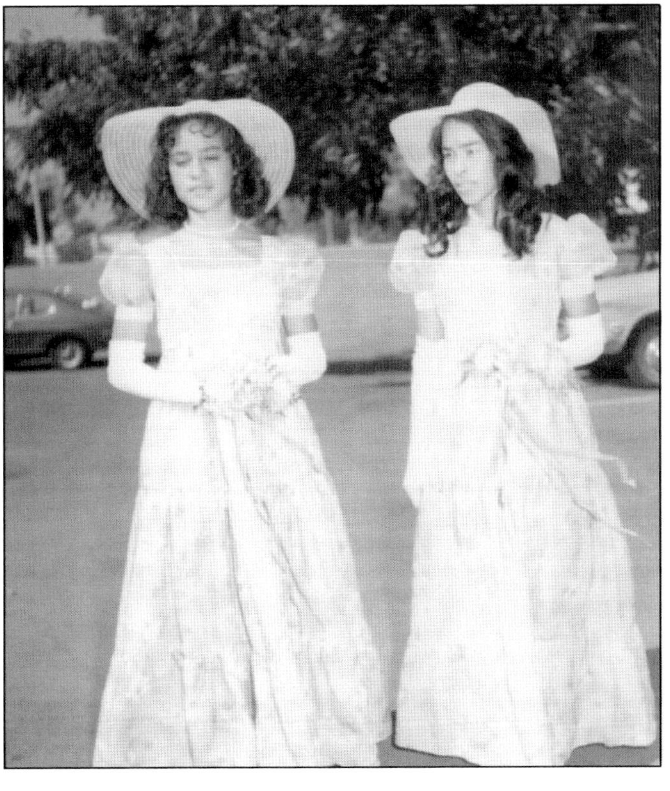

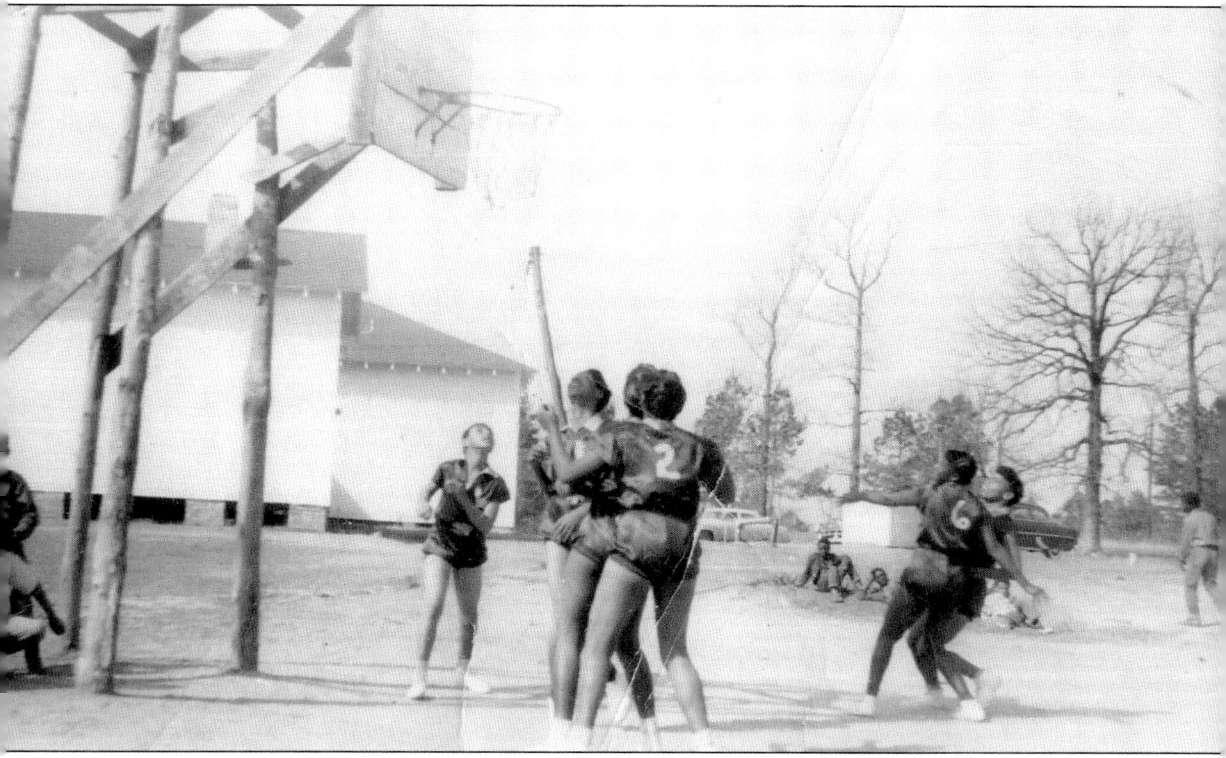

Early African American schools usually had an outdoor basketball court and homemade basketball goals. In the 1950s, the community was proud of the Washington Colored School and its teams. Under the supervision of the principal, parents and community members came together to build such items as the outside basketball goal shown in this image. (Courtesy of Mamie Rogers Hodge.)

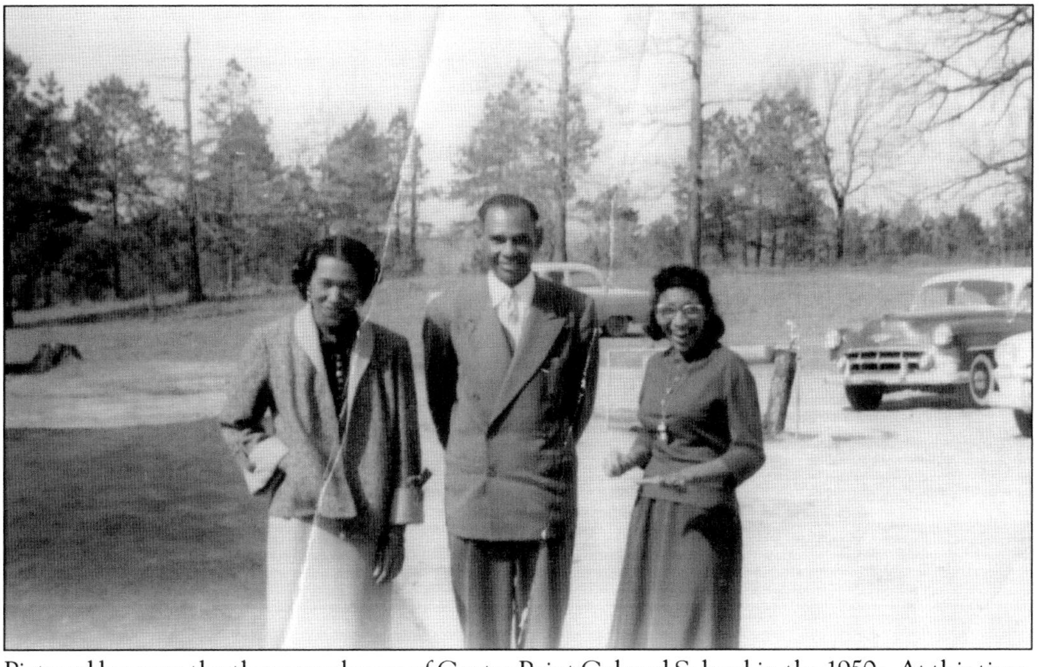

Pictured here are the three employees of Center Point Colored School in the 1950s. At this time, it was common for schools in Nacogdoches County to employ only three teachers. The teachers are, from left to right, Lorene H. Watson, J.W. Wilson (principal), and Mamie Rogers Hodge. (Courtesy of Mamie Rogers Hodge.)

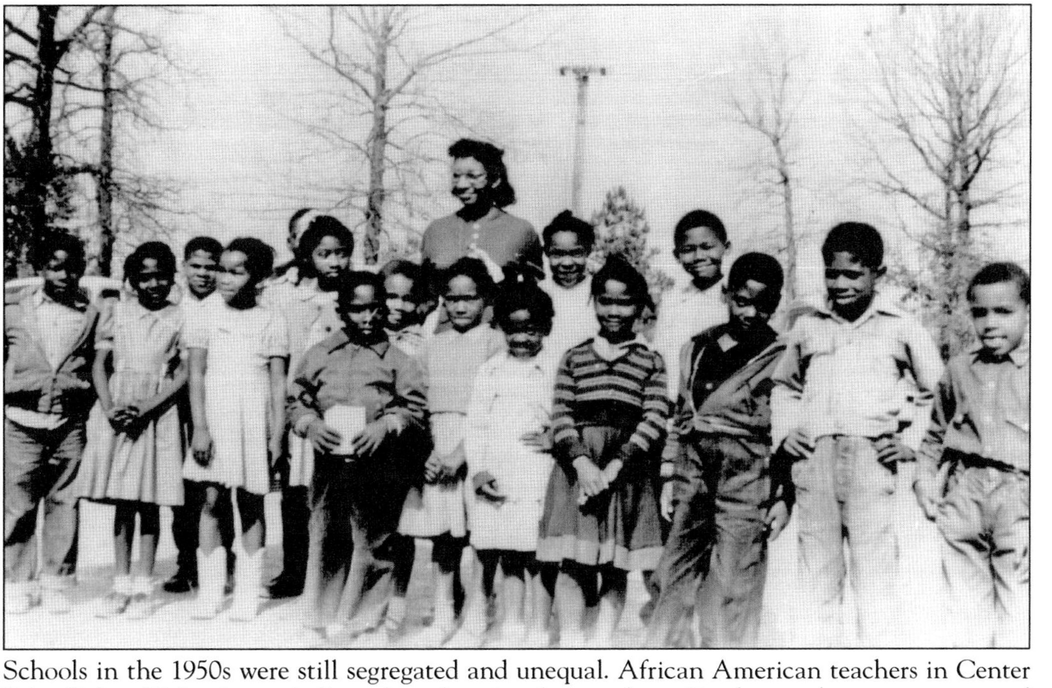

Schools in the 1950s were still segregated and unequal. African American teachers in Center Point Colored School were dedicated to educating their students. Teachers and parents encouraged students to pursue their education in order to have a better chance of succeeding in life. (Courtesy of Mamie Rogers Hodge.)

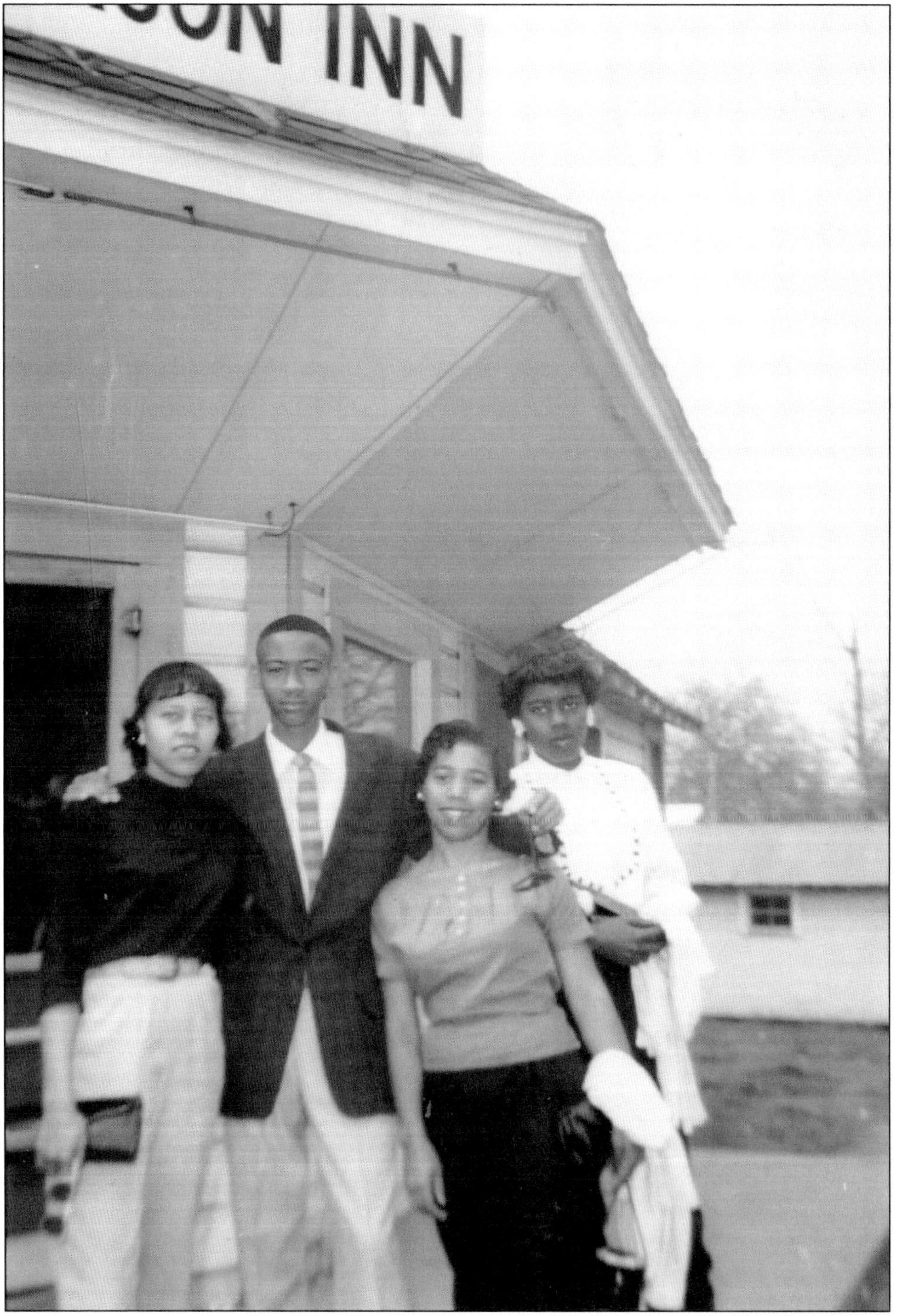

Pictured are unidentified students in the 1950s in front of the Dragon Inn, a popular restaurant and meeting place for young African Americans in the community. It was a place to meet and celebrate a victory of the E.J. Campbell Dragons. Other popular businesses on historic Shawnee Street were the colored movie theater, black hospital, and Hobart Powers Grocery Store. (ETRC.)

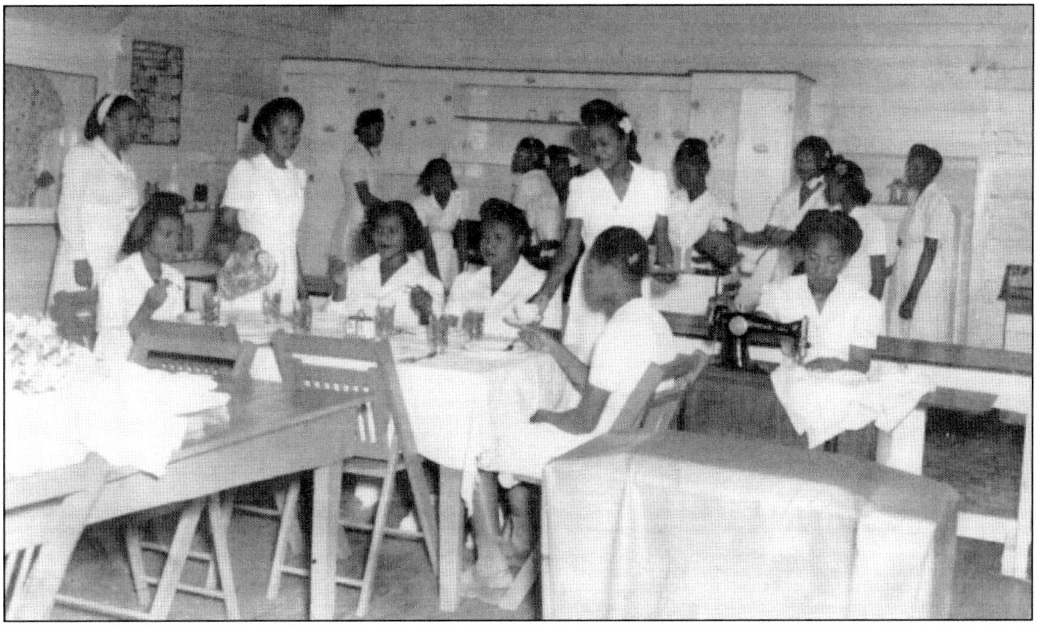

Pictured is a home economics class at Chireno Colored High School in the early 1950s. Because of segregation, black female students participated in New Homemakers of America while white female students participated in Future Homemakers of America. After the schools were integrated the two organizations merged and, by 1999, became Family, Career, and Community Leaders of America. (Courtesy of Jennie Rhodes Mitchell.)

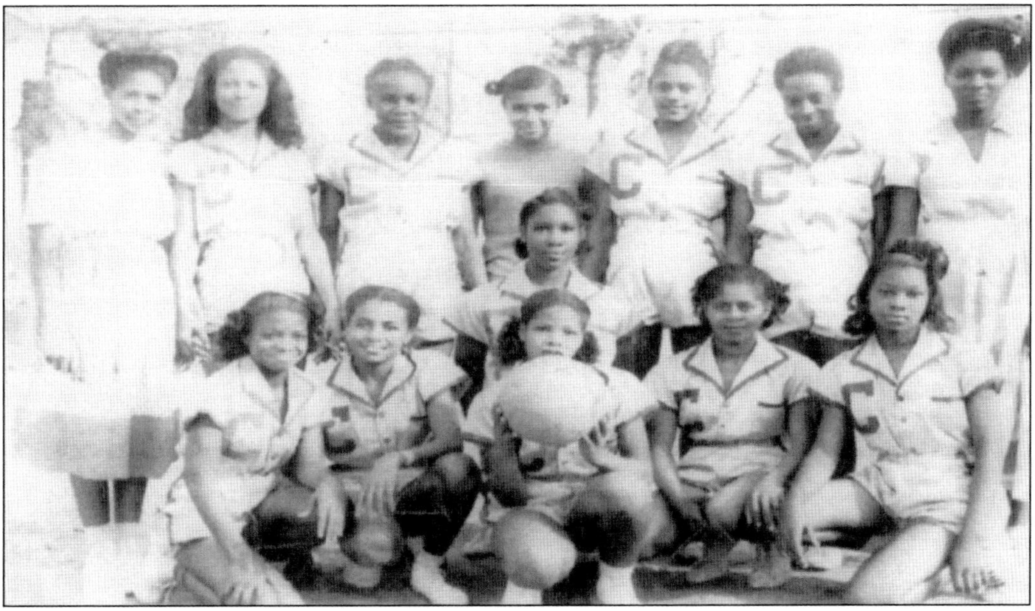

This is an image of Chireno Colored High School girls' basketball during the 1950s. African American girls were proud to participate in their segregated school sports. (Courtesy of Mable Ferguson Hall.)

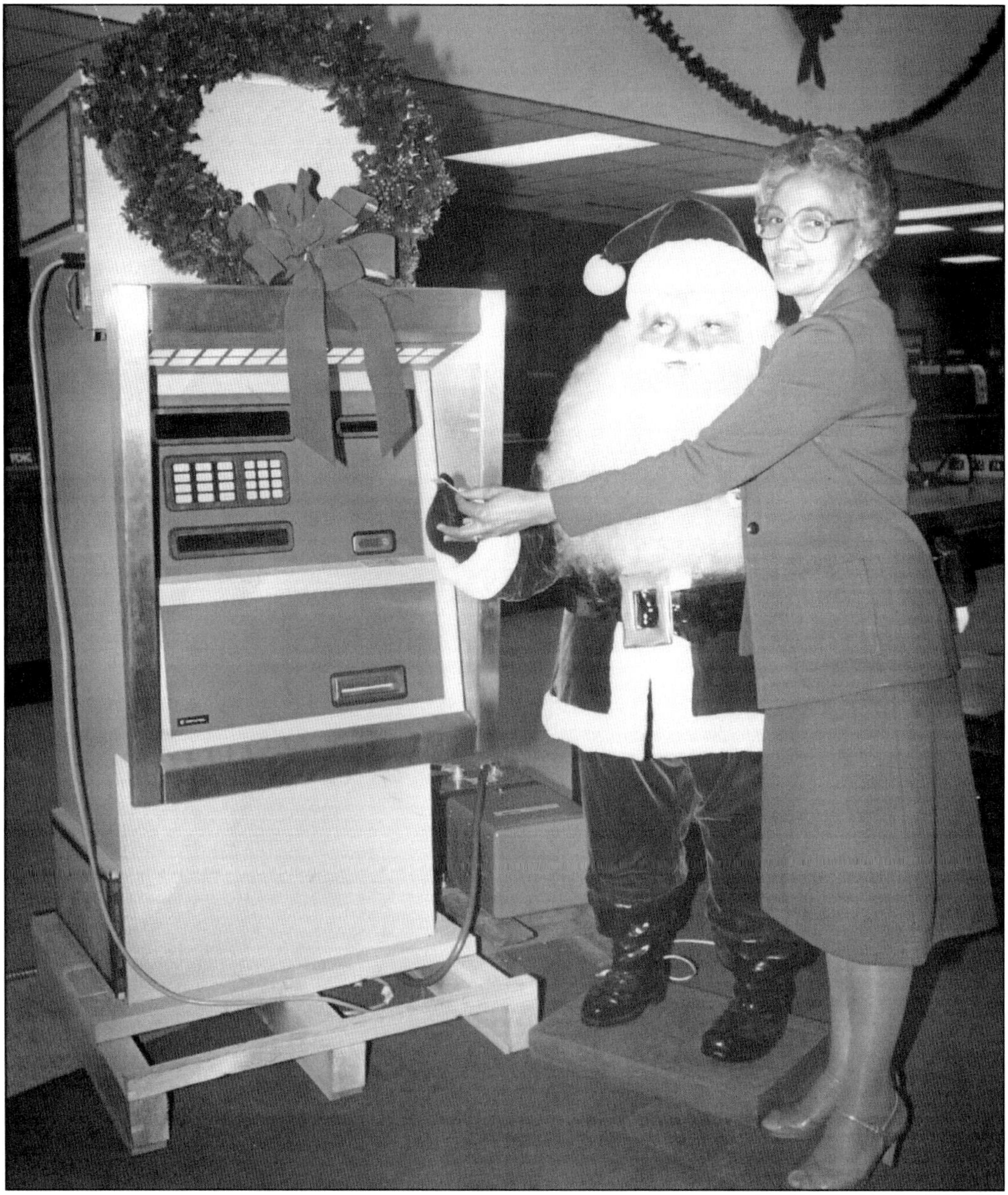

In 1970, Perlene Horton joined Fredonia State Bank as a female custodian when Nacogdoches was in the midst of civil rights unrest. Six months later, she accepted a position as a bookkeeper, and three years later, she accepted a position as a teller, retiring after 25 years of service in this position. (Courtesy of Perlene Horton.)

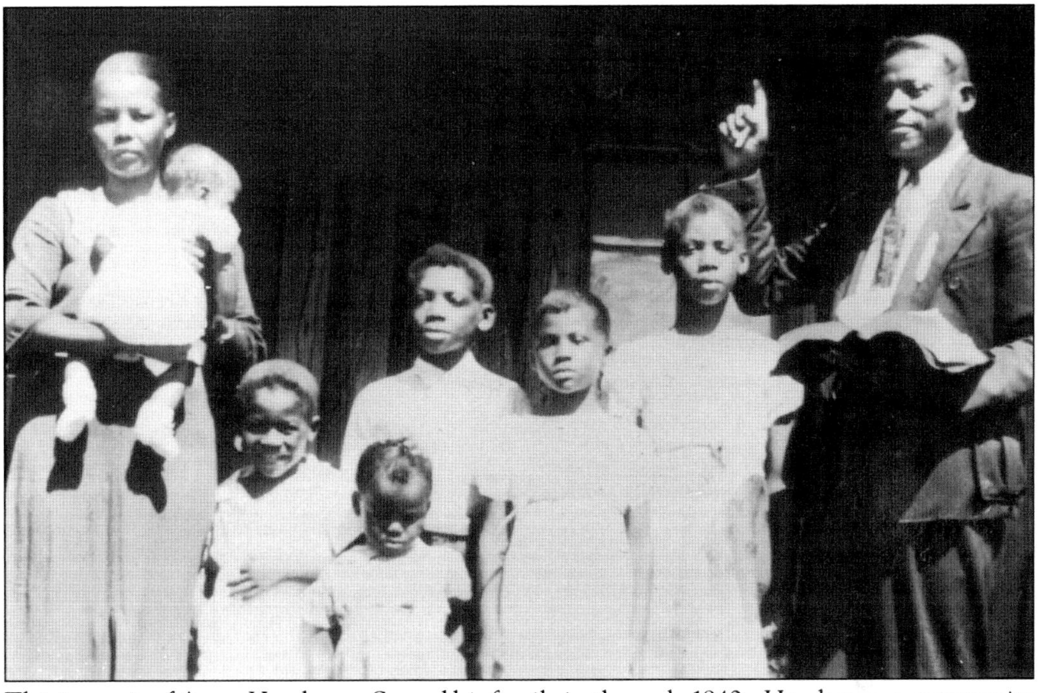

This image is of Amos Henderson Sr. and his family in the early 1940s. Henderson, a community leader, served as pastor of several area churches. In 1975, Henderson was elected the first African American county commissioner in Nacogdoches and in the state of Texas. (ETRC.)

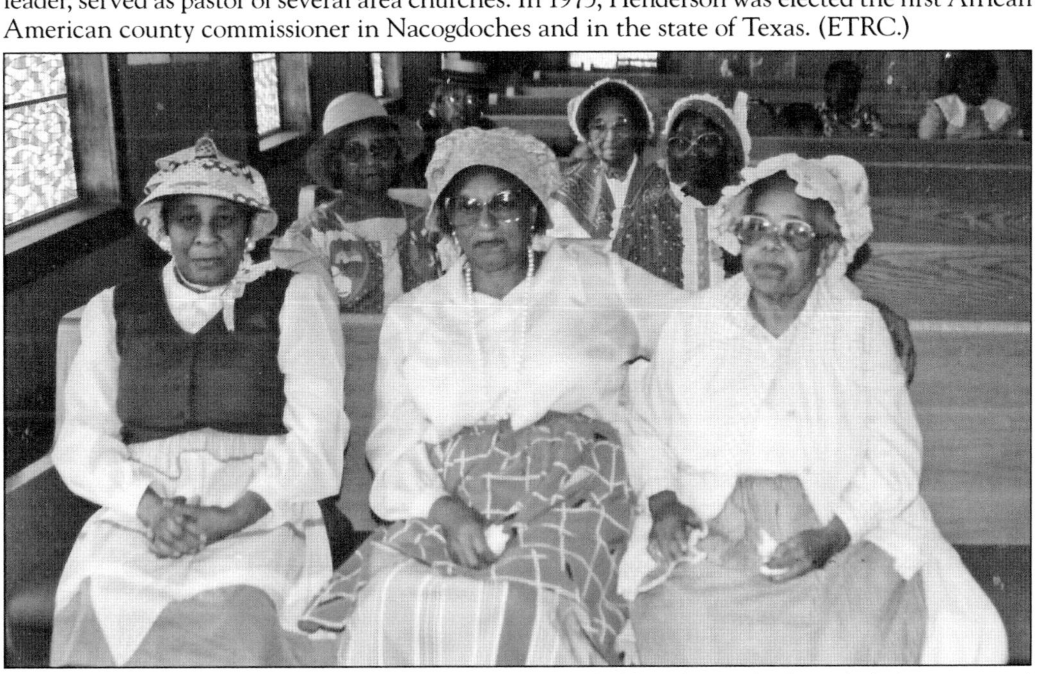

The ladies in this photograph are dressed in attire of olden days, which included aprons and bonnets. The bonnet was to protect the head from the sun or cold, and aprons protected their clothing and were also good aids for carrying various items in the pockets. After dressing in the mornings, the women put on their aprons before starting any task. It was hung on a nail in a special place waiting to be used the next day. (Courtesy of Mable Ferguson Hall.)

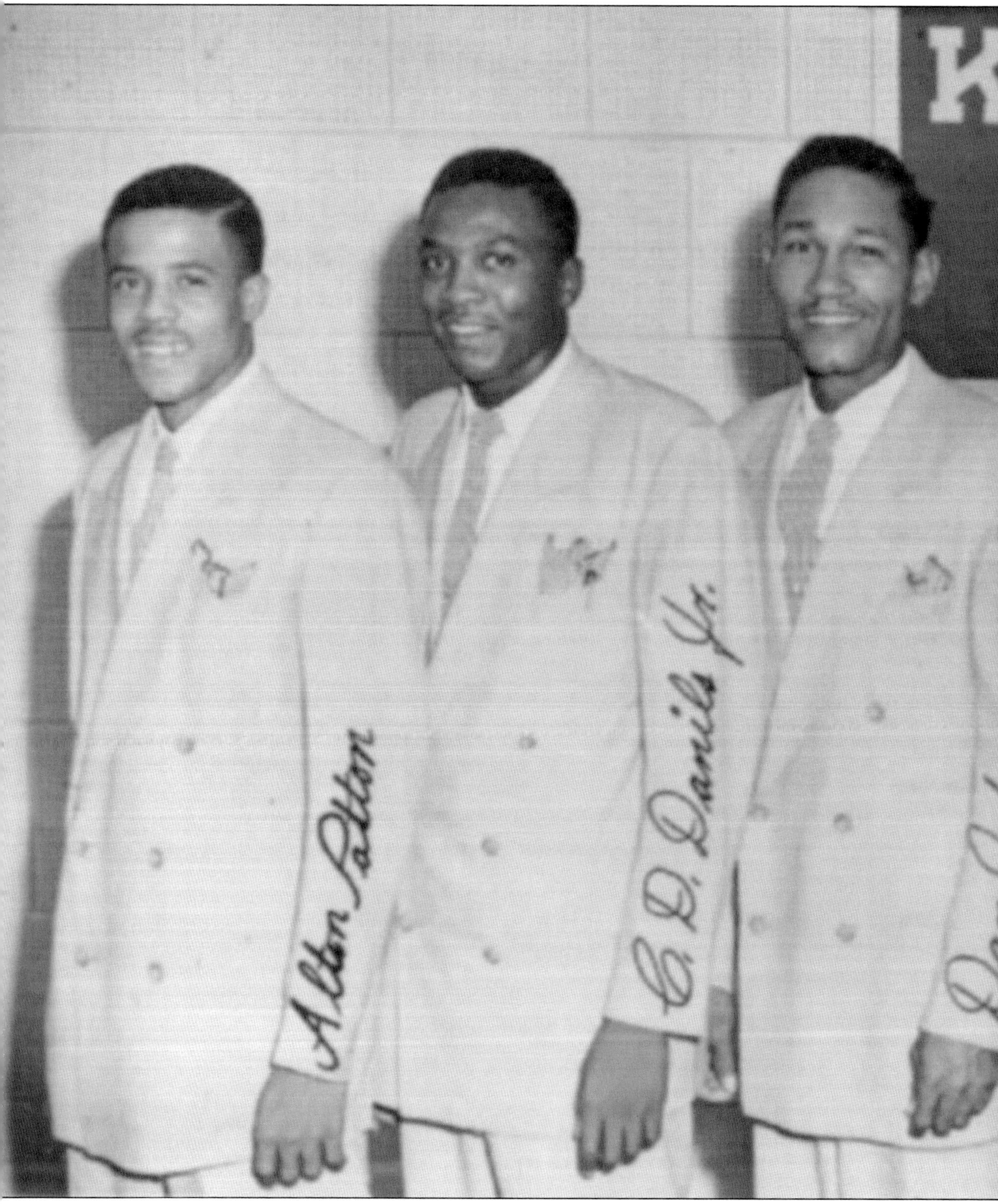

The members of the Rolling Five singing group were some of the first African American entertainers to have their own show on KSFA radio station. They were often invited to perform at churches in

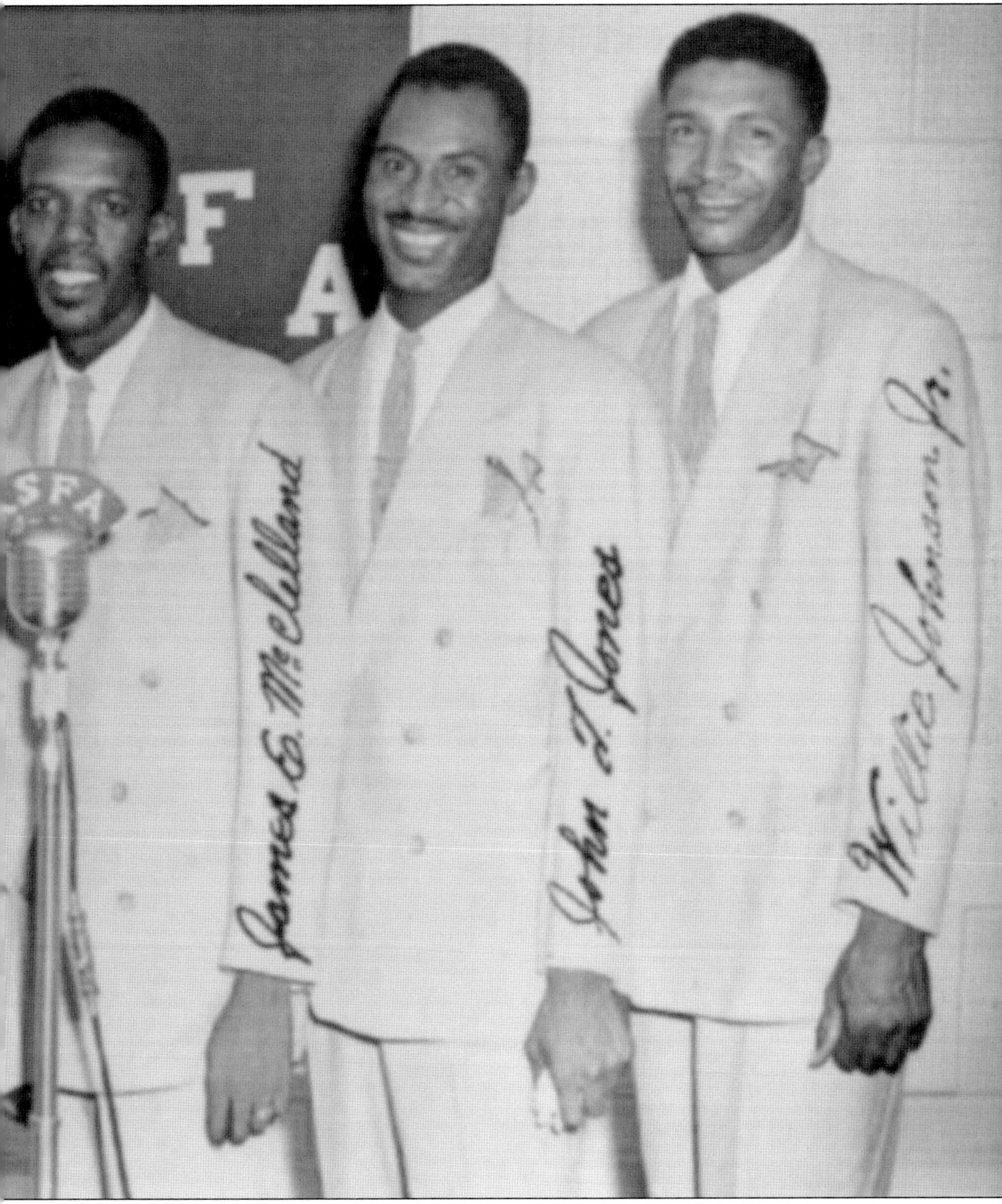

African American communities. They were Alton Patton, C.D. Daniels Jr., Dan Johnson, James E. McClelland, John F. Jones, and Willie Johnson Jr. (Courtesy of Obadiah Johnson.)

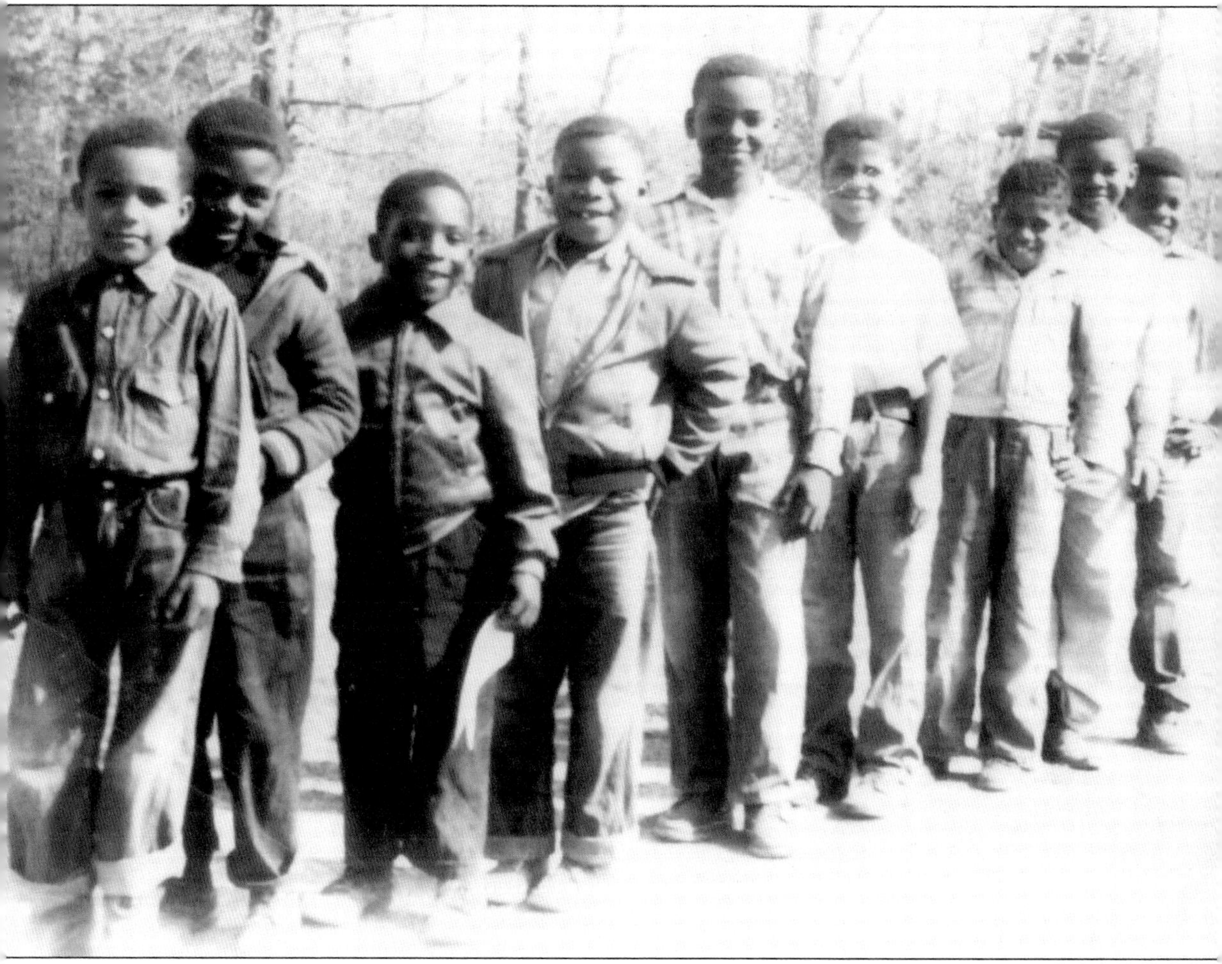

Until the 1950s, many African American students attended school for four months, arriving early in the morning and returning late in the evenings to help their parents in the fields. Many students had to walk long distances to attend classes. The young smiling students from the Center Point community in this image suggest that they are happy to be at school and away from the fields. (Courtesy of Mamie Rogers Hodge.)

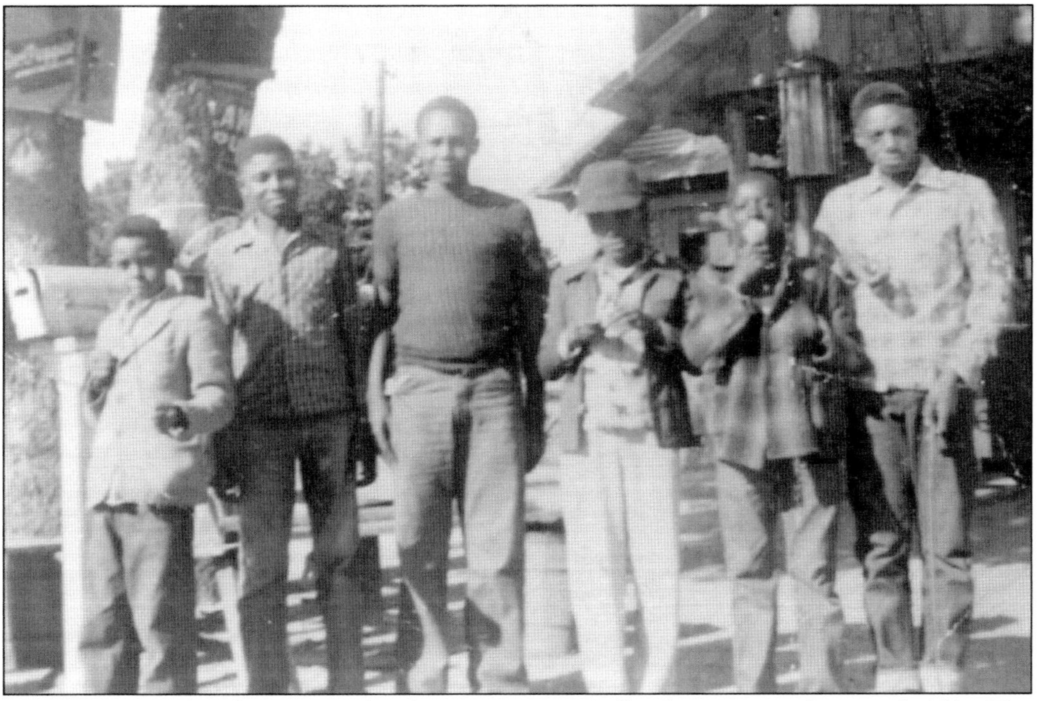

This image of schoolboys was taken by store owner Dollie Brown in early to mid-1950s. The boys would go there at lunchtime. Dollie Brown's store was one of two stores in the community. Everyone knew her as a kind and generous lady—she allowed credit to most anyone. (Courtesy of Mable Ferguson Hall.)

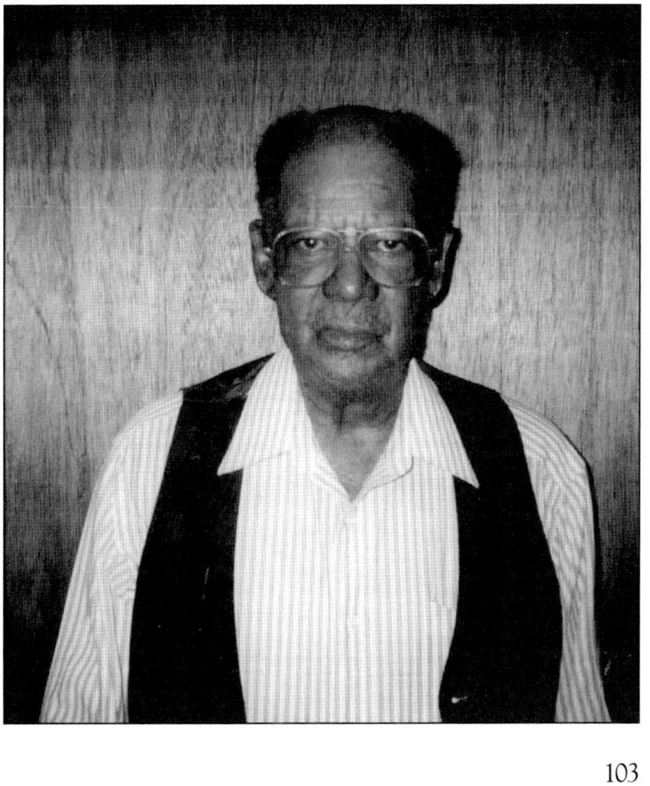

During the dark days of extreme segregation and violence, heroes like Arthur Weaver stood tall and bravely fought against Jim Crow laws, an unfair legal system, and separate and unequal schools. He established the first National Association for the Advancement of Colored People (NAACP) organization in Nacogdoches. He bravely endured threats on his life while taking a stand to help and encourage others. (Courtesy of Charlotte Weaver Stokes.)

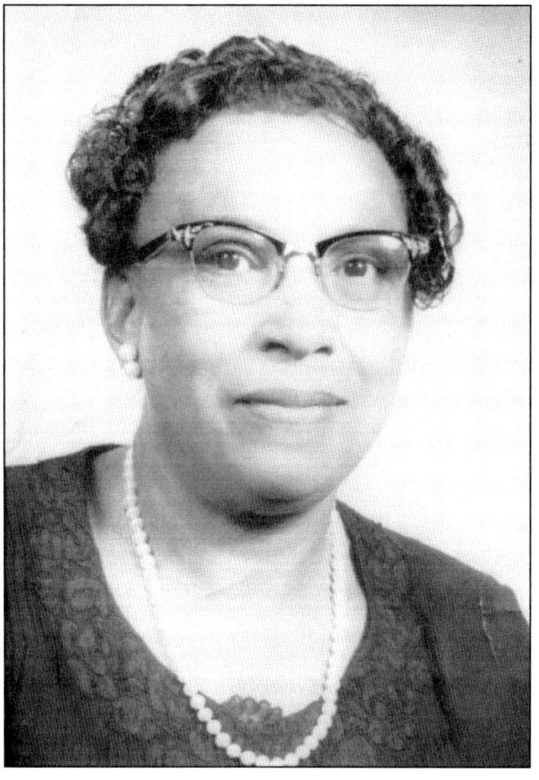

Helen Wright was an early educator in Nacogdoches, beginning her career in the early 1920s. She retired as a principal of Emeline Carpenter Elementary School after more than 40 years as an educator. She was the first black educator to be sworn in among the top-level 15-member Committee on Excellence in Public Education appointed by Gov. John Connally of Texas. (Courtesy of Barbara Govan and the Wright family.)

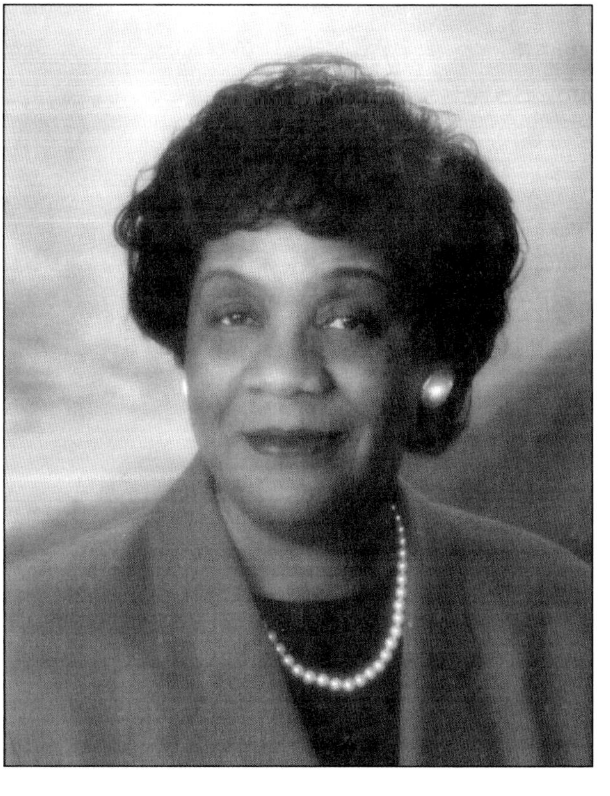

Charlotte Weaver Stokes took the original Head Start Program from one small building in the 1970s to an eight-building complex, from 65 students to 652 students, and expanding to seven counties, including Nacogdoches as the base home operation. She established Progressive Leadership Group, which serves the Nacogdoches community, and Project Turn Around, a successful program that helps dropouts return to school and graduate. (Courtesy of Charlotte Weaver Stokes.)

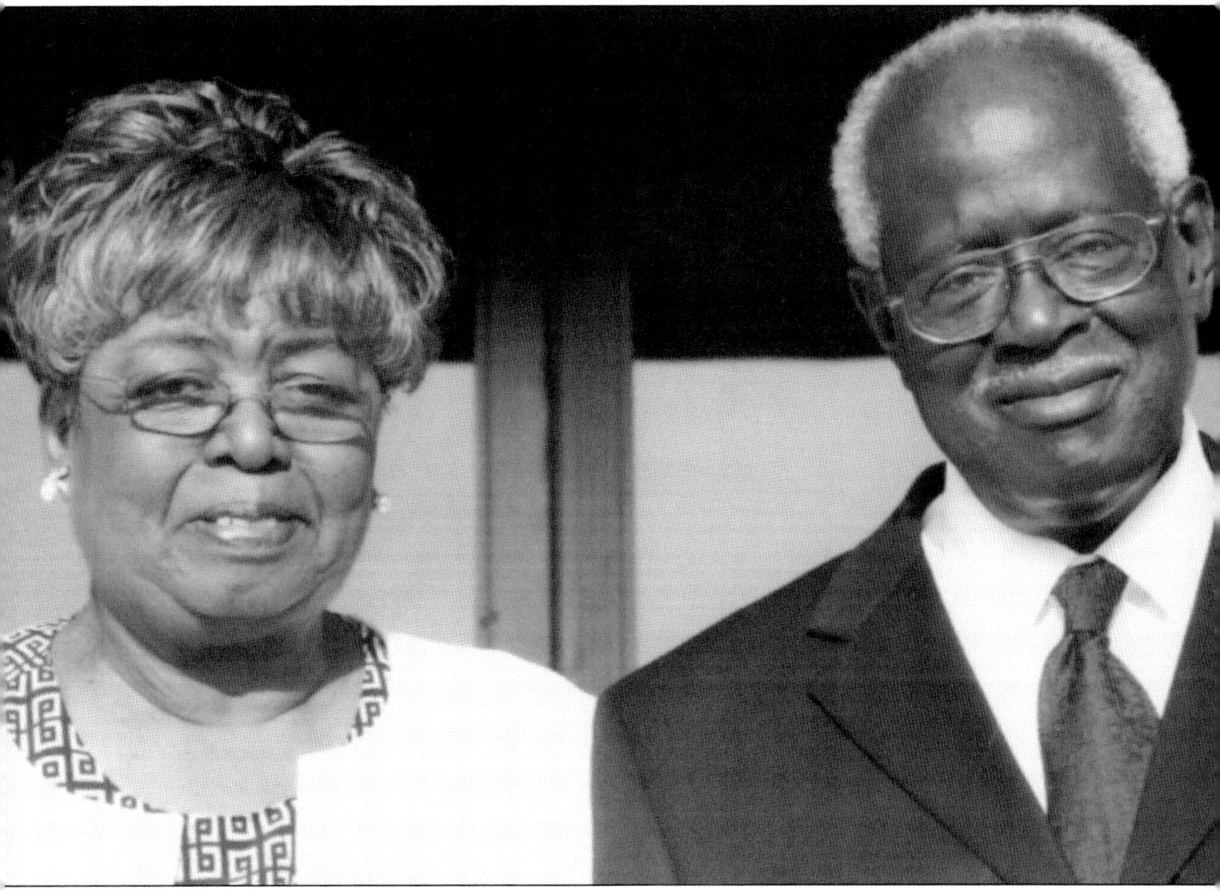

The late Rev. Larry Wade and his wife, Betty, came to Nacogdoches in 1959 as the first black pharmacists in the area; they established their drugstore on Shawnee Street. In 1979, he was called to pastor historic Zion Hill First Baptist Church, a post he held until his death in 2013. He served as a leader on many local, state, and national church organizations, including president of Texas State Missionary Baptist Convention, Inc. (Courtesy of Betty Wade and the Wade family.)

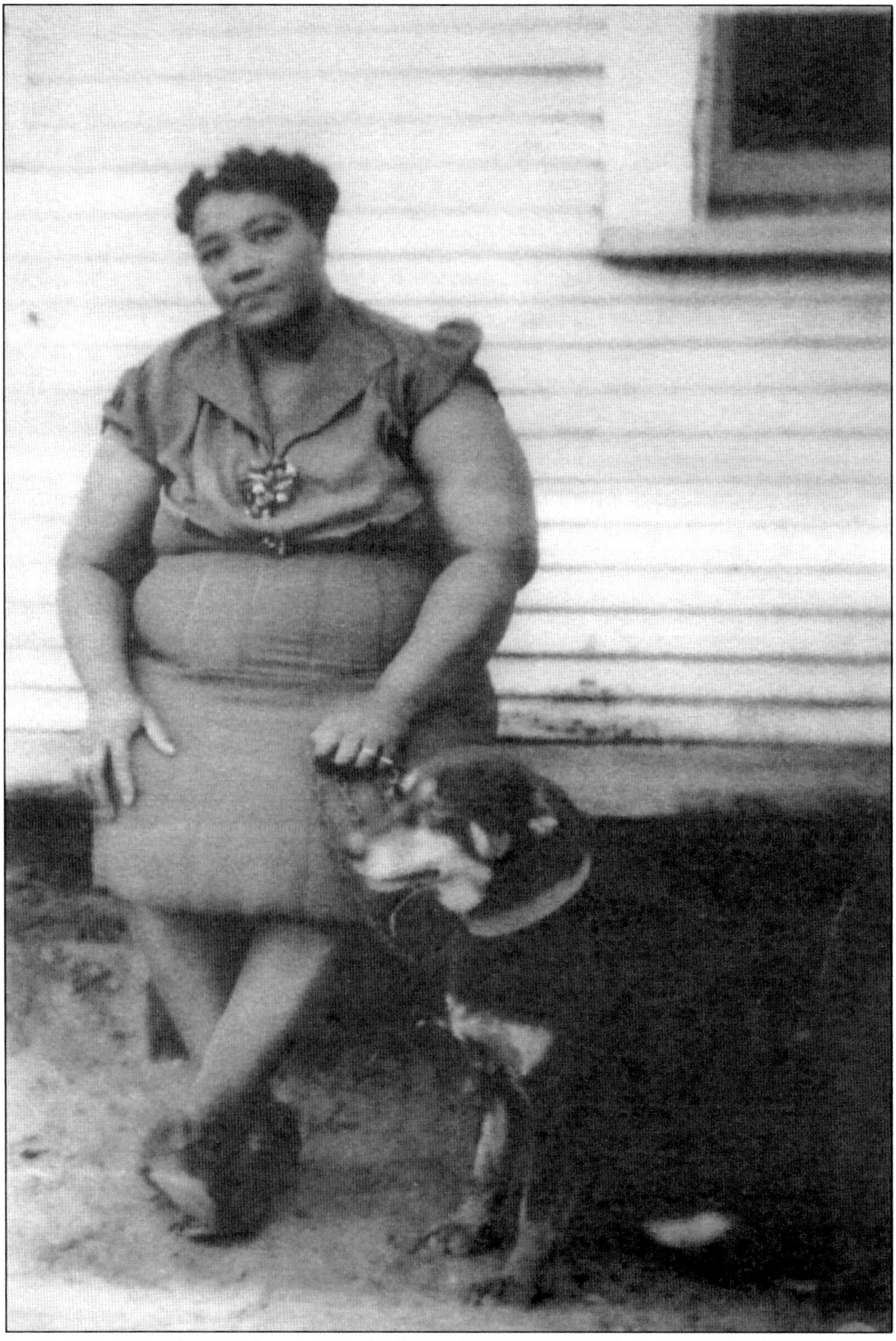

Jessie Mae Lewis-Taylor was known as the legendary operator of Big Sis Café, located near the Little Creek community in the area once known as the Hitch Yard. The "hot tamale man," Will Risper, pulled his tamale wagon to the Hitch Yard and drove his horse-drawn wagon through the neighborhoods selling the best hot tamales. (Courtesy of the Lewis-Taylor family.)

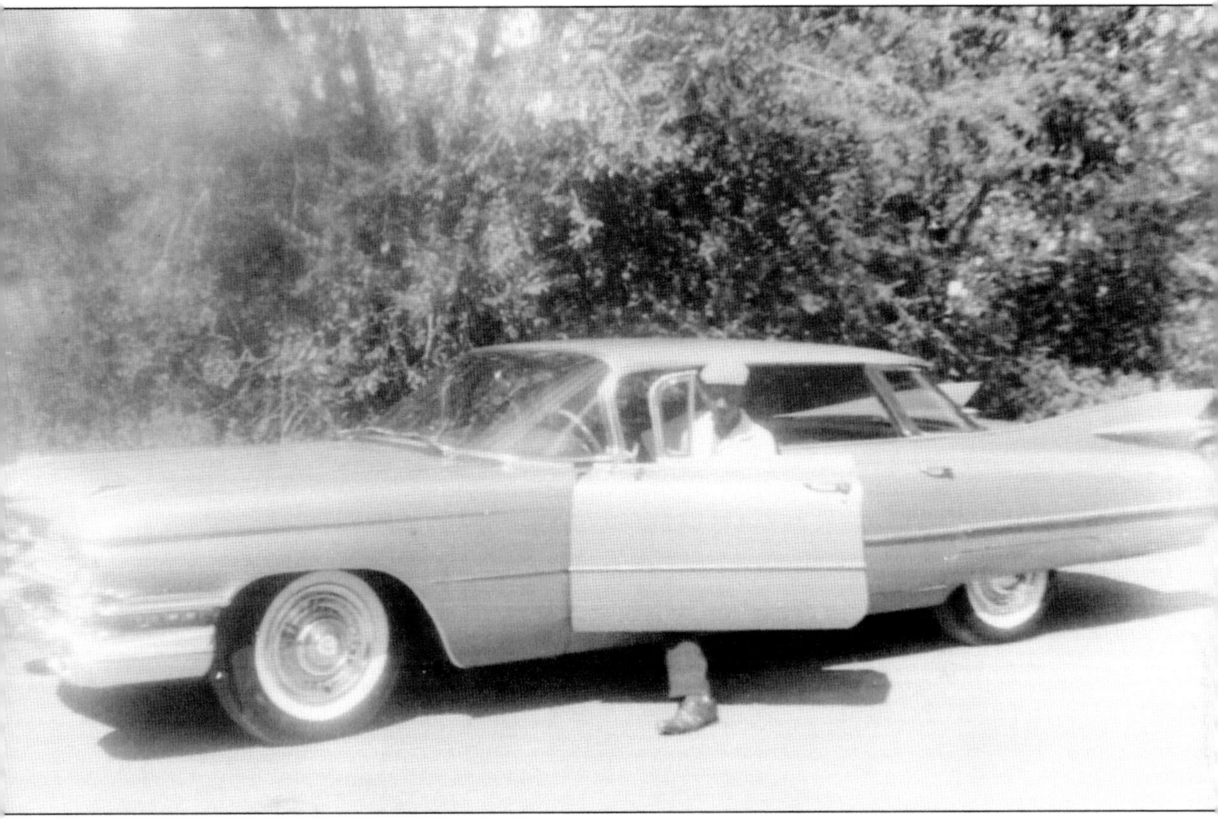

Cadillacs were popular cars for African Americans who could afford them during the 1950s and 1960s. One publication described this 1957 Cadillac as a luxurious "status" car for African Americans. (ETRC.)

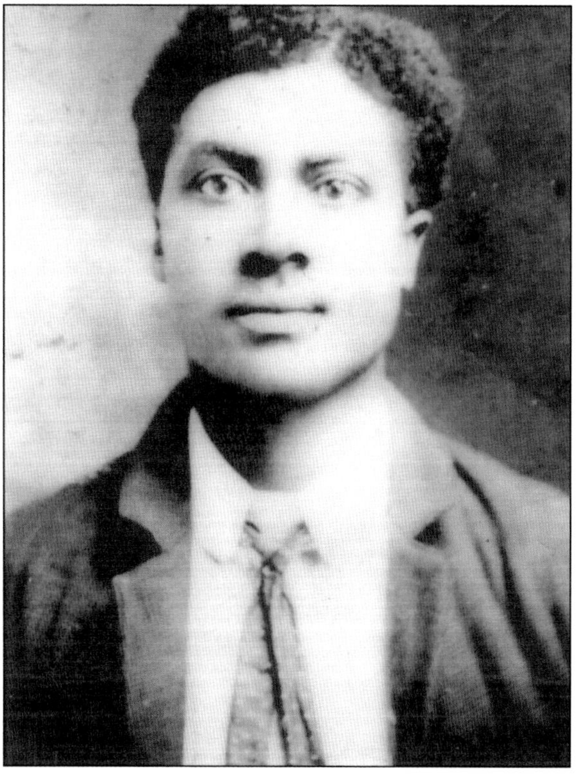

Erasmus Johnson II was born in slavery and brought to Texas around 1833 as the property of a slave-owner. After he became a freeman in 1865, he purchased 600 acres of land in what is known today as the North Redland African American community. He is considered the founder of this community and established Johnson Chapel Baptist Church in 1873. He is buried in the Old North Church Cemetery in Nacogdoches. (Courtesy of Robbie Johnson.)

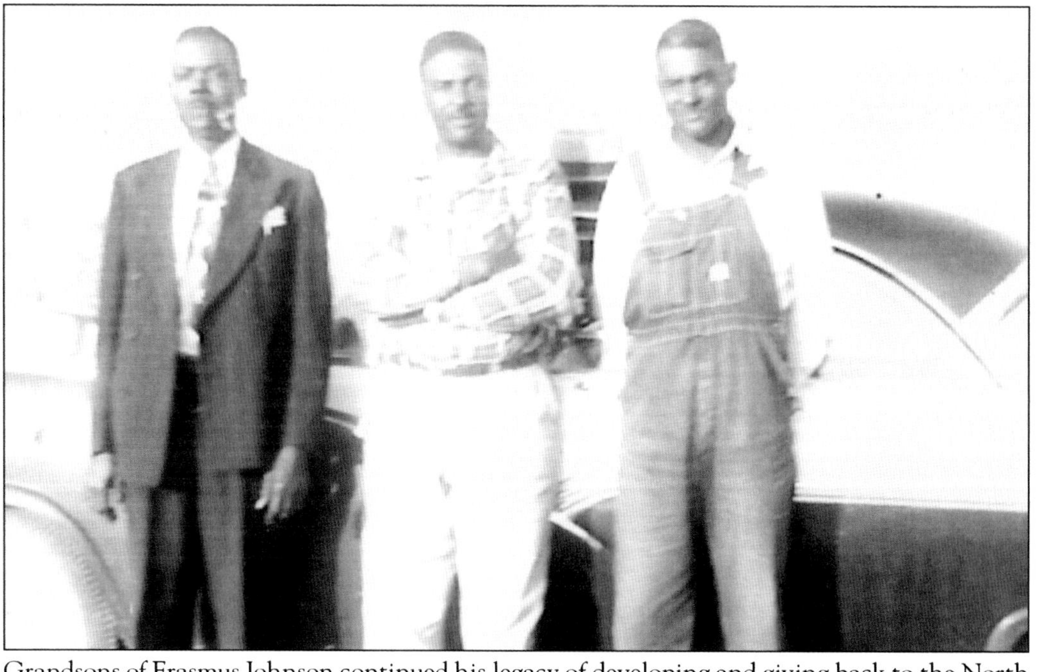

Grandsons of Erasmus Johnson continued his legacy of developing and giving back to the North Redland community. Brothers C.J. Johnson (left) and L.C. Johnson (right) are seen with cousin F.J. Johnson (center). Erasmus Johnson II, son of Nib Johnson and grandson of Erasmus Johnson I, donated a second cemetery in the North Redland community. (Courtesy of Robbie Johnson.)

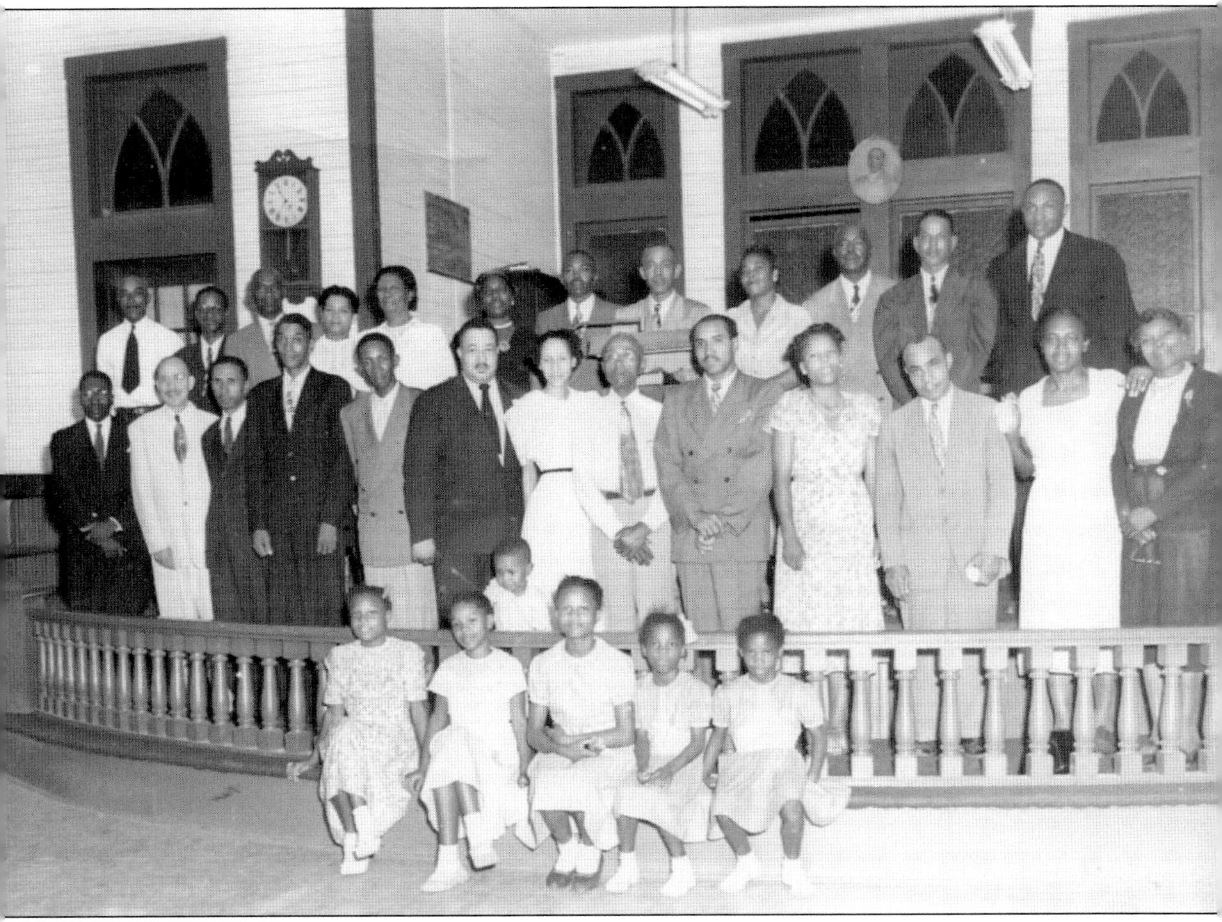

This image, taken between late 1940s and early 1950s, shows members of St. Paul Methodist Church, located on the historic Shawnee Street. Shawnee Street is where many black businesses thrived until the 1970s. Many of the church members worked primarily as service workers, servants, maids, cooks, and groundskeepers for affluent white families who lived nearby. (Mertie Mims Collection.)

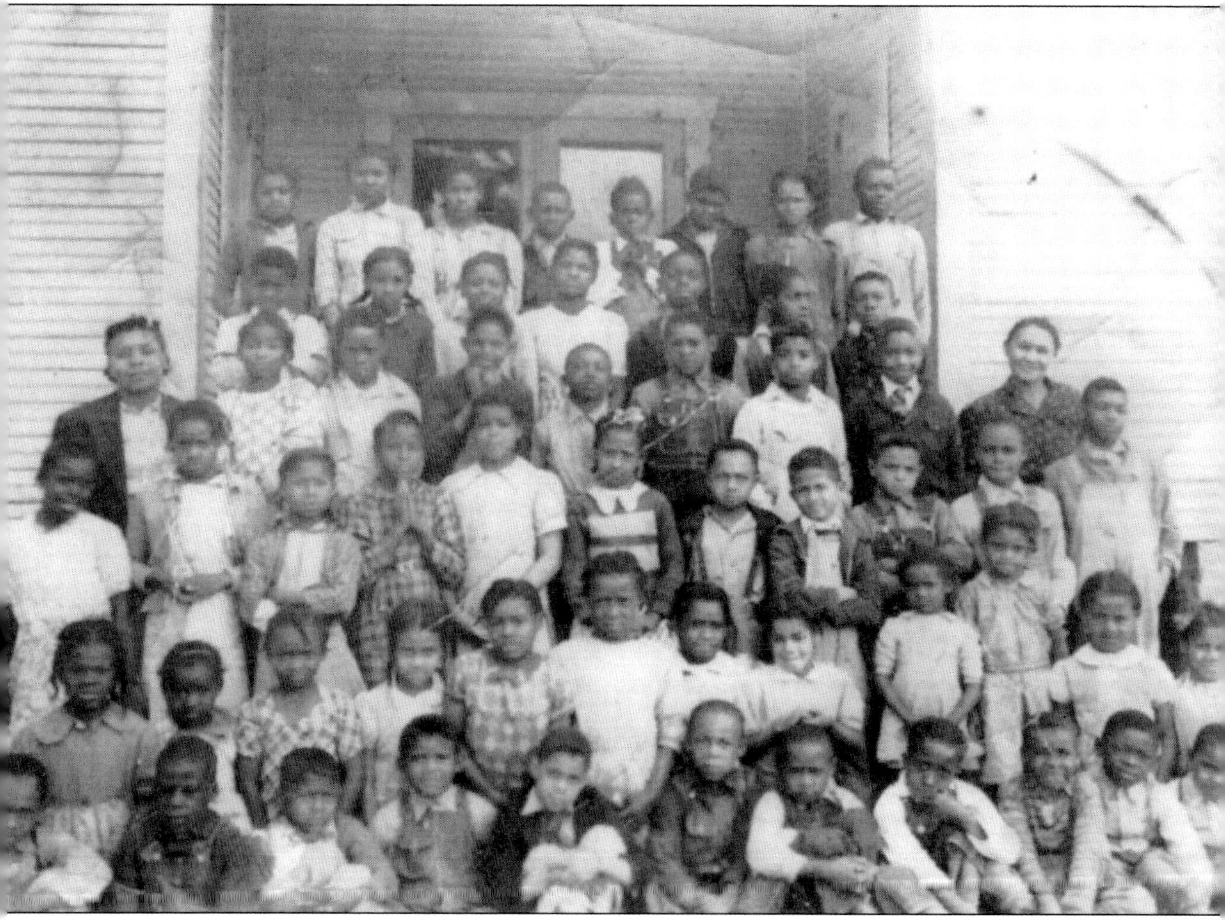

Sand Hill's c. 1940 mixed-level class is shown with teacher Marie Skillern, standing in the fourth row on right. In the 1870s, teachers were often paid with food and other commodities, such as feed for their personal livestock. Most students walked or rode horses and wagons to school. (Courtesy of Mable Ferguson Hall.)

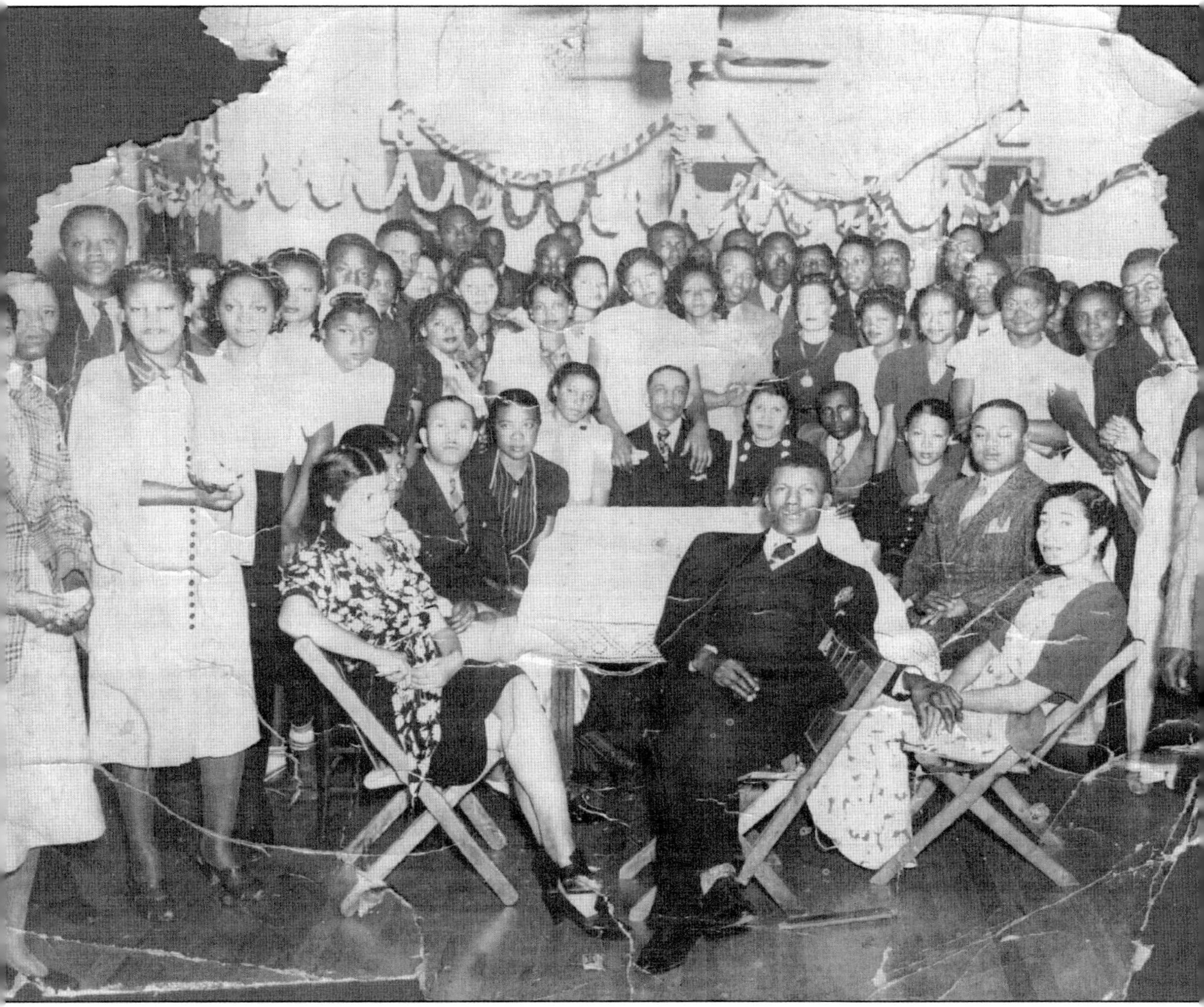

Many African American communities held social events in the churches, as shown in this 1930s image of Zion Hill First Baptist Church. Note the homemade paper decorations hanging from the ceiling, adding a bit of glamour to the festivities. (Courtesy of Clarence McMichael.)

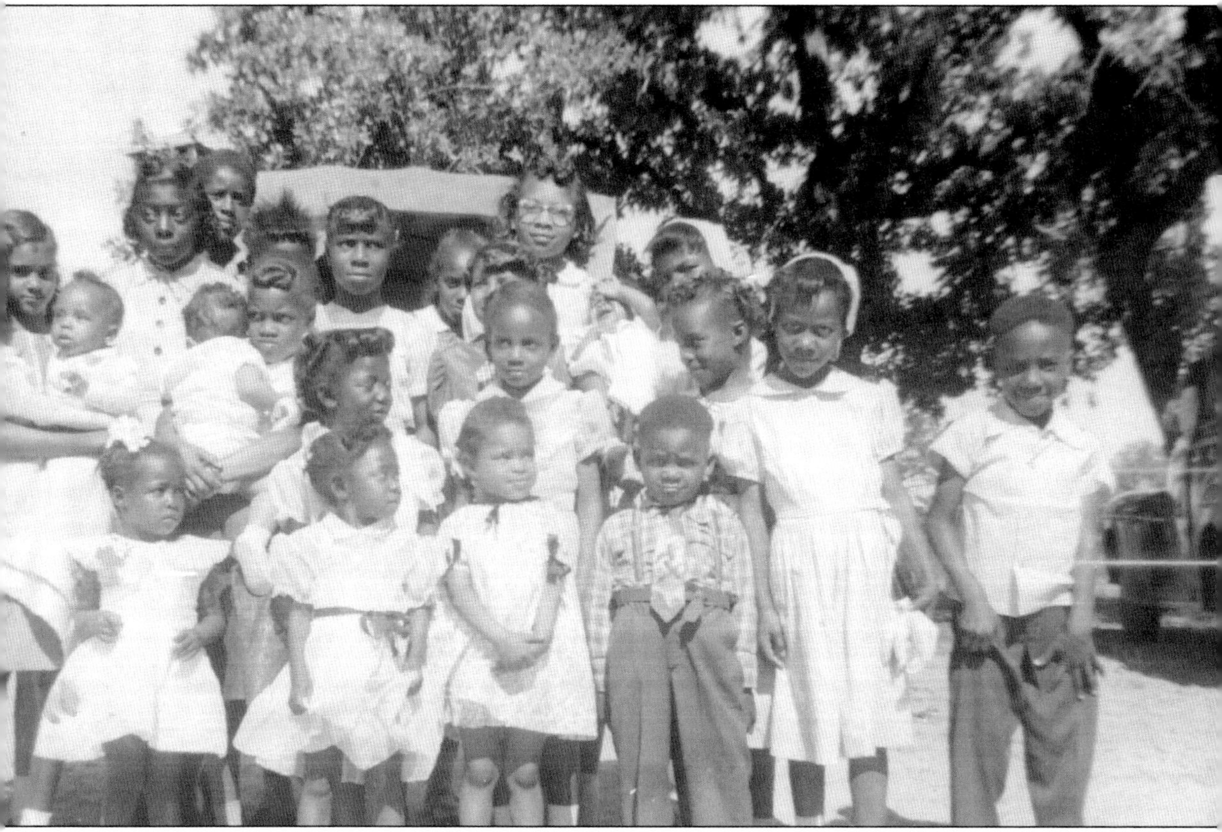

The young church members of Sand Hill Baptist Church appear to be dressed for the Easter parade. After the parade, the children enjoyed an Easter egg hunt, held on the grounds of the church and supervised by adult members of the church. (Courtesy of Mable Ferguson Hall.)

Clara Hill Corr, a native of Garrison, joined the ranks of many American women working in a defense plant in California; she helped build B-17 aircraft used in World War II. She was considered a true-life "Rosie the Riveter." Corr is shown here as a graduate of Garrison Colored High School around 1942. (Courtesy of Clara Corr.)

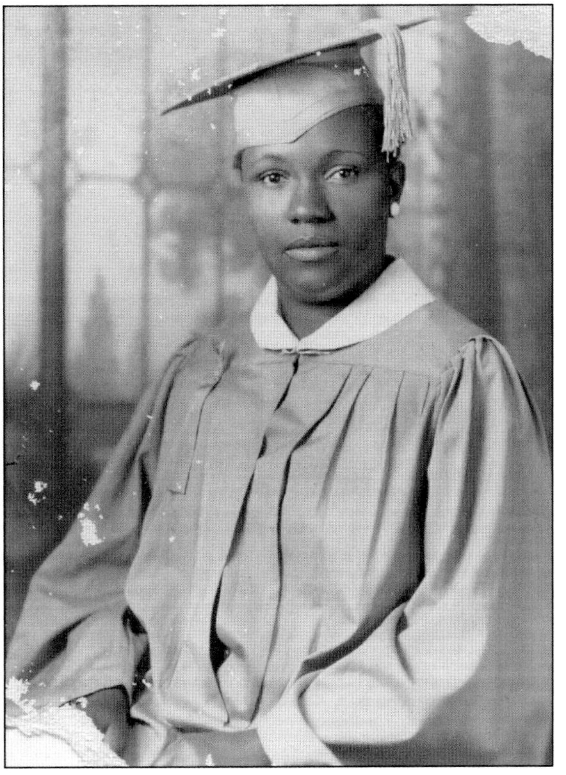

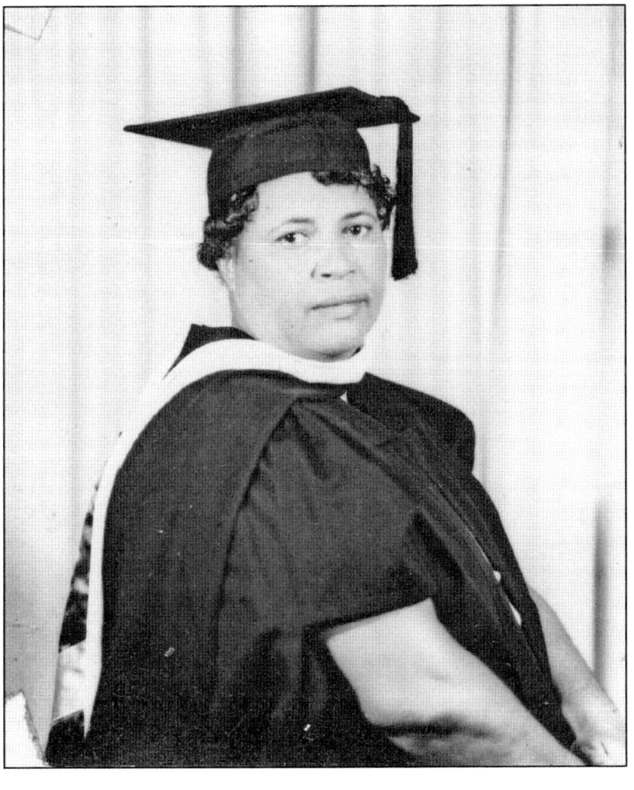

Mable Hill Blount of Garrison, Texas, joins other siblings from her family receiving degrees from Prairie View A&M College; she later served as an educator and music teacher in several Nacogdoches County and East Texas area schools. This image was taken in the late 1940s or early 1950s. (Courtesy of Clara and Cari Corr.)

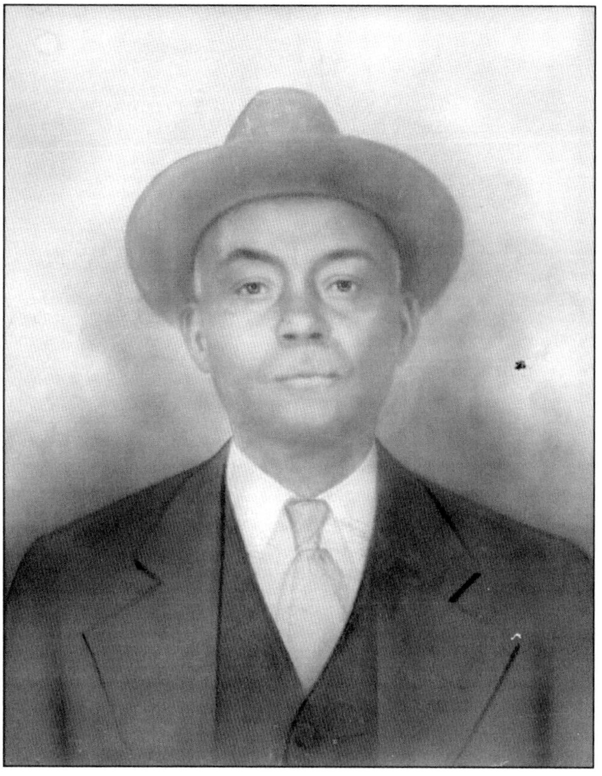

Nib Eli Hill, born in the late 1800s, was among the first African Americans in Garrison to own land. Daughter Clara Hill Corr and granddaughter Cari Corr currently live on the property that the family has maintained for more than 125 years. During the mid-1930s, a brick building for colored children was built on a portion a of Nib Eli Hill's property. (Courtesy of Clara and Cari Corr.)

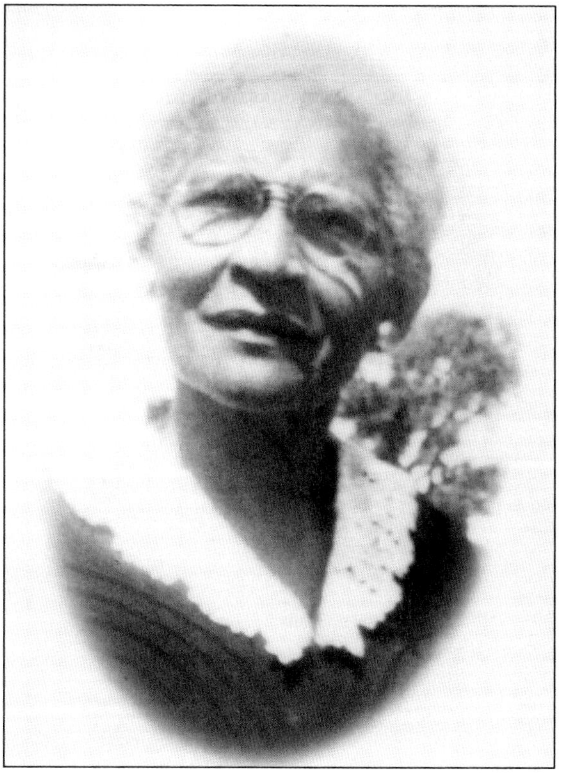

Frankie Davis Hill, the wife of Nib Eli Hill, is pictured around 1952. She is remembered by her children and grandchildren as a source of family oral history. She once told her granddaughters her skin was whiter than theirs because of the color of both her parents. (Courtesy of Clara and Cari Corr.)

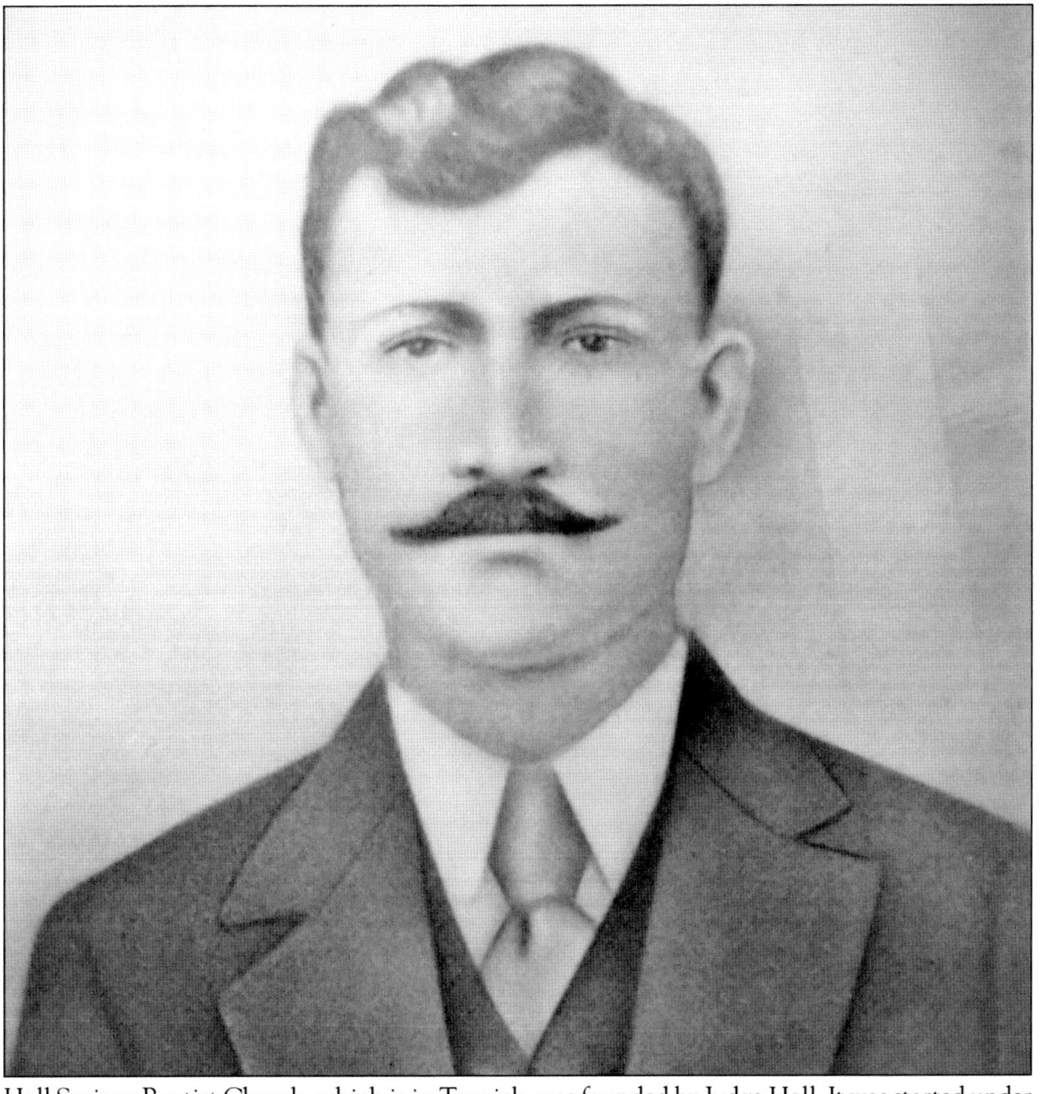

Hall Springs Baptist Church, which is in Trawick, was founded by Judge Hall. It was started under a makeshift arbor about 1901. The arbor was located near a spring, thus the church was named Hall Springs Baptist Church. A brush arbor is a rough, open-sided shelter constructed of poles, brush, cut branches, or hay. Around 1911, the church was moved to its present-day location in Trawick. (Courtesy of Earl M. Hall.)

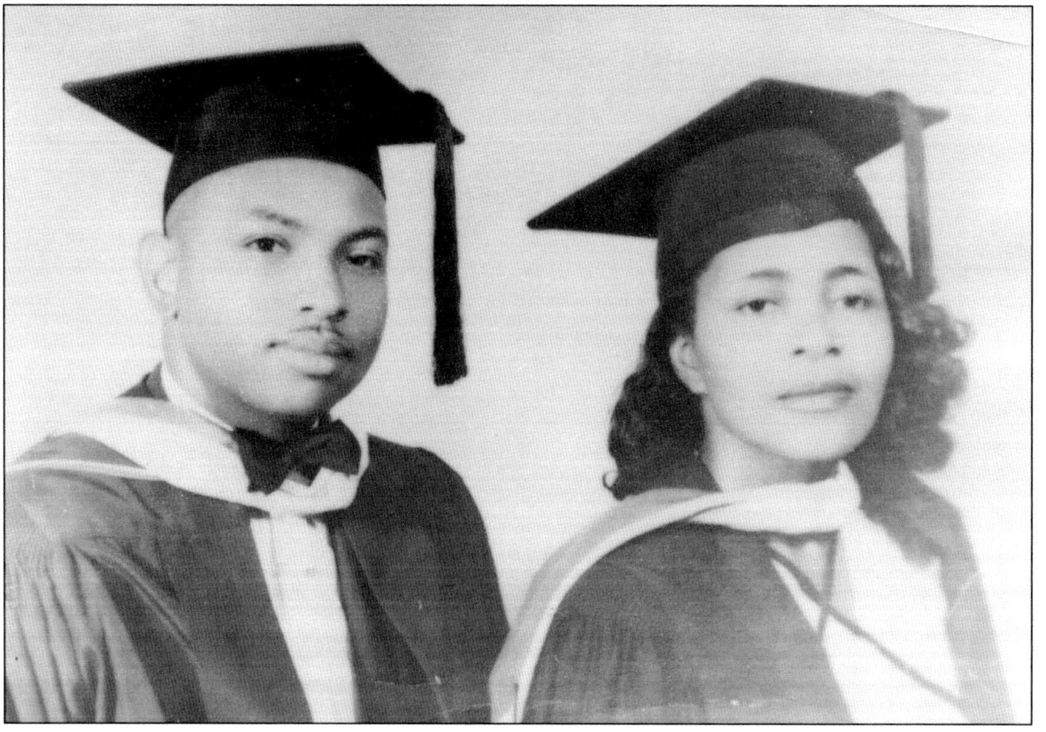

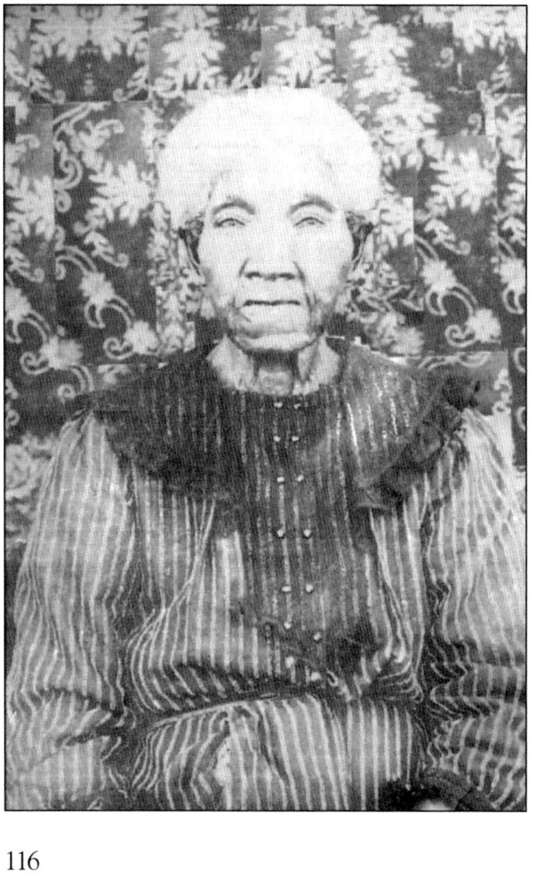

Rev. Garfield Hill and his wife, Eulalia Montgomery Hills, were both educators with long records of teaching success. Eulalia, a third-generation educator, and Garfield passed down their record of achievement to their children. Winston Hill is a college graduate and retired professional football player; Brenda Hill Cole is a judge for the state court in Fulton County, Georgia; Dr. Sharon Hill Cranford is a college professor and published writer; and Dr. Rhonda Hill Saldivar is a college professor. (Courtesy of Clara and Cari Corr.)

Charley Mast was born into slavery in North Carolina in 1829. The slave family of Charley Mast and six-plus children arrived in Texas with their slave owner Rueben Mast around 1860, settling near Center Point. His daughter Louisa Caroline is shown in this image. After freedom, Charley purchased 100-plus acres of land, later donating land for cemeteries and churches in Garrison and Center Point. (Courtesy of Clara and Cari Corr.)

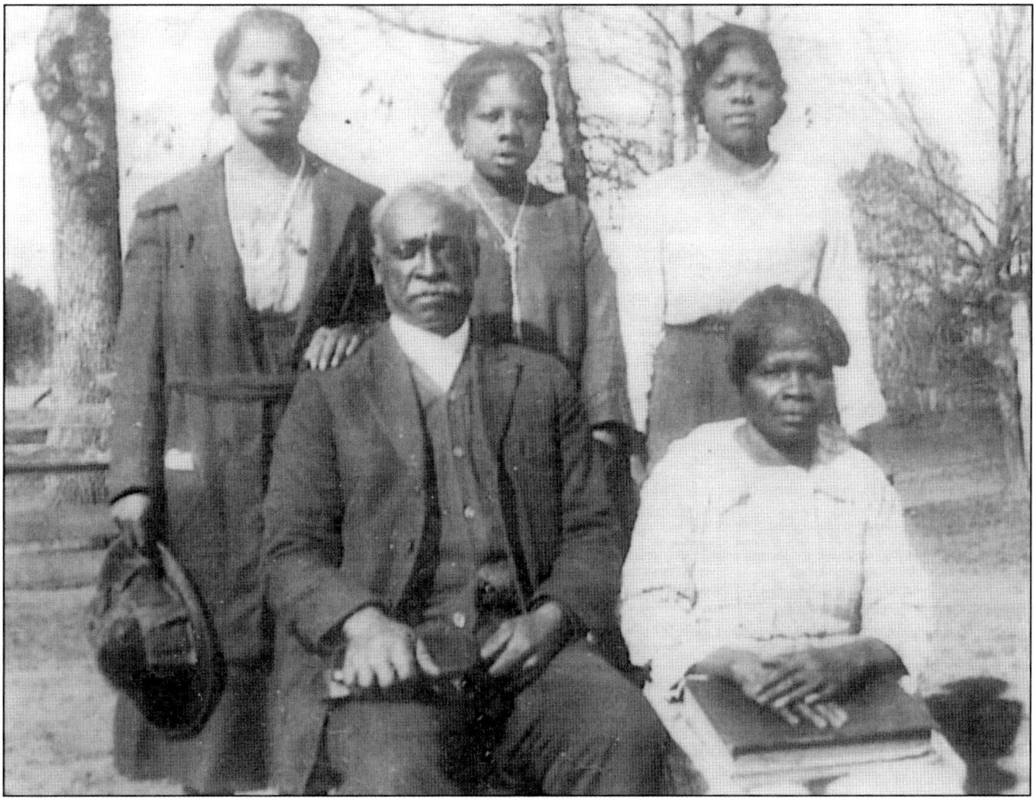

William Rogers, wife Lizzie Beth, and, from left to right, daughters Fannie, Arlea, and Eunice of the Center Point community are shown after church one Sunday around early 1900. William Rogers was the first known African American blacksmith in the Center Point community. (Courtesy of William Rogers Sr.)

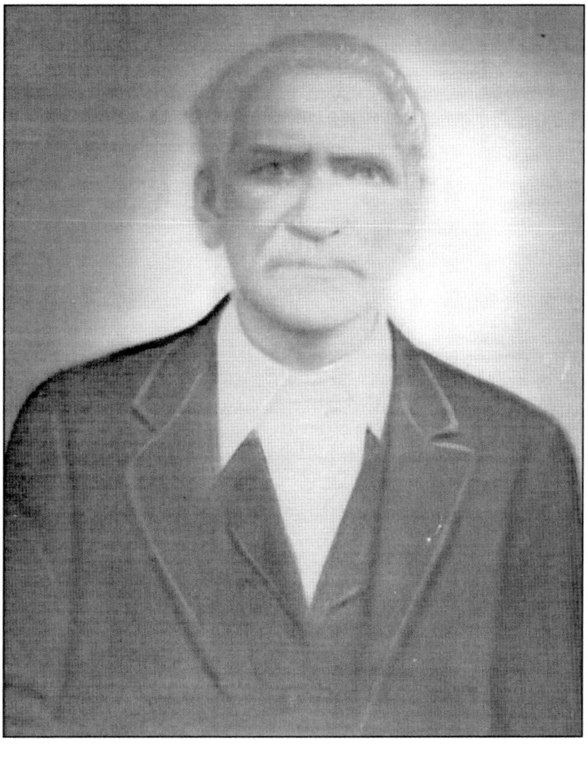

Born 1852, Alan Yarbrough was listed in the census as a mulatto. He lived in the Nacogdoches Center Point area with his wife, Dora, and their children. During the Civil War, Alan stayed back on the farm and took care of his family as well as his brother William Henry Yarbrough's family, which was very common during this period of history. (Courtesy of William Rogers Sr.)

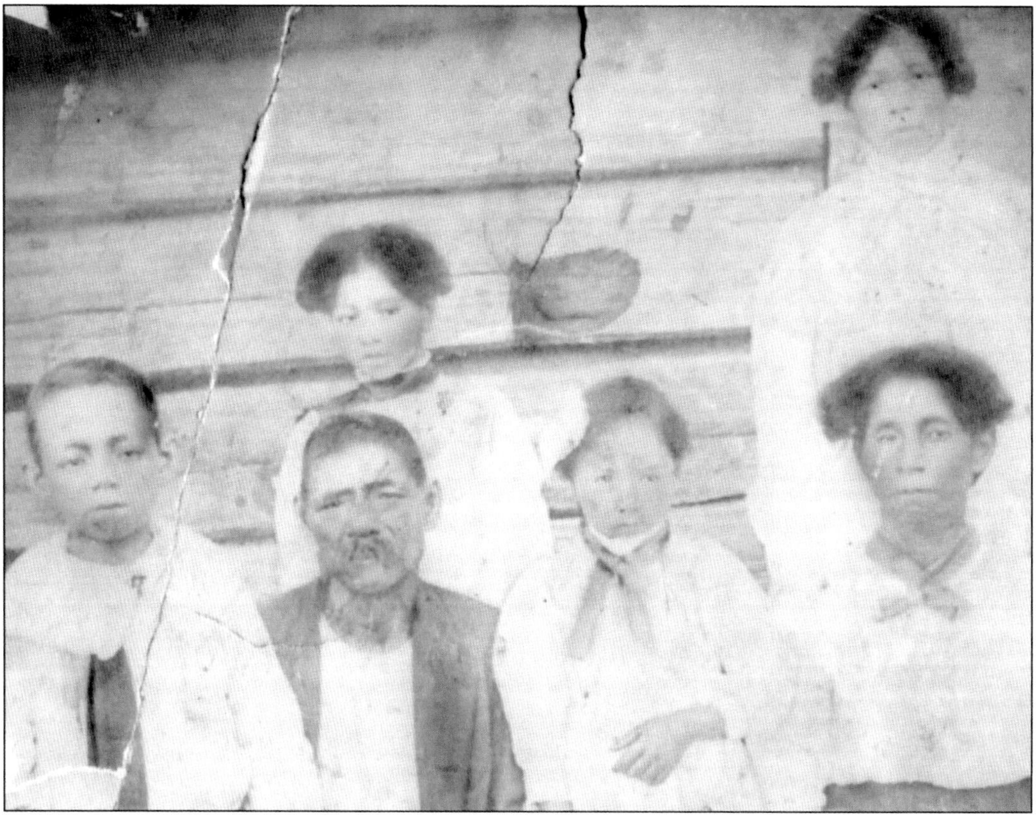

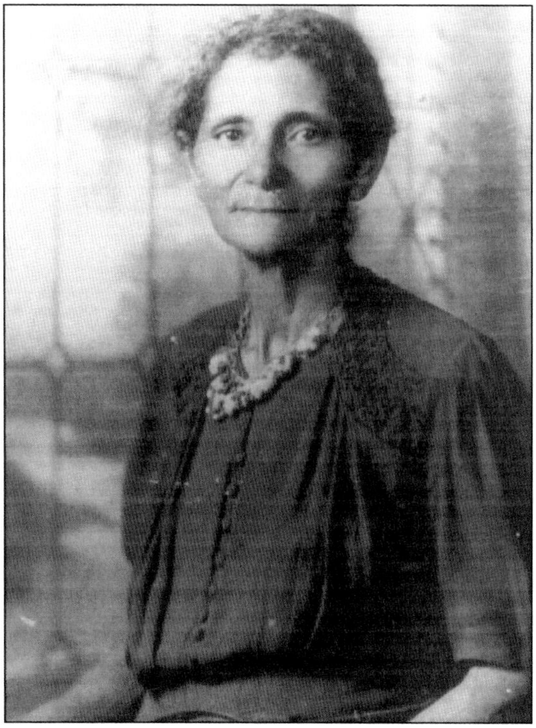

The George Watson family of Center Point is shown here in the early 1900s. Family members possibly identified are George; his wife, Emma Bell; son Robert; and daughters Jennie, Josephine, and Delilah. (Courtesy of William Rogers Sr.)

Born in 1883, Josephine Yarbrough, the wife of Will Yarbrough, is listed in the 1910 census with children Emma, Robert, and Homer. Later, in the 1920 census, the names Lillie, Evaline, Ruby, Ollie, and Oscar were listed as additional children. George and Josephine remained in the Nacogdoches County area, while most of the children moved away. (Courtesy of William Rogers Sr.)

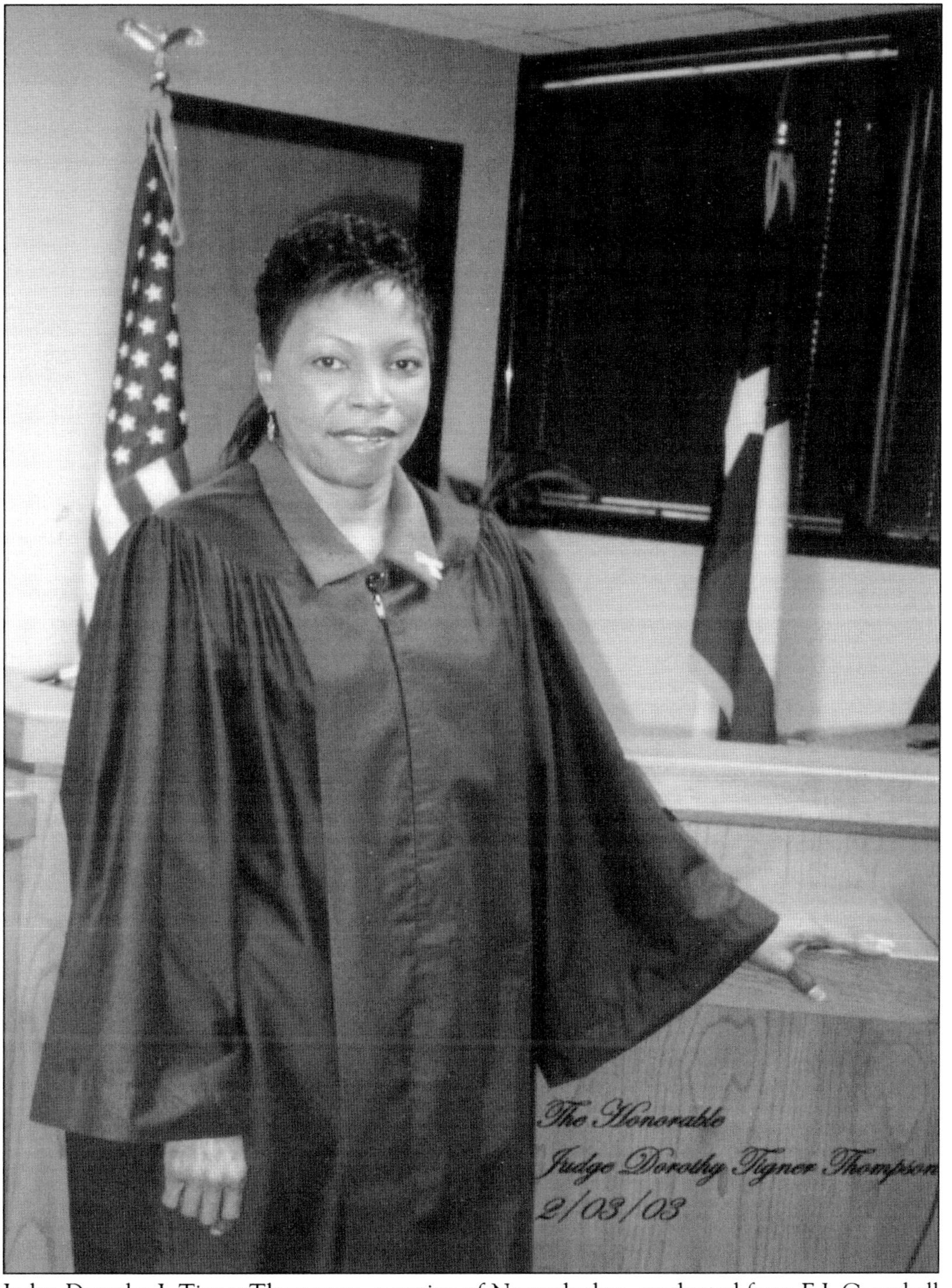

Judge Dorothy J. Tigner-Thompson, a native of Nacogdoches, graduated from E.J. Campbell High School. She was first appointed in 1998 to fill an unexpired term as justice of the peace for Precinct No. 2, Place No. 1 in Nacogdoches County. In 1999, she ran for this position and was elected, becoming the first woman and the first African American to be elected to this post. She has been elected for four consecutive terms. (Courtesy of Dorothy Tigner-Thompson.)

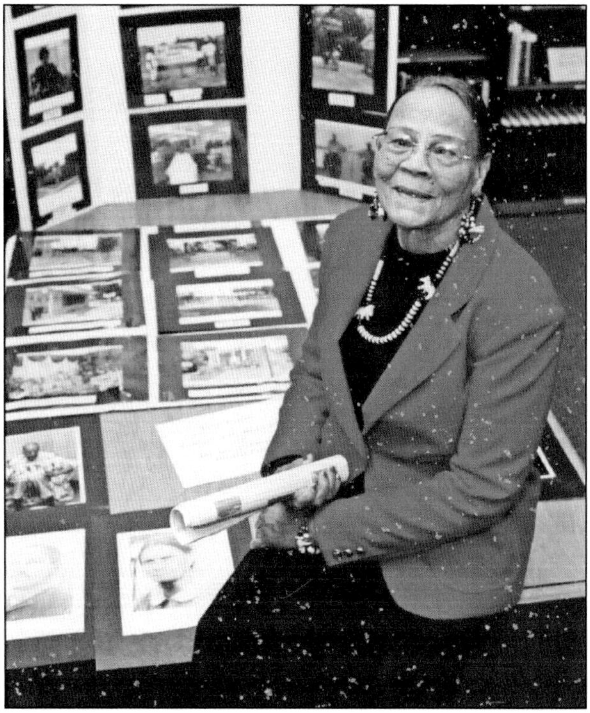

The late Birdie Wade earned her place in Nacogdoches African American history by establishing the African American Heritage Project with a mission to research and bring into knowledge the life and culture of the African American community. Her passion for education led her to enter college and graduate from Stephen F. Austin State University after rearing her family. She was involved in many community service activities and served as an inspiration for young women with families, proving it is never too late to get an education. (ETRC.)

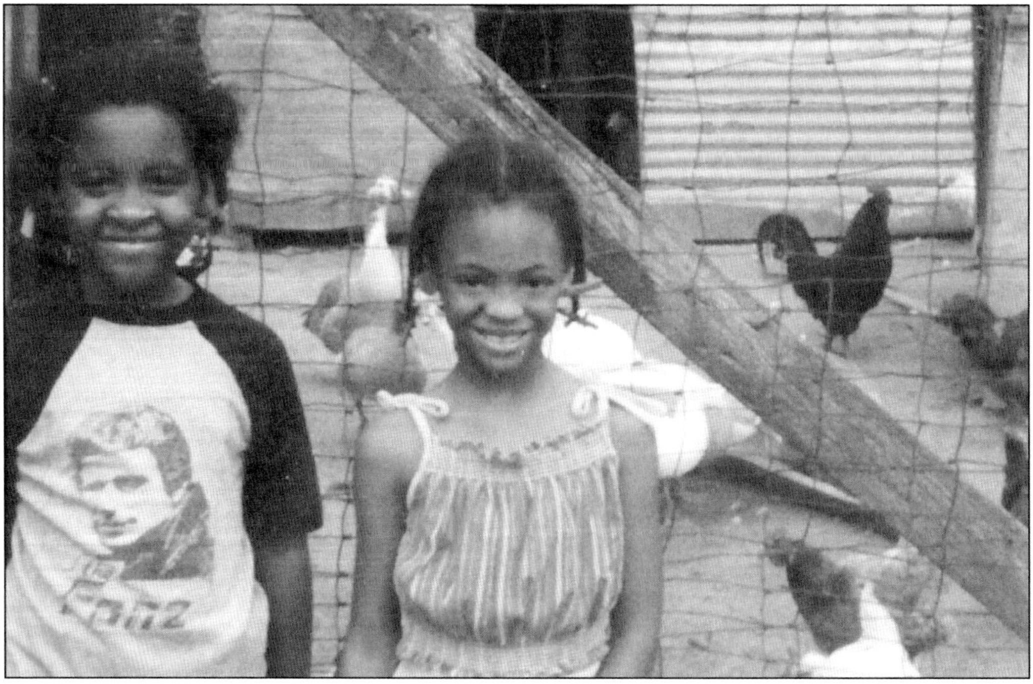

In the early rural communities, chicken feeding was a chore for young children growing up on farms. Rhode Island reds and Dominique chickens would be raised to eat, sell, or trade. Early black families raised chickens to produce eggs to sell or trade. The feathers could be used to make pillows and mattresses. Robin Johnson (left) and Terí Hamm (right) are feeding their grandmother's chicken in this image. (Courtesy of Maye Hamm.)

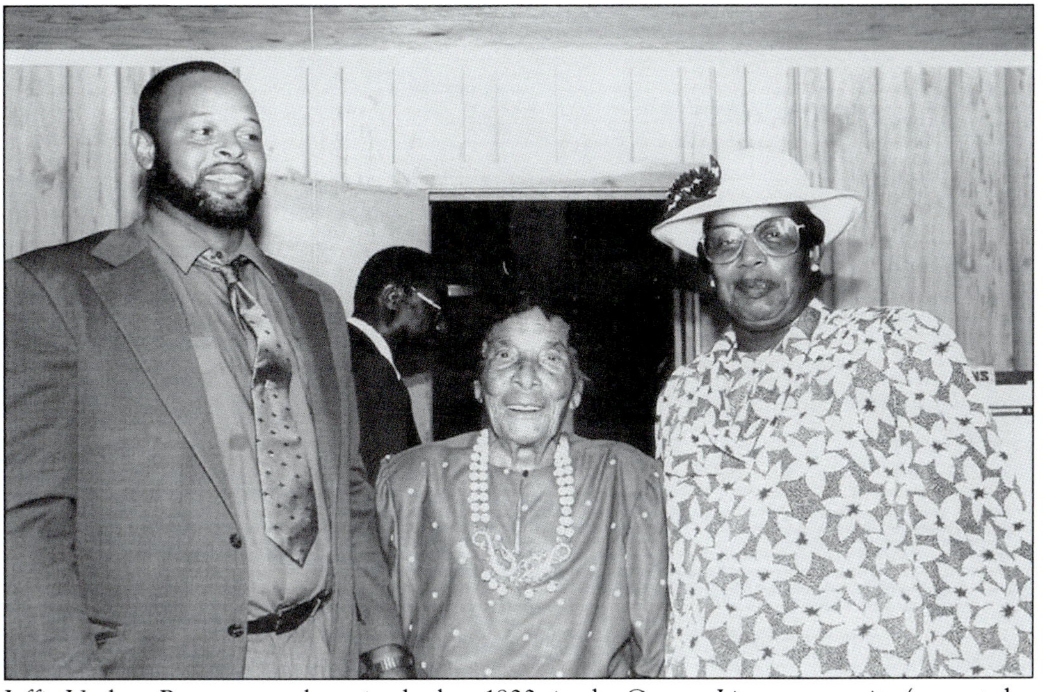

Jeffie Upshaw Ross, center, born in the late 1800s in the County Line community (present-day Upshaw), celebrates her 104th birthday with son "Sonny" and daughter Gladys around 2000. (Courtesy of Maye Hamm.)

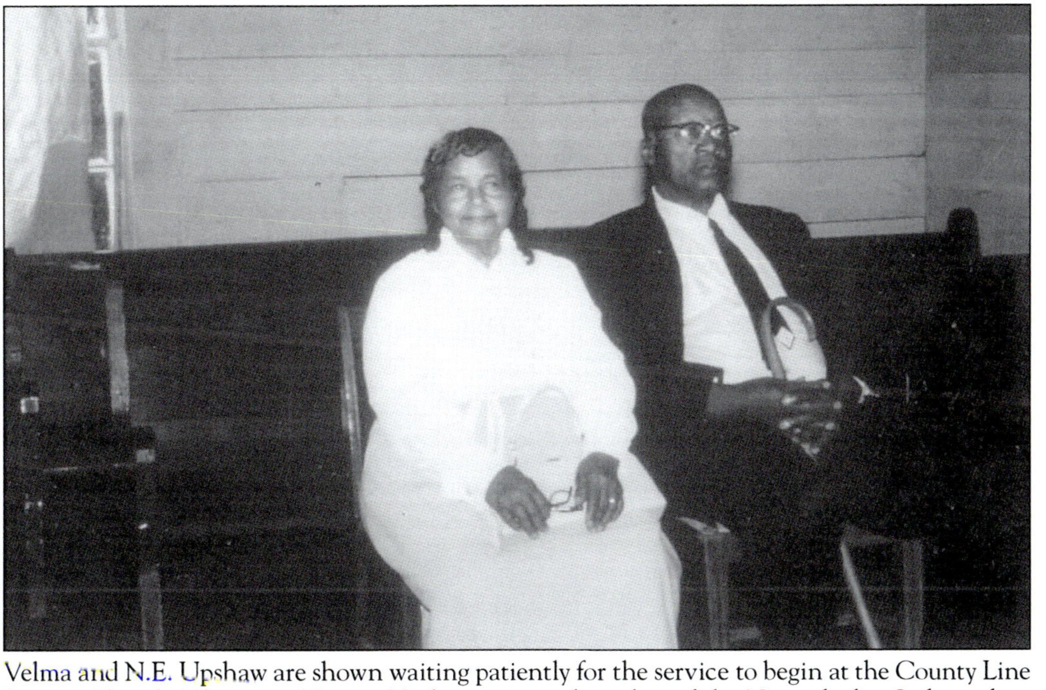

Velma and N.E. Upshaw are shown waiting patiently for the service to begin at the County Line Baptist Church. Their son Marion Upshaw, a retired teacher of the Nacogdoches Independent School District, was the first African American to have a radio talk show on KSFA AM radio, *Upshaw Talk Show*, which aired from 1992 to 1998. (Courtesy of Maye Hamm.)

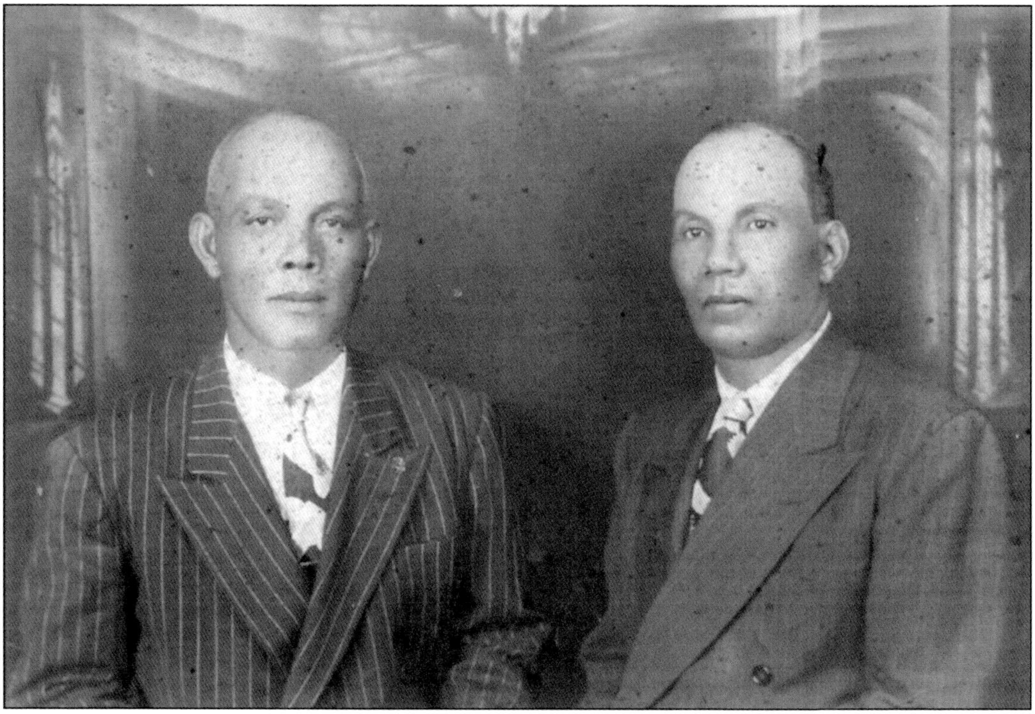

Rev. J.G. Upshaw (left) and his brother Eugene are shown here in an undated photograph. Historic documents reveal that they are related to the former slave brothers Felix, Jim, and Gus Upshaw, who founded the Upshaw community around 1870 after collectively purchasing over 1,000 acres in the County Line–Douglas communities. The brothers owned and operated the first blacksmiths, sawmill, gristmills, and cotton gins in the area. (Courtesy of Maye Hamm.)

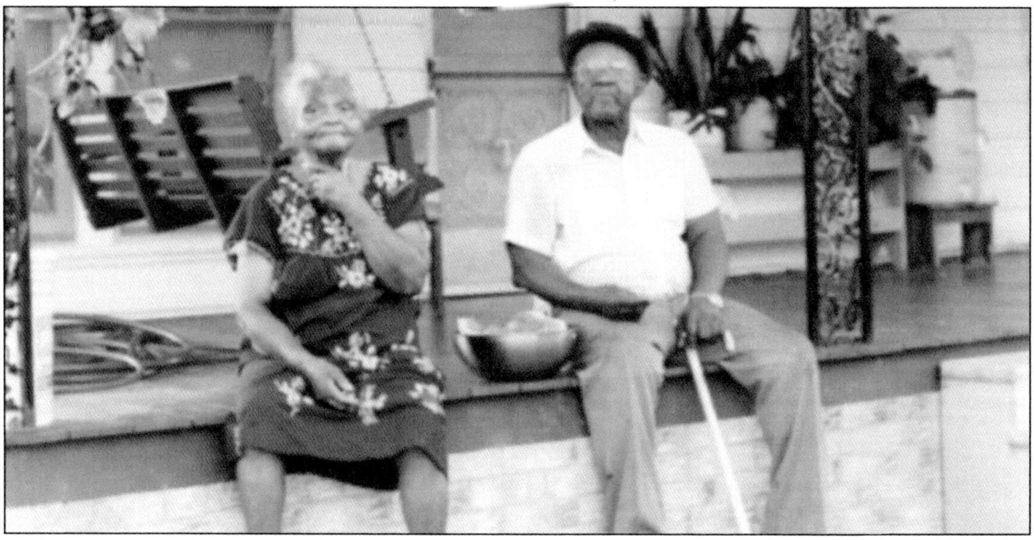

Porch sitting was an accepted and expected activity for people who lived in the country. During the 1940s and 1950s, televisions and air-conditioners were not available to most farm families, making porch sitting a popular pastime. Monel and Leota Upshaw are seen on their beautiful porch, enjoying watermelon on a pleasant summer afternoon. Note the flowers Leota took pride in growing on their front porch. (Courtesy of Maye Hamm.)

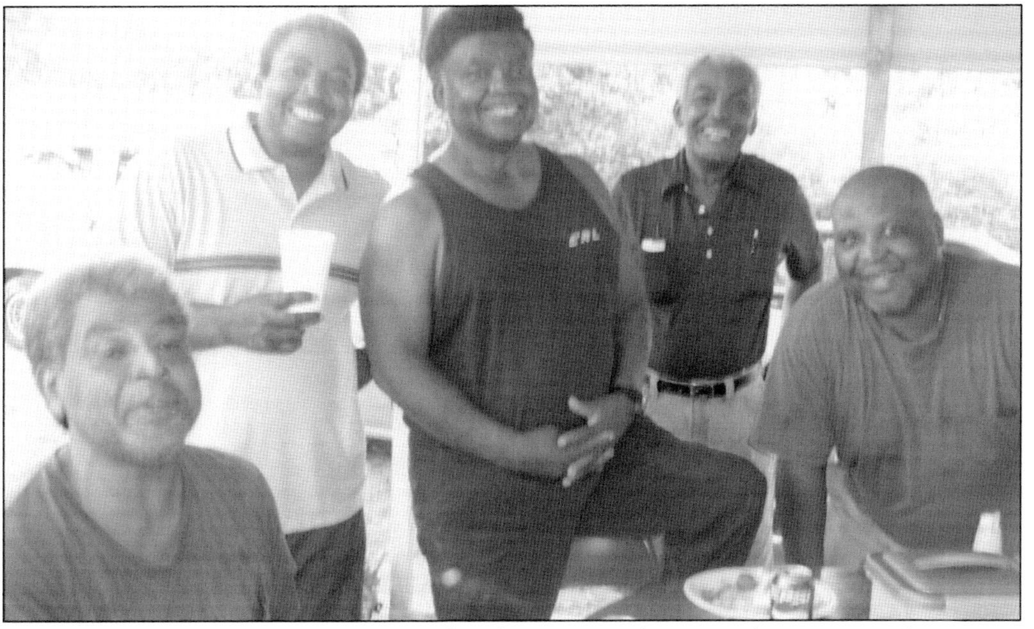

Smiling Upshaw brothers, sons of Monel and Leota, are shown in this image as they return annually to the County Line community for family reunion celebrations. This is typical of many African Americans making the pilgrimages back to the "home land" for homecomings and reunions, which symbolize obligations to remember ancestors that paved the way for them. (Courtesy of Maye Hamm.)

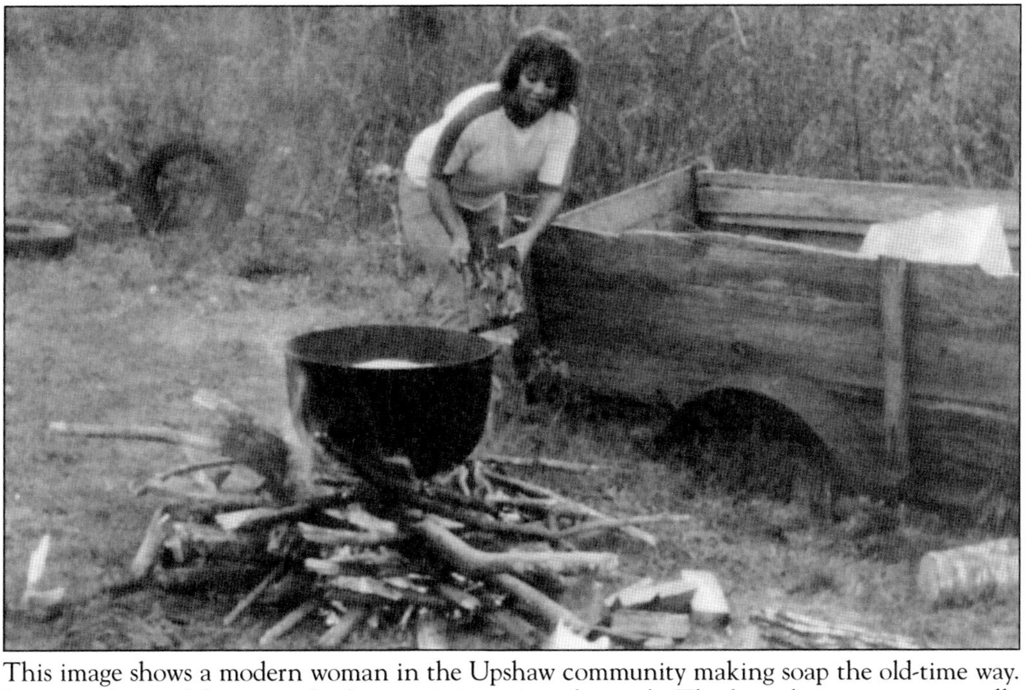

This image shows a modern woman in the Upshaw community making soap the old-time way. Lye was obtained from wood ash containing mineral potash. The lye solution was repeatedly poured over the ashes. The solution was stirred until it turned the animal fat into soap. (Courtesy of Maye Hamm.)

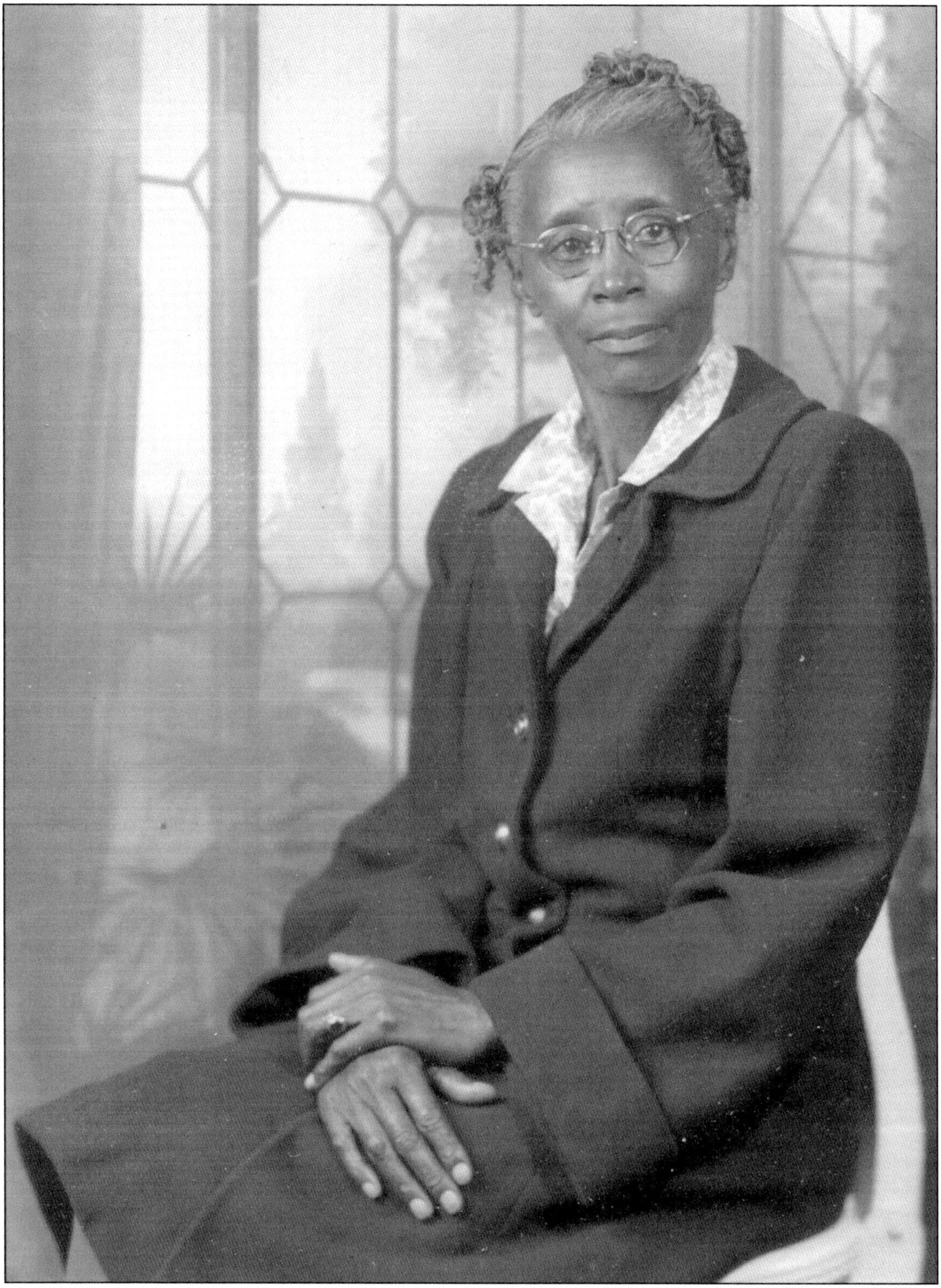

Isabella Gregory Teal, shown in this image, served as midwife in one of the early African American communities during the 1950s. Midwifery is a profession that is as old as the beginning of time. Even today, midwives are still used. African slave women in America made significant contributions to this role in the earliest years of America's existence. Many African Americans can recall a midwife being in their community. (Courtesy of Mable Ferguson Hall.)

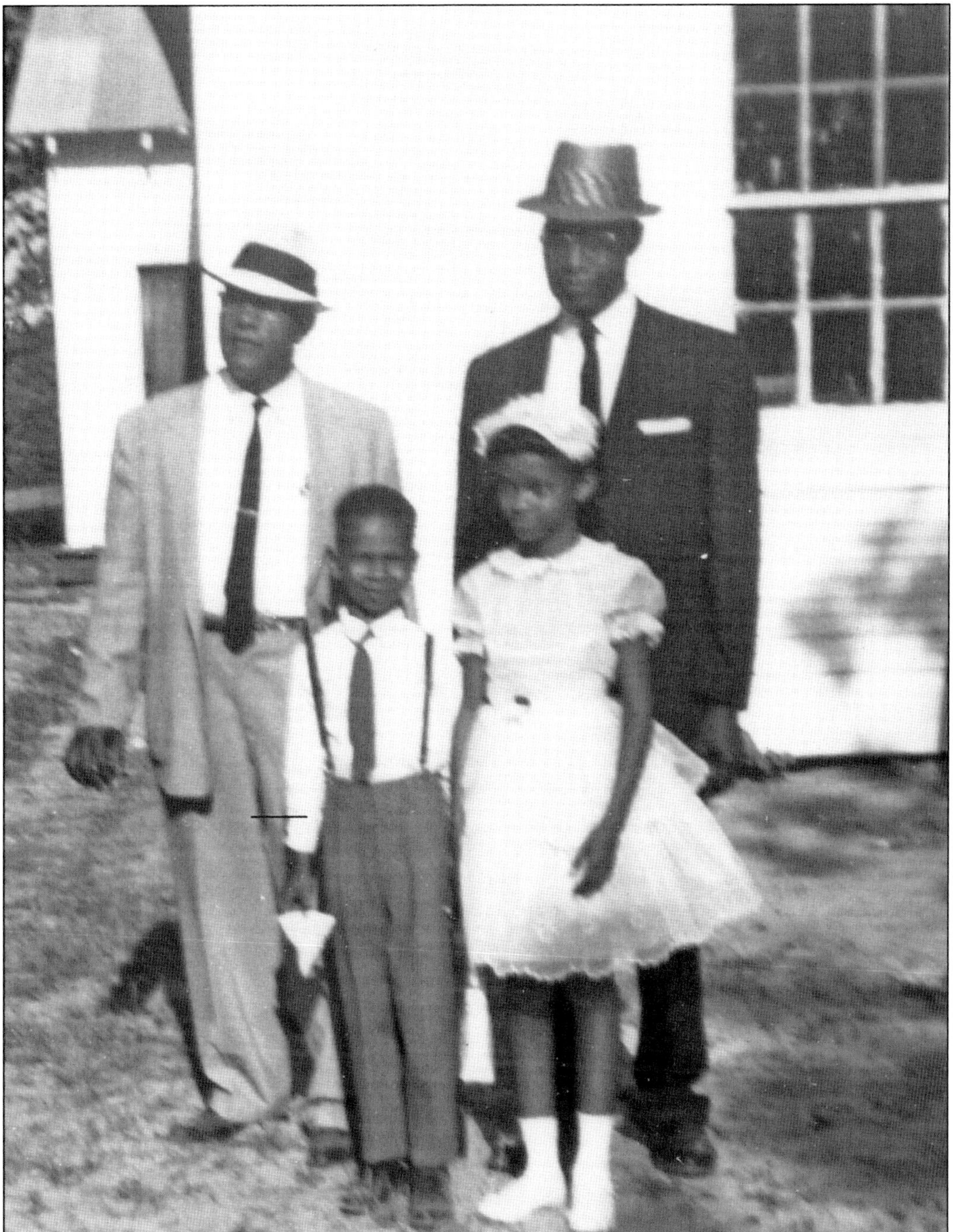

Pictured here are Chireno Colored High School faculty members B.J. Martin (left) and W.B. Freo (right) and Freo's children after baccalaureate service in the late 1950s to early 1960s. Baccalaureate is a centuries-old religious graduation tradition usually held on a Sunday. The service included a sermon and singing. It was a well-attended event, a time for people to dress in their finest attire and to celebrate with the graduates. (Courtesy of Mable Ferguson Hall.)

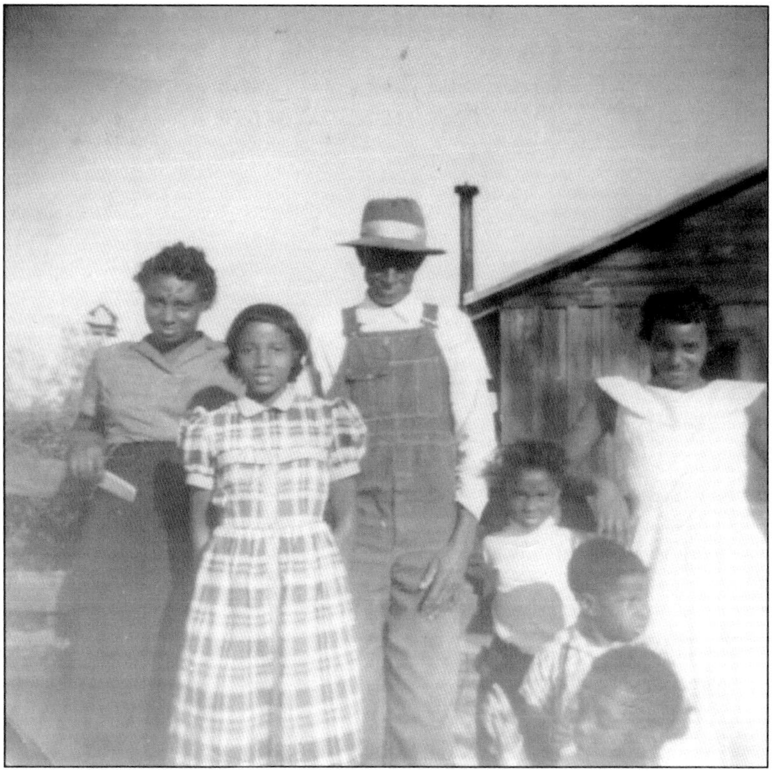

The Jake Ferguson family was a typical close-knit family in the Sand Hill community during the 1950s. The men typically worked in the fields, and women were homemakers. The children helped in the fields and had chores at home. Note the pipe coming from the roof, which indicated use of the wood-burning heater and stove. The tall gentleman is the father. (Courtesy of Mable Ferguson Hall.)

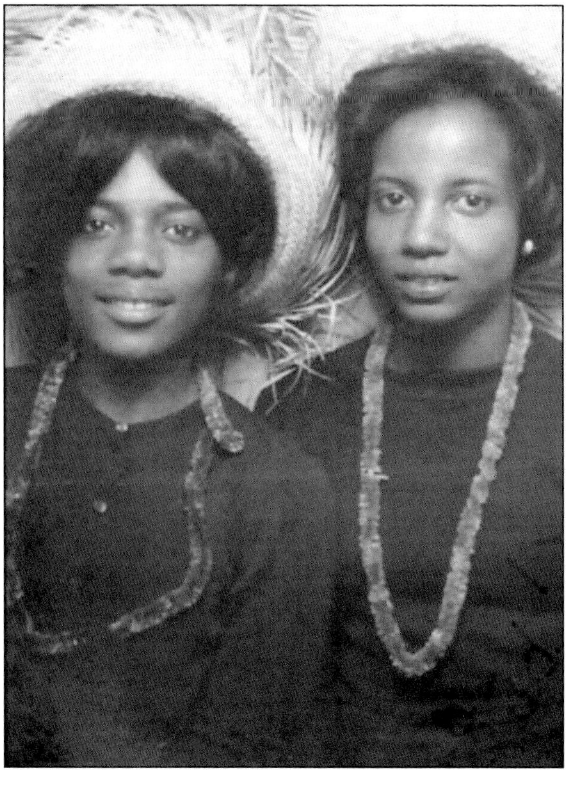

Taken at Nacogdoches County Fair between 1964 and 1966, this photograph is of Gloria Lampkin (left) and Mable Ferguson (right). The fair was held in October and was located down by Lone Star on Butt Street (present-day Martin Luther King Jr. Boulevard). It was an activity students looked forward to. Many students in the rural areas would pick cotton after school to make money to spend at the fair. The black and white schools each had a designated day at the county fair. (Courtesy of Mable Ferguson Hall.)

Bibliography

Barr, Alwyn. *The African Texans*. College Station: Texas A & M University Press, 2004.

Cranford, Sharon, and Dwight Roth. *Kinship Concealed: Amish Mennonite–African American Family Connections*. Winter Park, FL: Legacy Book Publishing, 2013.

Barton, Jan Dobbs and Peggy Arriola Jasso. Images of America: *Nacogdoches in World War II*. Charleston, SC: Arcadia Publishing, 2011.

Eby, Frederick. "The First Century of Public Education in Texas." *Texas Public Schools Handbook, Sesquicentennial Handbook 1854–2004*. Austin: Texas Education Agency, 2004. (www.tea.state.tx.us/WorkArea/DownloadAsset.aspx?id=6510)

Ericson, Joe E. *The Nacogdoches Story: An Informal History*. Westminster, MD: Heritage Books, Inc., 2008.

Hallman, P. *Psalm of Life*. Austin: Eakin Press, 1995.

Nacogdoches County Retired Teachers. *Nacogdoches County Schools 1864–1930*. Nacogdoches, TX, 1986.

The *Nacogdoches Daily Sentinel*. Nacogdoches, TX.

Nacogdoches County Retired Teachers. *Pioneer Women Teachers of Nacogdoches County, In a Historical and Anecdoctal History of the Schools in Nacogdoches County Before 1930*. Nacogdoches, TX: 1986.

Pruitt, Bernadette. *The Other Great Migration: The Movement of Rural African Americans to Houston, 1900–1941*. College Station: Texas A&M University Press, 2013.

Sitton, Thad and James H. Conrad. *Freedom Colonies: Independent Black Texans in the Time of Jim Crow*. Austin: University of Texas Press, 2005.